George Eliot's Religious Imagination

George Eliot's Religious Imagination

A Theopoetics of Evolution

✦

Marilyn Orr

NORTHWESTERN UNIVERSITY PRESS
EVANSTON, ILLINOIS

Northwestern University Press
www.nupress.northwestern.edu

Printed in the United States of America

10 9 8 7 6 5 4 3 2 1

Library of Congress Cataloging-in-Publication Data

Names: Orr, Marilyn, 1950– author.
Title: George Eliot's religious imagination : a theopoetics of evolution / Marilyn Orr.
Description: Evanston, Illinois : Northwestern University Press, 2017. | Includes bibliographical references and index.
Identifiers: LCCN 2017029797 | ISBN 9780810135895 (cloth : alk. paper) | ISBN 9780810135888 (pbk. : alk. paper) | ISBN 9780810135901 (e-book)
Subjects: LCSH: Eliot, George, 1819–1880—Criticism and interpretation. | Eliot, George, 1819–1880—Religion. | Evolution (Biology)—Religious aspects—Christianity.
Classification: LCC PR4692.R4 O77 2017 | DDC 823.8—dc23
LC record available at https://lccn.loc.gov/2017029797

It is perhaps the business of the commentator and critic to point to resemblances, as well as to differences, between the form of thought of a poet of the past, and our own, for it seems that unless this is done, and done repeatedly from generation to generation, works of the past cease to have significance for the ordinary reader, which is tantamount to saying they cease to live.

—Barbara Reynolds, "Introduction" to Dante, *Paradiso*, 15

Ring the bells that still can ring.
Forget your perfect offering.
There is a crack, a crack in everything.
That's how the light gets in.

—Leonard Cohen, "Anthem"

CONTENTS

PREFACE

I have always been finding out my religion since I was a little girl.
—Dorothea in *Middlemarch,* 4:39, 387

When I think of how I came to produce this book, I find myself encountering a number of friends, mentors, colleagues, and family members who have lighted my way. I think of Teilhard de Chardin's idea—whose affinity with George Eliot in reference to this and much else I discuss in chapter 5—that while each individual consciousness is an "absolutely original centre," each center becomes more and more itself as it is drawn constantly and increasingly "*into association with all the centres*"; each self becomes more and more, not less and less, itself "by convergence" with other selves.[1]

If I have become more myself by converging with other selves I have also come to understand, in the course of writing this book, more about convergence itself, a concept that increasingly delighted and enthralled George Eliot and is a key theme in her last novel, *Daniel Deronda*. Convergence, Teilhard would say, increases complexity, and increased complexity leads, for those who are open to it, to increased consciousness. Indeed, coming to understand this and learning how to act upon this awareness is one way of describing the evolution that Dorothea undergoes in *Middlemarch*.

George Eliot's ever-increasing understanding of and belief in convergence, which I explore mainly in chapter 4, is one of the key elements of what I am calling her "religious imagination." Convergence is crucial to her religious imagination particularly because she sees it as affirming the power of imagination in various forms. Along with convergence, the three main components of her religious imagination are inwardness, incarnation, and integration. All four of these elements develop according to evolution, which Teilhard calls "the light illuminating all facts."[2] Inwardness and incarnation are my two main themes in chapter 1, but in chapter 2 I show how George Eliot's understanding of them evolves such that they move from being themes in her work to becoming essential to her own being and practice. Another way to describe what she learns through her writing at this stage is the power of integration (my main focus in chapter 3), as she comes to experience her own integral relation with her characters and their stories. This insight comes at a cost, and underlying and informing George Eliot's religious imagination in all four of these elements is an ever-evolving understanding of suffering. From the start of her career she shares Kierkegaard's understanding that suffering, when turned inward, constitutes growth; she furthers this understanding until she arrives at the insight that Teilhard will later develop, that suffering, turned inward, produces energy for good.

These four elements—inwardness, incarnation, integration, and convergence, but in no particular order and often all at once—have also been fundamental to my experience of writing this book. That I was able to begin at all, at least as we conventionally understand beginning, was because of an insight that allowed me to recognize and to set free my own process of integration: this was the realization, initially only intuitive, that my scholarly journey and my spiritual journey were one and the same. Even the impulse to pursue that intuition until it became articulate and productive is a manifestation of the sense of convergence and the belief in a suprarational consciousness that George Eliot embraces. For key to my own process was the ongoing discovery of convergence between my work and hers.

Crucial to this insight into the convergence and integration of my scholarly and my spiritual lives was my compulsion—at first in spite of myself—to find spiritual retreats to be the sites of scholarly work and, conversely, to find in scholarly work much spiritual worth. On one such retreat, early in this process when I was working toward what turned out to be chapter 1, I was given instruction in inwardness by an unlikely teacher: walking meditatively and repetitively the winding, mulch-covered paths of the tiny but wondrous grounds of what was the Queenswood Centre in Victoria, British Columbia, I took a seat on a small makeshift wooden perch facing the pathway. Though my eyes were wide open all the while, it was nonetheless at least ten minutes before I realized that staring back at me from the other side of the pathway, nestled in his own comfy enclosure, was a large buck. Though it was not unusual to see deer even on the streets of Victoria (to the chagrin of gardeners and drivers), it was unusual to see a large, solitary buck, much less in peaceful repose. From this encounter I took the lesson that if I was intending to write about inwardness, I had better find out what it was.

There is no need to report on how I also needed to internalize and make my own the lesson I show George Eliot learning in chapter 2, that even failures can be prophecies, or the lesson of her whole career that suffering turned inward produces energy for good. It will already be clear, I think, that what I was learning in the course of my writing was the nature of my own religious imagination, or what a fellow traveler on another retreat called the spirituality of intellect.

It remains for me simply to thank those fellow travelers, dead and alive, who have played Virgil to my Dante and at times allowed me to do the same for them. Thank you for accompanying me on this journey, sharing your bread and wine with me and lightening my load by lighting my way with lots of alliterative love and laughter, mixed with tears too deep for words.

But as my sight by seeing learned to see
The transformation which in me took place
Transformed the single changeless form for me.

—Dante, *Paradiso*, 33: 112–14

ACKNOWLEDGMENTS

The lengthy time this project has taken to complete means that my list of people to thank is also lengthy, but I will restrict myself here to identifying only a few, trusting that the others will hear their names implied in my "Preface."

For generous encouragement and consistent support of my work over the years I thank my colleagues (and not least the secretarial staff) in the Department of English and the Faculty of Humanities at Laurentian University. I am especially grateful to those who mapped out with me and enjoyed the territory where collegiality and friendship overlap. To Rachel Haliburton of the Department of Philosophy at the University of Sudbury at Laurentian and to Michael John DiSanto of the Department of English at Algoma University I offer thanks for their generous and incisive readings of a draft version of the major portion of this book; their comments helped sharpen and develop my analysis throughout. To Bruce Ward of the Department of Religious Studies at Thorneloe University at Laurentian I am grateful for practical advice and support when the project was little more than an idea. I am also grateful for the LURF grant I received from Laurentian University to help with costs related to publication.

My many long-suffering students also deserve thanks for their endurance of my George Eliot passion; their insights and questions often helped to sharpen and deepen my reading, and their enthusiasm fueled mine. My own teachers also deserve grateful acknowledgment, but for special merit in this regard I must recognize Ina Ferris at the University of Ottawa, who has supported and encouraged my work since we first met as student and teacher decades ago. She continues to model for me what it means to be a fine scholar and a good friend. I am also grateful to the late D. Ruth Etchells, with regret that it was only with her loss that I began truly to recognize her gifts.

Over the years I have tried out ideas I was developing for this book on many academic audiences. I would particularly like to thank the members of the Christianity and Literature Study Group, which always provided a supportive and stimulating environment for my work. I also have benefited tremendously from the work of the George Eliot Fellowship. Particularly wonderful was a Study Day devoted to *The Mill on the Floss*; I am grateful to the Fellowship for allowing me to use material in chapter 2 that appeared as "'Even our Failures are a Prophecy': *The Mill on the Floss* and the 1860s" in *The George Eliot Review* no. 42 (2011): 38–48. I would also like to thank the editors of *Christianity and Literature* for giving me permission to reproduce here as chapter 1 a piece that appeared as "Incarnation, Inwardness, and Imagination in George Eliot's Early Fiction," *Christianity and Literature* 58, no. 3 (Spring 2009): 451–81.

Like any profession, I suppose, academia is a mysterious domain to those outside of it. For this reason it is especially wonderful for me to have experienced support, encouragement, and even serious interest in my work from my family. I dedicate this book to the memory of my parents, Owen and Josephine, and to my four siblings, their spouses, and their offspring, with love.

George Eliot's Religious Imagination

INTRODUCTION

Writing is part of my religion.
—George Eliot, *Letters*, Haight edition, 2:377

This book reexamines religion and related questions in the work of George Eliot. It is conceived as a study of her "religious imagination" because at the center of the argument is the conviction that George Eliot's idea of religion is an outgrowth of her imaginative work, which is in turn an outgrowth of her mind and life. One of the key principles of the present study imitates one of the key principles of George Eliot herself: integration. *Middlemarch*, generally held up as her masterpiece, represents the climax of her fictional work because it embodies this principle of integration almost as perfectly as any novel could. The web has long been noted as a predominant metaphor of *Middlemarch*, and it is so important exactly because it figures so beautifully the impossible complexity of the task before any writer—of George Eliot to explore the world of the recent past without unraveling it, and of the present writer to explore the world of George Eliot's writing life with a similar delicacy.

The project I have set myself is to take seriously George Eliot's own words, first, as in the epigraph above, her deep conviction that her calling as a writer is a religious one. This book is an exploration of what she means by "religion." At least as challenging is to take seriously her conviction of the unknowability of human beings, including herself, even to herself. In her first story, "The Sad Fortunes of the Reverend Amos Barton," her narrator exposes the myth of self-knowledge and the corresponding need for "dear friendly illusion" to allow us "to dream that we are charming." Here too she expresses the subjectivity of all of our knowledge and our reliance on one another's faith: "no miracle can be wrought without faith—without the worker's faith in himself, as well as the recipient's faith in him. And the greater part of the worker's faith in himself is made up of the faith that others believe in him."[1] This epistemological paradox helps explain the intense difficulty of her writing process; this too speaks of integration in that "the mystery of human sorrow" she speaks of in her first novel and explores throughout her career is also her own.[2]

I focus on George Eliot's religious imagination because she implicitly accepts the Romantic view of the imagination as the predominant human faculty, famously defined by Coleridge as the great repeater of the creator's power and the unifying force of all experience. Indeed, it is because of this imagination that George Eliot's work can be both realistic and idealistic. It is because of this imagination, with its compulsion to think and feel together, that she has always been criticized by some purists for importing philosophy into fiction. Like Coleridge she sees life as an integrated whole, refusing to make a separation between mind and soul and heart. I call her work "theopoetical" because, rather than writing theology, she can be numbered among poets such as Coleridge, Shelley, Hopkins, Blake, and Dante, whose imaginative work shapes and expresses their response to God.

George Eliot's understanding of imagination is remarkably consistent throughout her career. In several of her early essays, as I discuss in chapter 1, she castigates writers who mistake weakened, fanciful intelligence for imagination. And in her very last essays, collected as *Impressions of Theophrastus Such*, she is only more articulate and pointed about this. In "How We Come to Give False Testimonials, and Believe in Them," George Eliot uses the voice of Theophrastus to try once more to clarify that a "fine imagination" is not opposed to intelligent perception but is instead dependent upon it.[3] Her reiteration of the point could readily pass for a gloss on Coleridge's definition of imagination:

> It is worth repeating that powerful imagination is not false outward vision, but intense inward representation, and a creative energy constantly fed by susceptibility to the veriest minutiae of experience, which it reproduces and constructs in fresh and fresh wholes; not the habitual confusion of provable fact with the fictions of fancy and transient inclination, but a breadth of ideal association which informs every material object, every incidental fact with far-reaching memories and stored residues of passion, bringing into new light the less obvious relations of human existence.[4]

To illustrate this understanding of imagination, Theophrastus turns to Dante, further supporting the idea that George Eliot belongs among practitioners of theopoetics.

The principle of integration that undergirds the Coleridgean sense of wholeness of being and Dante's artistic practice is fundamental to George Eliot's religious imagination. Equally important is the notion of incarnation, both in its ethical and sacred modeling of integrated humanity and in its modeling of the aesthetic goal of making the words of her art become flesh, in a figurative sense. For, despite her withdrawal from the institutional church, she continues to believe in the incarnation as the basis for human values and relations. As an artist she believes not only in the ethical imperative to live one's beliefs but also in the aesthetic imperative to "show, not tell" one's ideas.

The interrelation of integration, integrity, and incarnation reveals itself as a deeply personal idea in the course of George Eliot's writing: in the process of bringing her characters and ideas to life in fiction, she discovers that she herself, as their creator, must bear their suffering in her own body. This process is fundamentally integrating because it is not an idea that she decides to demonstrate; instead it is an experience that she learns to believe. In Christian terms, one might say that belief in the incarnation is fundamental to the possibility of integrated humanity; George Eliot lives out this notion in the course of her career. In the deepest sense then, her imagination is religious and her theopoetics is comprised of and energized by love.

The principle of integration also explains the deceptively simple design of this book, which takes seriously George Eliot's own understanding of her career as a developing continuum. While interspersing comments on works from every period of her career, I trace the growth of her religious imagination as it evolves, with the exception of reserving my analysis of the early work *Silas Marner* for chapter 5. As I will try to show, her central beliefs—always founded on a sense of ultimate mystery—change only in the sense of growing and deepening, thereby demonstrating again the fundamental importance of integration.

Indeed, the other essential element of George Eliot's religious imagination is her belief in evolution as fundamental to all of life, including consciousness. Failure to understand the importance of George Eliot's belief in evolution is responsible for the notion that she "lost her faith" as a young woman, a view that has been the mainstay of a secular dismissal or misunderstanding of her serious religious concerns. Basil Willey seems to have lost the argument he took up in his *Nineteenth-Century Studies*, published in 1955, when he famously disputed Lord David Cecil's claim that George Eliot was "not religious." Willey argued that religious was "just what she was," contending that "the whole predicament that she represents was that of the religious temperament cut off by the *Zeitgeist* from the traditional objects of veneration, and the traditional intellectual formulations."[5] His voice was drowned out in the secularizing tide, however, such that much critical work on George Eliot is founded on the assumption that Cecil was correct. As recently as 2001, for example, Barry Qualls's chapter "George Eliot and Religion" in *The Cambridge Companion to George Eliot*, while thorough and subtle, began by stating that George Eliot maintained her connection to biblical texts and language "when she lost her faith," without his feeling the need to defend or explain this premise.[6] Willey supported his claim by citing George Eliot's sustained attention to "righteousness," "renunciation," and "reverence."[7] These are key themes for my argument as well, and in a way I am able to take up where he left off because the Zeitgeist has shifted toward more openness to exploring religious experience and beliefs.

Indeed, while it is true that the discovery of evolution constituted the major challenge to traditional Christianity in the nineteenth century, this was only the beginning of a process of revisioning religious beliefs, experience, and consciousness in the context of scientific discoveries. For some, it is true, the scientific challenge led to abandoning religion, as belief in reason replaced religious faith. The climate of intellectual skepticism did become widespread and came to feed the pervasive secularism following the World Wars; it is only now in the twenty-first century that what has been called "the religious turn" has given us a wider perspective in which to consider the nineteenth-century response to evolution. One of my aims is to contribute, along with such books as Peter Hodgson's *The Mystery Beneath the Real: Theology in the Fiction of George Eliot* and J. Russell Perkin's *Theology and the Victorian Novel*, to a reconsideration of the complexities of nineteenth-century religion, in the hope that we might begin to recognize that it is just as complex as that of our own century.

It is in the context of an evolutionary understanding that I try to clarify what George Eliot meant by faith and religion. By examining the way that she lived out their meaning in her writing, I wish to show how inadequate, even useless and misleading, is the concept of a lost faith as applied to George Eliot. Fundamental to my argument is the idea that in her work George Eliot is anticipating ways of reconciling faith and reason, mainly through the action of imagination, which had yet to be theorized or adequately understood. I therefore enlist the aid of several thinkers whose work she did not know, most because she predated them and, in the case of Kierkegaard, because she never happened (as far as I know) to encounter his work. Kierkegaard's arguments for the truth of subjectivity and the subjectivity of truth are fundamental to my approach.

Since one of the most important catalysts of George Eliot's evolution with regard to religion occurred when she encountered Roman Catholic art in Europe, it seems apt that most of the thinkers I invoke are from that tradition. My work benefits greatly from the insights of the Catholic philosopher Richard Kearney. I particularly draw from his understanding of imagination as a force that, in allowing for the possibility of the unseen, awakens the human potential for change by actualizing goodness, beauty, and truth, as well as his theory of "anatheism"—the process by which one may come back to God in a new way. Kearney's teacher, Paul Ricoeur, helps me develop an idea of George Eliot's "narrative identity" in chapter 2. For chapters 3 and 4 I rely on Karl Rahner and Evelyn Underhill (the latter a member of the Church of England) for their understanding of mysticism.

Perhaps most controversial is the use I make of the work of Pierre Teilhard de Chardin, since it is here that I act upon Kierkegaard's affirmation of the subjectivity of truth to claim that Teilhard's reconciliation of science and faith might have effected George Eliot's own "anatheistic" return to a newly understood God. In my effort to support this claim I am grateful for the work of Dorothy L. Sayers and Barbara Reynolds on Dante's *Divine Comedy*, as well as, of course, the work of the great Italian master himself. George Eliot did read and love Dante's work, a fact that I read as testament to her intuition concerning what there was to believe and what it meant to believe.

Chapter 1, "Incarnation and Inwardness: George Eliot's Early Works in the Context of Contemporary Religious Debates," begins with an outline of the early life of Mary Anne Evans—later George Eliot—and her movement from the evangelical Christianity of her youth toward the noninstitutional religious attitude of her mature life. I discuss several key essays she wrote before venturing into fiction. I refute the standard view that George Eliot accepted Strauss's demythologized Jesus and embraced Feuerbach's "religion of humanity"—both of whose key works she famously translated—by showing the importance to her of the individual as a spiritual being. While acknowledging that George Eliot did not know his work, I propose Kierkegaard's idea of the individual as a better model. The chapter argues that two key concepts of Christianity, incarnation and inwardness, inform George Eliot's work from the start. The importance of integration is evident from the beginning as well, as I show by introducing the notion of incarnation as a principle that underlies the understanding of fiction as well as the understanding of faith at this time. My main focuses for illustrative analysis in this chapter are "Janet's Repentance" (the last story in the *Scenes of Clerical Life*), *Adam Bede*, and *The Mill on the Floss*.

Chapter 2, "'Even Our Failures Are a Prophecy': Toward a Post-Evangelical Aesthetic," covers George Eliot's middle period between two major successes, the publication of *The Mill on the Floss* in 1860 and that of *Middlemarch* in 1871–72. Generally understood as a time of experiment if not outright failure, this period sees the publication of two major works that deal directly with religion in a historical, European context—the novel *Romola* and the long dramatic poem *The Spanish Gypsy*—as well as a novel, *Felix Holt, the Radical*, which seeks to create a secular saint in near-contemporary England. This is also the period when George Eliot writes lesser-known poetical works, several of which investigate the value of art and the role of the artist. My argument in this chapter is that, having finished in *The Mill on the Floss* with the evangelical Christian landscape of her youth, George Eliot is seeking in this period a new terrain for her fiction. Because, as quoted above, writing is part of her religion, this means seeking a religious terrain and a way to affirm the artist as a kind of religious figure. In this context, these works take on a profound importance in helping her to work out the implications of her calling as an artist and in mapping out the landscape of future works.

Central to this chapter is a consideration of the idea of suffering, which, while a key theme from the beginning, takes on a new meaning in this context. The major figure here is that of the martyr, and, as throughout the study, integration will be seen to be an important clue to how George Eliot's religious imagination is developing in this period. Integration will also provide the clue as to why she begins to explore different literary forms: not only does she write more and more poems, but she also writes about tragedy. Incarnation again comes into play in that, though she keeps at bay any suggestion that her own physical and emotional suffering has an ultimate meaning, we see her own view of suffering change as her experience grows to embrace what might be seen as artistic failure.

In chapter 3, "Religion in a Secular World: *Middlemarch* and the Mysticism of the Everyday," I argue that *Middlemarch*, as an almost flawlessly integrated whole, demonstrates how central integration is to George Eliot's religious imagination. *Middlemarch* not only explores the way in which integrity manifests as integration but also itself represents George Eliot's own achievement of personal and artistic integration. Even its status as both a critical and popular success demonstrates a triumph of integration. As in the previous chapter, I turn first to two poems of this period—"The Legend of Jubal" and "Armgart"—in this case poems that focus on the role of the artist. In them George Eliot expresses a Romantic, idealistic view of the artist so that she is able to ground her prose—or, in other words, to subordinate her own need for idealism—in order to incarnate her ideas and ideals in realistic characters and situations. This approach sets the pattern for her novel *Middlemarch* as Dorothea must learn a similar kind of grounding, which involves a shift in her understanding of religion when her experience with Casaubon drives her from the apostolic, idealistic, doctrinally pure Christianity of her youthful dreams to a religion that is based on love in action and practical goodness. I argue that in this Dorothea is learning what might be called the theology of integration that is the basis of the mysticism of everyday life.

This chapter also includes a brief survey of the clergy of nineteenth-century Britain and their representatives in George Eliot's novelistic world. The theology of integration is crucial again in that fundamental to her religious imagination at this time is the belief that religion is an integral part of society. Through her fictional clerics in *Middlemarch* George Eliot demonstrates that the clergy are at their best integrated into society and that, like men and women of every profession and role, they are called to manifest integrity by living out their faith in their daily lives and integrating themselves into the life around them.

Chapter 4, "'The Religion of the Future': *Daniel Deronda* and the Mystical Imagination," shows George Eliot further pursuing the ideas and concerns of *Middlemarch* as she sets a novel for the first time in her own time and city, confronting the sense of jaded purposelessness and anxious hopelessness that pervades her culture in the wake of its loss of a religious center. She offers religion as a solution by reclaiming three kinds of religious life—the everyday mysticism modeled by Dorothea, the ancient Jewish mystical tradition, and the Romantic understanding of imagination. All three of these attitudes exemplify the mystical notion that faith transforms the ordinary world into a realm of poetry and possibility. With these three mystical possibilities George Eliot gestures toward "the religion of the future" that she refers to in a letter of this time. Her sense of the future clearly incorporates religious ideas from the past, is grounded in present action, and envisions the future as something other than the afterlife that is present-day religion's preoccupation. In *Daniel*

Deronda we also see George Eliot furthering her efforts toward integration by writing a novel in which religion, poetry, art, and music are thematized.

In chapter 5, "Evolutionary Spirituality and the Theopoetical Imagination: George Eliot and Teilhard de Chardin," I move to the conclusion of this study by speculating about how very deeply evolutionary and religious George Eliot's attitude was. I do so by placing her in a continuum of theopoetical thinkers, with Dante as her ancestor and Teilhard de Chardin as her heir. I show in *Daniel Deronda* three specific cultural illustrations of the religious imagination at work, and I analyze *Silas Marner* in light of Teilhard's evolutionary spirituality in order to show that underlying George Eliot's novels is her appeal to ways of religious being that are at once ancient and ever-evolving. The discussion in this chapter is framed by my contention that Teilhard's ideas on evolutionary spirituality, particularly those concerning the convergence of science and faith and the evolution of consciousness, along with his radical perspectives on interpretation and on the meaning of suffering, can help us to understand George Eliot's religious imagination. As I have argued from the beginning, George Eliot's affirmation of subjective, individual, evolving ways of knowing is central to her religious imagination. Here, I develop this notion by briefly exploring some of the ways in which subjective, individual, evolving ways of interpretation have always been central to Christian thought.

In a brief "Conclusion," I suggest that George Eliot's ever-evolving religious imagination finds an echo in the contemporary understanding of "The Word Continuously Incarnated."

Chapter 1

Incarnation and Inwardness

George Eliot's Early Works in the Context of Contemporary Religious Debates

> The secret of our emotions never lies in the bare object, but in its subtle relations to our own past: no wonder the secret escapes the unsympathising observer, who might as well put on spectacles to discern odours.
>
> —George Eliot, *Adam Bede,* 2:18, 180

> Is there not a spiritual existence that belongs to individuals?
>
> —Søren Kierkegaard, *Repetition*

In the great age of religious questioning, which U. C. Knoepflmacher says was "obsessed with epistemology,"[1] George Eliot's importance was such that an early reviewer could call her "the emblem of a generation distracted between the intense need of believing and the difficulty of belief."[2] In the "conflict of interpretations" that David Carroll rightly sees as central to her narrative situations, George Eliot's fiction reveals, I will argue, her own exploration of faith and imagination and her discovery of their inseparable connection as hermeneutical mind-sets.

It is impossible to read George Eliot's novels without thinking about religion, one would think, since, even when they do not directly concern religious clerics, they focus on characters engaged in deeply religious struggles. George Eliot's work is rich enough that astute readers can find material for almost any sophisticated reading, and it is perhaps not surprising that while critics in a secular culture have tended to follow the standard view that Marian Evans "lost her faith" as a young woman, there is increasing interest in the necessary complexities of any such trajectory. While there have always been critics and readers speaking against the tide, the pervasive tendency has been to acknowledge her early piety and reiterate the "conventional wisdom"[3] that after her encounter with Higher Criticism, firstly through Charles Hennell and then Strauss and Feuerbach, and with the Comte school, her Christian beliefs were replaced by a Feuerbachian version of the religion of humanity. While the crucial influence of all of these is undeniable, I agree with Peter Hodgson when he argues that George Eliot never became a disciple of any system or ideology.[4] Instead, I will argue, her views were deeply evolutionary. Rather like one of the mollusks which were the subject of her husband's study, she accreted these beliefs like so many layers, with each new level of knowledge adding to and adapting, rather than displacing, her earlier views. While it is easy enough to find comments in her letters declaring her rejection of conventional forms of Christianity, it is not much harder to find as many comments that modify and complicate these declarations of unbelief.[5]

In his book, Hodgson briefly analyzes each of George Eliot's novels for their Christian content, and extrapolates from this the principles of what he calls George Eliot's "future religion," a form of "revisionist postmodern" theology that he aligns with various theologians from Schleiermacher to Ricoeur.[6] Hodgson's idea that George Eliot practiced a "faith, which kept the reality of God in suspense"[7] echoes ideas of the philosopher Richard Kearney, himself a student of Ricoeur. Kearney's recent work, as suggested by the title of his book *The God Who May Be*, analyzes the ways that modernist writers such as Joyce and Woolf invoke sacramental language that shadows forth a "possible" God. Kearney's work on "narrative imagination" as the basis for the "narrative identity" that is acquired "in large part by receiving others' narratives and re-narrating itself in turn to others" informs my whole argument.[8] It seems to me that we might put George Eliot in the company of Kearney's modernists of sacred possibility, for George Eliot's religious imagination took her beyond Feuerbachian humanism toward a far more complex understanding of religious experience. The first stage of this development is enacted in her early fiction, in which she constructs an aesthetic that is deeply rooted in two fundamental elements of her early experience among Evangelical Christians, incarnation and inwardness.

A brief sketch of her religious history is in order. Mary Anne Evans (as she was christened) grew up in a middle-of-the road Anglican household but as a schoolgirl came under the powerful influence of intense Evangelicalism with a Calvinist/Puritan streak in the persons of a teacher and fellow students. Her youthful letters, which sound cringingly pious to most modern ears, reflect what one biographer calls an "unforgiving, damnation-conscious form of religion"[9] and are a convenient source for any who are on a quest for evidence of the pathologies of adolescent faith. For my purposes, they point to the way in which faith and imagination were already at odds in her thinking, for in them she records a suspicion of "imaginative literature, particularly fiction," which she overcomes out of a conviction of the necessity to be familiar with common references,[10] and of musical settings of biblical passages, which she at once revels in and deplores.

The next landmark on her intellectual journey was her meeting with a warm and intelligent family of free-thinking Unitarians. While the Hennell sisters became Mary Anne's close and lifelong friends, their brother Charles Hennell's *Inquiry concerning the Origin of Christianity* (1838) began what became the sea change in her thinking, as he carefully explained Christianity in entirely natural terms. The result was a temporary but hugely significant rift with her beloved father, whose housekeeper she was, when she refused to accompany him to church. Mary Anne relented after several weeks because, characteristically, her relationship with her father was more important to her than the principle of truth, once she had made sure to demonstrate it to him.[11] But the break was made, and not the least important development was her determination to become financially independent from her father and brother.

In 1851 she moved to London and became Marian Evans, writer of reviews and essays, the shadow editor of the *Westminster Review*, reading and writing prodigiously. The two most famous landmarks in her religious life bracket this move: her translations of Strauss's *Life of Jesus*, published after almost two years of painstaking labor in 1846, and of Feuerbach's *Essence of Christianity* in 1854. For now, I will just say in a sentence that Strauss's work demythologized Christianity, taking earnest, sympathetic pains to do so, and Feuerbach's work situated the origin of God-ideas in the human mind: "All religious cosmogonies," writes Feuerbach, "are products of the imagination."[12]

Before moving away from biography, it is important to note the most important presence in Marian Evans's adult life, the man she would call her husband, George Henry Lewes, whom she met between the translating of these two tomes. And it is important to say as well that in the case of George Eliot, the intimate personal relations of her life as Mary Anne and then Marian Evans must be seen as the ground of her intellectual life. In other words, her ideas were always inseparable from her feelings, and from her body in the world: there were no words without flesh. This sense of the necessity to incarnate ideas is the basis of the embodied aesthetic of her fiction. For what early reviewers saw as what Carroll calls her "dissociated sensibility"—a conflict between George Eliot the artist and George Eliot the philosopher[13]—is what might also be called a paradoxical effect of her effort to incarnate her aesthetic.

In this study I am taking up George Eliot's works more or less chronologically because, as others have recognized, there is a deeply evolutionary quality to George Eliot's career. Like many writers I suppose, she is loathe to repeat herself and, while readers might recognize characters and situations that she is revisiting, she always needs to believe in her own development as a writer. In her letters she repeatedly champions her first stories, for example, largely because they contain "ideas" that she doubts she "can ever embody again."[14] This is an important idea in a broader sense too in that her philosophy was grounded in a belief in the idea of progress. This is most neatly exemplified in *Silas Marner*, which is often called a fable, but is a fable not just of one man's life but of the progress of humanity and civilization, as reflected in the growth of a single consciousness and community. (I will save further comment on *Silas Marner* until chapter 5, in which I will discuss more fully George Eliot's work in the context of evolutionary ideas.)

Two of her earliest reviews reflect the importance of this belief in progressive thinking. In 1849, writing of Froude's *The Nemesis of Faith*, she affirms "its suggestive hints as to the necessity of recasting the currency of our religion and virtue."[15] In an important essay of 1851, her review of R. W. Mackay's *The Progress of the Intellect*, George Eliot explicitly refutes the Comtean view that "human progress" means "devot[ing our] energies to the actual rather than to the retrospective," affirming instead Mackay's "survey of the past," which shows "how each age and each race has had a faith and a symbolism suited to its need and its stage of development."[16] It could be said, I think, that George Eliot's whole opus demonstrates this view with regard not only to her characters but to herself. In the same essay she affirms "Mackay's faith" in what theologians came to call progressive revelation, which he sees, she writes, as "co-extensive with the history of human development."[17] She quotes Mackay at length on the alliance between religion and philosophy. Sounding very much like a prosaic version of the "Prologue" to Tennyson's *In Memoriam*, Mackay writes:

> Religion and science are inseparable. No object in nature, no subject of contemplation is destitute of a religious tendency and meaning. . . . Faith [is] the inseparable companion and offspring of knowledge . . . Faith, as opposed to that blind submission to inexplicable power which usurped its name in the ancient East, is an allegiance of the reason; and as the "evidence of things unseen," stands on the verge of mysticism, its value must depend on the discretion with which it is formed and used.

In a statement resonating with Kearney's ideas, Mackay states, "True faith is a belief in things probable."[18] Equally important to George Eliot's work is Mackay's criticism of the pervasive understanding of religion as having "nothing to do with the head" but rather as "exclusively an exercise of the heart and feelings" meant to train moral character yet leaving the feeling "uneducated," abandoned by reason.[19] It might not be overstating the case to cite this essay as the central text of George Eliot's philosophy, except that to do so would contradict the philosophy it states. For, as I mentioned above, it is crucial to recognize how vital to her work is this belief in progress.[20] And it is interesting to note that in her last novel, *Daniel Deronda*, as we will see in chapter 4, her religious revisioning finds her back before her own time, in a kind of mystical Judaism. In her own way, then, George Eliot was engaged in the work that Carlyle called retailoring the tailor, refashioning the myth for a new age. And as with Carlyle, Mackay's mention of mysticism is apt, in that this is about a new way of seeing the "evidence of things unseen" which is faith.

Incarnation

Another way of talking about this is in terms of "incarnation," in Christian terms the doctrine that God took on human nature in Jesus Christ: the Word became flesh; the Idea became actual. This is of course the central doctrine of dispute at this time. Strauss takes enormous pains respectfully to debunk the possibility of a historical Jesus and reaffirms the Idea of Jesus despite his lack of historicity; he redefines the incarnation as the idea of humanity as a whole incarnating Christ, pointing to the evolution of an ideal human type. Feuerbach famously turns theology into anthropology, seeing the idea of God incarnate as a projection of human need and desire. It is primarily in her response to various works, mainly in the form of reviews and, in the case of Strauss and Feuerbach, in her translations, that the writer who would become George Eliot (hereafter referred to by that name) articulates her own understanding of the incarnation, but essential to her response is what Kierkegaard would call "indirection." This approach is evident in two main ways: first, in her refusal to articulate a positive doctrine. As she writes in a letter in 1870, "I have an unreasonable aversion to personal statements. . . . I shrink from decided 'deliverances' on momentous subjects, from the dread of coming to swear by my own 'deliverances' and sinking into an insistent echo of myself."[21] Secondly, implicit throughout her fiction is the kind of secular faith expressed in my epigraph from *Adam Bede*: the belief that finding the truth of things is a matter of discovering and interpreting what has been revealed to the individual heart and remains otherwise hidden. In Hennell and Strauss she found an articulation of her own understanding of faith as a matter of mythical rather than historical truth, and this understanding of the power of story soon led to her own creation of stories that speak of and indeed seek to incarnate human and divine truths, their language redolent with biblical echoes. But even when she agreed with them on important matters, none of the writers she studied satisfied her. While convinced of the merit of the scientific view of the fundamental power of nature, for example, she famously refused to embrace Darwin's *Origin of Species*: "But to me the Development theory and all other explanations of processes by which things come to be, produce a feeble impression compared with the mystery that lies under the processes."[22]

It is possible, then, to trace what we might call the progress of George Eliot's own intellect and her understanding of faith through her works, and I would like now to highlight views that point to her understanding of incarnation. First, however, it is important to clarify how I am using the term "incarnation" for, as Gerald O'Collins points out as he begins his book of that title, the primary theological meaning of incarnation—that God became a man—needs to be distinguished from the common usage by which we describe someone as incarnating a particular quality.[23] Yet, as the writer Kathleen Norris makes clear—beginning with her pointed indefinite article in "A Word Made Flesh"—incarnation can be seen as the task of all writers, who are advised to "show, do not tell": good fiction-writing aims to embody and reveal the truth, rather than argue it discursively.[24] Further, related to this is the common understanding of the importance of matching actions to words, commonly called practicing what one preaches—an ethical demand that carries greater weight for writers, who, after all, live by words. It is for these reasons that, as A. S. Byatt notes in her discussion of George Eliot's understanding of fiction, the question of how to write fiction—because it is a question of bringing together form and substance—became so pressing in the century that challenged the meaning of the Christian concept of the incarnation.[25]

As I hope will become clear, George Eliot's struggles over the form of her fiction were always struggles to incarnate her ideas in Norris's sense and were always, at least implicitly and often explicitly, deeply entangled with her own beliefs regarding the incarnation of Christ. In what follows I will highlight four main ways in which George Eliot's complex understanding of incarnation emerges in her work: first, as suggested above, in the sense of nature itself manifesting the immanent presence of God; second, in her conviction that genuine Christians will put their beliefs into action in the form of love; third, in the way that she affirms the value of the lives and the words of ordinary folk; and, fourth—the foundation for her entire incarnational aesthetic—in the way that she affirms empathetic understanding and ultimately suffering for others as the basis of ethical and fully human living.

George Eliot's sense of the importance of incarnation and her struggles over its implications are evident in one or more of these four ways in all of her nonfiction. As I mentioned above, she takes from Hennell a completely naturalized, and then from Strauss a demythologized, view of the divine, but in the same year as her translation of Strauss's *Life of Jesus* is published she speaks with conviction of "the grand law which God has impressed on all nature—the production and development of life."[26] While this is far from a belief in the incarnation of Christ of course, it does testify to her fundamental sense of nature's giving physical form to the divine. More telling is George Eliot's conflicted response to Strauss's deconstruction of the idea of God becoming a man: throughout her work on Strauss George Eliot famously grieved for the image of Christ she was abetting him to desecrate. As her biographer Gordon Haight reports:

> [She] had a cast about twenty inches high of Thorwaldsen's "Risen Christ" standing in her study, and on the wall an engraving of Delaroche's *Christ*, which she had once thought of using for a frontispiece. She told the Brays that "she was Strauss-sick—it made her ill dissecting the beautiful story of the crucifixion, and only the sight of her Christ-image and picture made her endure it."[27]

It is interesting to note that her very body rebelled against the words that sought to demythologize the notion of an embodied God.

It is noteworthy that George Eliot's reviews of Froude and Mackay, with her implied affirmation of their understanding of the incarnation in terms of progressive revelation, follow her Strauss translation in 1849 and 1851 respectively. One can surely speculate that she was seeking a way to reconcile current knowledge with ideas of faith. It is widely understood that she found this a few years later in Feuerbach's religion of feeling, and I certainly agree that his translation of the theological question of incarnation into anthropological terms and his focus on human feeling as its source and ground—particularly since her work of translating Feuerbach coincided with her becoming intimately involved with the decidedly godless Lewes[28]—satisfied for a time her need to reconcile her rational views with her feelings. But, as with Strauss, her endorsement of Feuerbach was measured according to her determination not to allow her desire for faith to override the truth of experience.

I will speak more of George Eliot's response to Strauss and Feuerbach when I discuss her early fiction, but it is worth noting here the shift in her theological interest that took place around this time, owing partly at least to her happiness with Lewes and the consequent or at least concurrent move farther away from the Unitarian Bray/Hennell family, with whom she had conducted lively debates about pressing matters of faith. Now, and increasingly as she submerges herself more deeply into her fiction and into her relationship with Lewes, she responds to Sara Hennell's earnest efforts to clarify doctrines of faith as a mildly interested observer of her friend's work rather than as a participant in the debates.[29] For a time, indeed, George Eliot shifts attention beyond Christianity to broader theological concerns as she begins translating Spinoza, thus engaging in a more strictly philosophical way in questions of theology, ethics, and metaphysics.[30]

All of these efforts turn out to be significant stepping-stones toward the emergence of George Eliot the novelist, and I want to mention three essays of the time in the context of her developing understanding of incarnation. The first two, "Evangelical Teaching: Dr. Cumming," published in 1855, and "Worldliness and Other-Worldliness: The Poet Young," published two years later, are mainly taken up with the second meaning of incarnation mentioned above, the failure of these two clerics to incarnate their faith in love. The first is a scathing rebuke of an evangelical preacher, whose "*absence of genuine charity*" and "*perverted moral judgement*" incur the wrath of a vitriolic pen.[31] More fortunate than Dr. Cumming in being a century dead, the poet Edward Young comes under her scrutiny as "a remarkable individual of the species *divine*," whom she charges with "*radical insincerity as a poetic artist* . . . deficient intellectual activity and deficient feeling."[32] Throughout this piece, as in this comment, we note George Eliot's understanding of the interrelation of the two senses of incarnation that Norris speaks of, in her conviction that, for a Christian writer, bad poetry—both intellectually vapid and emotionally false—follows from an inadequate expression (one could say incarnation) of love. Interesting as well is the fact that both Cumming and Young serve as foils for her to express a truer idea of Christianity. "The best minds that accept Christianity as a divinely inspired system," she writes, "believe that the great end of the Gospel is not merely the saving but the educating of men's souls, the creating within them of holy dispositions, the subduing of egotistical pretensions, and the perpetual enhancing of the desire that the will of God—a will synonymous with goodness and truth—may be done on earth."[33] "The highest state of mind inculcated by the Gospel," she goes on, "is resignation to the disposal of God's providence . . . it is to dwell in Christ by spiritual communion with his nature, not to fix the date when He shall appear in the sky."[34] In contrast to Young's "deficiency in moral, i.e., in sympathetic emotion," she celebrates Cowper's *The Task* "in the genuine love that it breathes."[35] George Eliot's wrath is provoked against both Cumming and Young for their hypocrisy and the superficial thinking that goes along with a lack of genuine charity and sympathy; like a latter-day Chaucer, she lays bare their failure to practice what they preach, as the saying goes, or, in other words, to demonstrate the word incarnate.

Norris's idea that incarnation for a writer means "show, do not tell" also comes to mind in considering an essay George Eliot published between these two. "Silly Novels by Lady Novelists" is even more caustic but also hilarious, not only perhaps because the object of her rebuke is her own sex but because she was soon to become a "lady novelist" herself. The lady novelists are charged with failings similar to those of the writer clerics above, particularly since their pious aim is to represent Christian ideas. Concerning their attempts to describe human beings, George Eliot charges them with a complete lack of experience "in every form of poverty except poverty of brains" and the consequent complete "want of verisimilitude."[36] The lady novelist of the "*oracular* species" fails to convey spiritual truths, a failing which is not surprising since "the means by which she usually chooses to conduct you to true ideas of the invisible is a totally false picture of the visible."[37] Interesting here again, then, is her sense that bringing ideas to life in fiction requires a full intellectual and emotional engagement with real-life experience, a notion that suggests her conviction of the interrelation of incarnation and realism.

Even more amusing is George Eliot's send-up of these poor ladies' attempts at philosophical reflection in their fiction: "Lady novelists, it appears, can see something else besides matter; they are not limited to phenomena, but can relieve their eyesight by occasional glimpses of the *noumenon*, and are, therefore, naturally better able than anyone else to confound sceptics, even of that remarkable but to us unknown school, which maintains that the soul of man is of the same texture as the polypus."[38] Further, as poor as the lady novelist is at representing chivalry, "we like the authoress much better on her medieval stilts than on her oracular ones—when she talks of the *Ich* and of 'subjective' and 'objective.'"[39] The humor here is of course all the more delicious when we realize that George Eliot is making great fun at the expense of the "lady novelists" who fail at doing just what she wants to do: to dramatize in fiction the philosophical and theological ideas that were in the air by incarnating these ideas in the persons of clerics and their female parishioners, a desire that was soon to bear fruit in the three *Scenes of Clerical Life*.

I will talk in more detail about one of these *Scenes* later in this chapter when I focus on the idea of inwardness, but here I want first to follow the theme of incarnation. No one could fail to notice the change in tone from these essays to the stories, which, while anatomizing in sharp detail the failings of various specimens of the divine, never revert to what Rosemary Ashton calls the "magnificent malice" of the essays.[40] Flawed as these clergymen are, riddled as Amos Barton, for example, surely is with the egotism, shallowness, and vanity that would place him firmly among the evangelical preachers she describes in the opening sentence of the essay on Dr. Cumming, the storyteller moves from satirizing and bemoaning Barton's faults to sympathizing with, perhaps we might say forgiving, his weaknesses and vulnerabilities and even appreciating his few and feeble strengths. Whereas the essayist might herself have been accused of the "lack of genuine charity" she identifies in her targets, the novelist promotes and reflects the kind of fellow feeling that becomes one of the markers of her aesthetic, as she encourages readers to forgive as they would be forgiven. Indeed, particularly in the first story, many find an excess of sympathizing and an overflow of sentiment.

As Elizabeth Jay points out, it is perhaps not surprising that George Eliot should be more careful in writing her stories, since, while she could count on her essays being read by like-minded radicals, who would expect a critique of Christianity from the *Westminster Review*, her stories are meant for the general reading public, and she would be careful not to offend.[41] While this is undoubtedly likely, to me a more important idea emerges here: in writing fiction, I believe, George Eliot encountered a different kind of truth. Bringing characters to life in words demanded a kind of entry into human experience that commanded sympathy.[42] And here it is interesting to look behind the scenes. Because George Eliot published these first stories anonymously, there was much discussion in the reading world about who the author could be. Most readers guessed a cleric, some a cleric who was also a man of science, some crediting his wife with the so-called feminine touches. Much of the speculation fed on trying to identify the real models for the characters. Of interest at this stage in George Eliot's life is the great drama that would ensue, which came to a head after the anonymous publication of her first novel, *Adam Bede*, when characters in the novel and stories were identified—some of them accurately—with actual people. The drama intensified when a certain Mr. Liggins was widely held to be the real George Eliot and when *Adam Bede, Junior*, a sequel to her novel by another pretender, was announced.

Here was a real confusion between reality and imagination, which soon led George Eliot to disclose her true identity. Obviously, the stakes were high, if a woman—and a freethinking woman at that—came to be revealed as the author of these stories of clerical lives and Christian themes.[43] But more interesting for my purposes here is the struggle one reads of in the letters of this time, when George Eliot seems genuinely surprised to find that some of her characters are recognizable as based on actual people. While she staunchly and eloquently argues for the authenticity of the artistic imagination, in several cases she maintains silence, presumably rather than lie. What seems to be unfolding here is her own understanding of the nature of imagination; she learns that she is bringing to life on the page not abstractions but real persons. The source for her characters is not, as she had supposed, only her imagination, but her imagination drawing from her memory. Of course she always had known that she was writing about what she remembered, but this controversy was crucial in furthering her sense of the mysteries of imagination, and central to this realization was her understanding of incarnation.

I referred above to A. S. Byatt's edition of George Eliot's essays, in which she dedicates a whole section of her introduction to "Incarnation." It begins:

> The long nineteenth-century debate about the precise meaning, or lack of meaning, of the Christian concept of the Incarnation, the meeting-point of the divine and the human, the infinite and the finite, is inextricably connected, consciously and unconsciously, to the development of the form of the novel.[44]

Byatt's thesis certainly is borne out in George Eliot's case. Despite turning away from the church of her youth, she continued to follow Christian themes and characters in all of her fiction, beginning with a whole volume dedicated to "clerical life." For, while she abandoned religion in the institutional sense, she not only promoted what she saw as the essential truths of Christianity but proclaimed in a letter, "writing is part of my religion."[45] Indeed, it might be said that writing became her religion, and that its most recognizable tenet was the living out of the incarnation. Byatt quotes a letter George Eliot wrote during a correspondence in 1866 with the Positivist Frederic Harrison, who wanted her to use her fiction to represent his philosophy, with which she was in some agreement at the time. In this letter George Eliot explicitly speaks of her incarnational aesthetic, as she writes of having "gone through again and again the severe effort of trying to make certain ideas thoroughly incarnate, as if they had revealed themselves to me first in the flesh and not in the spirit."[46] Here George Eliot echoes Kathleen Norris's understanding of the writer's practice: even as the incarnation was the Word made flesh, her job as an artist was the Word (or spirit) made word (fiction) in the incarnate "flesh" of her characters. This has huge implications for the doctrine of her so-called realism, which she is claiming here was never about imitating real people. The origin, rather, is "in the spirit."[47]

I want to show now how George Eliot's realist aesthetic, most explicitly articulated in chapter 17 of her first novel, *Adam Bede*, which was published a year after *Scenes of Clerical Life*, is at the same time a doctrine of incarnation, by illustrating the four main ways (cited above) in which George Eliot's understanding of incarnation is manifest. Concerning the first point, the immanent presence of God in nature, George Eliot's fullest response to Darwin (mentioned above) comes in the "indirect" form of her fiction. Throughout her early works in particular many have noted a Wordsworthian celebration of nature and of ordinary human nature, an approach that reflects as well what Erich Auerbach calls the *sermo humilis* that characterizes the language of the Bible, in whose heroes "humiliation and elevation" meet.[48] One example from "Janet's Repentance," the third "Scene," represents many. Commenting on how the restoration of Janet's spirit lends wonder to "the flowerless monotony" of an ordinary walk, the narrator says: "A very commonplace scene indeed. But what scene was ever commonplace in the descending sunlight, when colour has awakened from its noonday sleep, and long shadows awe us like a disclosed presence?"[49] Extending this view, *Adam Bede,* her novel of the same year as Darwin's *Origin of Species*, positively revels in the power of nature and its Ecclesiastes-like imperviousness to human woes. But for George Eliot's narrator the facts of evolution and natural selection are the text for a lesson: as "children" of nature's "large family," we must learn "to be content with little nurture and caressing, and help each other the more."[50] In other words, the inexorable inhuman power of nature calls human beings to be all the more human. *Adam Bede* reflects the understanding that pervades George Eliot's early fiction that the natural tragedies of human experience are the site of a kind of natural redemption that carries hints of an underlying supernatural "mystery."

The second way in which George Eliot demonstrates the mutually reinforcing doctrines of realism and incarnation in *Adam Bede* is to promote an anti-doctrinal form of Christianity that is lived out in the form of love and sympathy (what we would call empathy or compassion) for the weak among us. The two main clerics here are the Anglican Reverend Irwine and the Methodist Dinah Morris, who show their true Christian character by putting doctrine aside in favor of love. Despite Dinah's rather otherworldly, asexual character (eventually modified when she falls in love), George Eliot convinces readers to see past Dinah's prim exterior to the genuine faith and love that pervade her spirit. Like Adam, we might not accept her words except that we see her acting on them: "I don't know what I should ha' thought of her and her letter if I'd never seen her,"[51] he says, thus testifying to a faith in her words because of the genuineness of her actions, the incarnation of her words. Extending this one step further, we could say that George Eliot wants us to believe, not what Dinah believes, but in the Dinah who believes it.

With Reverend Irwine, George Eliot produces another in her lifelong series of flawed but in this case highly admirable Anglican clerics. As is her wont, she interrupts the flow of her narrative about a third of the way through with the famous chapter 17, entitled, à la Fielding, "In Which the Story Pauses a Little." By this time, we have already been introduced to Mr. Irwine by her characteristic method (of which more later) of taking us into his home, where he lives with his mother and unmarried, dependent sisters, one of them ill in the irritating way of nineteenth-century ladies, and we have seen him treat his family members and a semiliterate pompous parishioner with deep respect and consummate courtesy. The narrator even makes sure that we notice that he takes off his shoes upon entering the sickroom. But we have also seen him, with huge consequences, miss the opportunity to hear the confession of a young gentleman who visits him, thereby failing to avert the tragedy that is the story's center. This clerical failure is the catalyst for the narrator's interjection, as he[52] feels the need to persuade his readers of the worthiness of his cleric. Here follows the famous manifesto of realism in which George Eliot, echoing Wordsworth's "Preface," declares her dedication to "the faithful representing of commonplace things."[53] While much has been made of the realist's commitment to represent "vulgar details," it is clear that George Eliot sees "Art" as called to be representative of ordinary life in the context of a love of beauty, not just for its own abstract sense (which she seems to mock as "the divine beauty of form"), but in the form of its "secret of deep human sympathy."

> Therefore let Art always remind us of ["these common, coarse people"]; therefore let us always have men ready to give the loving pains of a life to the faithful representing of commonplace things—men who see beauty in these commonplace things, and delight in showing how kindly the light of heaven falls on them.[54]

This dual commitment pervades her whole career: as she proclaims here, "paint us an angel, if you can, with a floating violet robe, and a face paled by celestial light; paint us yet oftener a Madonna," but do not "banish from the region of Art those old women scraping carrots."[55] Indeed this is, I think, more than an aesthetic code to her; it is a religious doctrine.[56]

Years later, in the letter to Harrison quoted above, George Eliot states this in her own terms: "I think aesthetic teaching is the highest of all teaching because it deals with life in its highest complexity. But if it ceases to be purely aesthetic—if it lapses anywhere from the picture to the diagram—it becomes the most offensive of all teaching."[57] What is most interesting to me is the way that her discussion of art in chapter 17 of *Adam Bede*, which we might see as a violation of her own doctrine, in that she feels compelled to speak in abstract, diagrammatic terms of her belief instead of letting her "picture" express itself through story and character, in a larger sense does exactly represent her belief, in that her defense of Mr. Irwine is also a defense of her art, and vice versa. She moves seamlessly from the outline of her aesthetic to Adam's defense of Mr. Irwine and his non-doctrinal brand of religion that spills over from the pulpit into the mundane activities of his life. In other words, Mr. Irwine is like George Eliot herself, whose art loves her characters despite what they believe or even how they behave. When she talks about her art, she is also talking about religion; when she tells her reader, echoing the Book of Common Prayer, that here is a man "with whom I desire you to be in perfect charity,"[58] she is also echoing Mr. Irwine himself, who would not only speak the words of Common Prayer but would speak the words and perform the acts of charity to everyone. She would have her readers do unto him as they would be done by, as she is doing by him and by every one of her characters, in charity. It is supremely logical, then, that George Eliot moves in one chapter from a defense of her aesthetic to a defense of her cleric. The relation between the two is essential; her job as an artist is to represent her cleric as he really is and to treat him with the same loving care that he treats his parishioners. Understanding that "the true and the good are one," as she says in her essay on Mackay, is "the essential element of religion."[59]

Language is important to this aesthetic—as central as it is to Wordsworth—and while George Eliot might be seen to violate her own code when she soars off into a eulogy of art, her true love for the common folk comes out when she speaks their language, always a moment of genuine sympathy and pleasure for the reader. When the narrator says, for example, that Mrs. Poyser "thanked God she never had any of your varnished rubbish in her house," George Eliot has thoroughly entered into the canny, honest pride of the farmer's wife.[60] Likewise her immersion in biblical culture is clear when she has her characters speak the language of Methodists. She too, then, is practicing what she preaches in using "loving pains" to bring her characters to life, thereby exemplifying the third way in which her incarnational aesthetic takes realistic shape. And here we touch on the key element in George Eliot's understanding of the incarnation, which underlies her whole aesthetic and provides the major theme of *Adam Bede*: the necessity for and the meaning of suffering, or, as she calls it in that novel the "mystery of human sorrow."[61]

Feuerbach's description of the God who is made in the image of man turns on the human desire for a God who loves us to the point of excruciating suffering and painful death. He writes eloquently of the idolatry of feeling that produces the idea of an incarnated god. "But the proposition: God is a feeling Being," Marian Evans translates him as writing, "is only the religious paraphrase of the proposition: feeling is absolute, divine in its nature."[62] In another famous section (chapter 25), Feuerbach celebrates the value of bread and water as purely physical substances, thereby naturalizing the elements of Christian sacraments. Both of these ideas have been widely used to support readings of a Feuerbachian *Adam Bede*. And generally critics see in the novel either a naturalizing of the sacred or a sacramentalizing of the natural. Both of these perspectives are valid, I think, because they are rather mutually illuminating than oppositional. As I noted before, George Eliot represents her two key religious characters as genuine embodiments of their beliefs, meaning that they practice what they believe in (although Rev. Irwine's beliefs are stated as expressions of his church affiliation, rather than in more personal terms). And she affirms the faith of these characters as being founded in what has been seen as a Feuerbachian kind of religious feeling. Dinah's faith, for example, is expressed in terms of the kind of Methodist "inner light" which she experiences as a deep feeling of God's presence and guidance. And Adam, likewise, expresses his own non-Methodist faith and affirms that of Rev. Irwine in terms of "deep, speritial things in religion" that are matters of "feelings," not "doctrines and notions."[63] Throughout, George Eliot affirms feeling as an expression of human participation in "an unfathomable ocean of love and beauty" that makes human love "hardly distinguishable from religious feeling."[64] Adam, for example, in trying to win Dinah away from religious feeling to feeling for him, says, "feeling's a sort of knowledge"[65] and Dinah's ultimate affirmation of the incarnation, one might say, is expressed in her ability to love God and Adam.

But the fullest expression of this capacity for feeling is through sympathy with weaker fellow beings and the suffering this entails. The whole novel is based on a demonstration of what must be seen as the essence of the Christian doctrine of incarnation, the transformative power of suffering,[66] as George Eliot implicitly argues against the hated doctrine of compensation on the one hand and the notion of meaningless pain on the other.[67] The most explicit reference to the Christian interpretation of suffering in the novel comes in a curious incident when the narrator notes how he has come across, in foreign lands (never in his own Loamshire) "an image of great agony: the agony of the cross." He speculates that a traveler who did not know the meaning of "this image of agony" would "find it strangely out of place in the midst of this joyous nature," not knowing that it pointed to the sufferings of some "foolish lost lamb," such as the wayfaring Hetty. He goes on, "No wonder man's religion has much sorrow in it: no wonder he needs a suffering God."[68] This moment echoes the much-repeated report (cited above) that while Evans was translating Strauss "it made her ill dissecting the beautiful story of the crucifixion, and only the sight of her Christ-image and picture made her endure it."[69] George Eliot continued to have a strong attraction to the story of a suffering savior. And, while it is easily possible to read *Adam Bede* as a revisioning of the incarnation in Feuerbachian terms, the image of Hetty as a straying lamb is one of many allusions to Christ's parables that points to Eliot's non-Feuerbachian response. For George Eliot could not think of God as what Feuerbach calls "a commonplace book, a nucleus of aggregation" from which humans derive "an aim" for moral action.[70] And, perhaps in spite of herself, her own stories reflect an aesthetic that is grounded in an incarnational approach that is modeled after the parables and stories of the incarnated God.

As I mentioned before, it is crucial to recognize George Eliot's indirection as essential to her approach. Like Kierkegaard, I would argue, she uses stories, not to tell the reader what to believe, but to inspire in the individual reader a belief in her or his own "capability of an altered vision." Like Kierkegaard's parables, as described by the theologian Thomas Oden, her stories "intend to communicate an enriched capacity for self-examination leading to increased moral sensitivity and intensified spirituality."[71] As the theologian and storyteller John Shea puts it, "A Christian culture must always generate secondary forms. The imagination must play with the story of Jesus and resymbolize it under the influences of the present experiences of the Spirit."[72] Like Jesus, in fact, Christian storytellers must release their stories and allow for this kind of "play" of interpretation. It is important, then, to affirm for George Eliot's stories the possibility of differing interpretations, because just such hermeneutic openness is essential to her aesthetic, even as it was essential to Christ's storytelling. One reader may in fact see her stories as affirming Feuerbach's religion of humanity, and another reader may not. The only thing one can say with certainty is that she leaves the theological meaning a matter of interpretation, demanding only that readers recognize the personal message of love and charity. And perhaps in this regard, oddly enough, she is imitating the message of the Gospel: as Adam says, it isn't notions and doctrines, but actions and feelings that count.

Inwardness

George Eliot's understanding of incarnation is knit together with her understanding of inwardness. Firstly, in a way that I have already been suggesting, incarnation—in religion and in art—is a matter of revealing what will remain hidden to those who do not have eyes to see (and various forms of the trope of vision and blindness, as has often been noted, are rife in her work). While George Eliot is clear that her call as an artist is to represent the "commonplace things," it is at the same time "to see beauty" in them: women peeling carrots need to be represented alongside angels and madonnas. In this respect she is explicit about the fact that the manifest superiority of her major characters—Adam, Dinah, and Rev. Irwine—is based on the extraordinary perceptual ability that they share with their creator: the ability to see beauty and worth in apparent unworthiness. Throughout her career George Eliot represents social groups in need of a special person. What qualifies these characters as special is their capacity for inwardness. Inwardness is the corollary to incarnation, in that while incarnation makes the idea visible (though as noted above, infinitely debatable), inwardness is a matter of a hidden, invisible, "unfathomable" space of engagement.[73]

Most readers associate George Eliot with the idea of inwardness in the form of her masterful psychological approach to character, and Michael Davis's recent book situates her skill in the context of nineteenth-century psychology, showing her conversance with a complex and erudite mass of contemporary works on psychology, most importantly those of her husband. Davis includes a chapter on religion and science, focusing on *Daniel Deronda*, but the extent of the interplay in George Eliot's work between religious consciousness and psychological consciousness has not, to my knowledge, been explored. Davis finds abundant evidence in George Eliot's works for two points that are fundamental to what I want to argue here: he reiterates how important to George Eliot is the fact of individuality, including the individuality of each consciousness; and the fact of unknowability: that each mind is to a great extent an unknown, not only to others, but, I would argue, to itself.[74] In light of the wave of philosophical debate on this issue—notably, as I have mentioned, Strauss's argument for a universal human and Comte's idea of a kind of social salvation—George Eliot's adherence to the belief in an ultimately mysterious individuality is important. In fact, I want to argue, her belief in individuality, and the inwardness that is its marker, is profoundly religious.[75]

Charles Taylor speaks of the idea of inwardness when he traces the development of the modern sense of the self, showing that it is Augustine who first invokes "the language of inwardness," thus creating what Taylor calls "a stance of radical reflexivity."[76] Augustine takes this step from ontology to epistemology to show that "God is to be found in the intimacy of self-presence,"[77] but Descartes later concludes that what we find in this space is not God, but our selves. I turn again here to Kierkegaard, the great prophet of inwardness and individuality. Although George Eliot never knew his work, so far as I have been able to discover, Kierkegaard's response to the great Hegelian wave, including Feuerbach, is useful to establish the ground of my argument because it is based on an aversion to Hegel's dismantling of the importance of individuality, an aversion which George Eliot clearly shared. Feuerbach turns the space of inwardness—human subjectivity—into a reflector of and projector onto the outer world. "I unconditionally repudiate *absolute*, immaterial, self-sufficing speculation—that speculation which draws its material from within," he asserts; "I hold *that* alone to be an object which has an existence beyond one's own brain."[78] Feuerbach wants to turn the gaze of religion "from the internal to the external," from "the sign to the thing signified."[79] The supposed object of religious feeling, he claims, is also its subject: "thy own being."[80] There is only our perception, he would say, which claims to find outside what is really just inside of us; we would understand this if we truly appreciated what is really outside of ourselves, natural elements such as bread and wine, for example.[81] (No wonder the "silly ladies" were confused.)

In opposition to such ideas, Kierkegaard's consuming passion was to restore authenticity to contemporary Christianity by rescuing the essential ingredient that he saw as being destroyed in Hegel's philosophy—the individual—and to do so by redefining the individual as the religious subject. Kierkegaard identifies the meaning of existing as a human being with existing religiously; that is, with a sense of what he calls inwardness.[82] For Kierkegaard, "subjectivity," for individuals located in time, "is the truth" and "the truth exists for them in inwardness."[83] Also relevant to my argument here is Kierkegaard's understanding of the meaning of suffering: it is only when suffering "turns the person inward," he says, with Keatsian resonance, that a person can "*become an individual.*"[84]

George Eliot's attention to inwardness, in terms very similar to Kierkegaard's, constitutes a virtual epistemology, if not a theology, of interiority. Indeed, it seems to me that her understanding of inwardness takes her away from Feuerbach and toward Kierkegaard. In writing to a friend to explain how she could have written in *Adam Bede* of Evangelical Christianity from the inside, as it were, George Eliot writes that, despite her rejection of "dogmatic Christianity," her experience from the ages of 15 to 22 among Evangelicals left her with "the profoundest interest in the inward life of sincere Christians."[85] And though she acknowledges here that "that inward self" of her own has changed since those years, it is clear that, as Gordon Haight writes in his "Introduction" to her *Letters,* "Without her intimate knowledge of the Evangelical mind George Eliot would have lacked part of the experience on which her wide sympathy was founded."[86] It is in fact her insistence on interiority that is the basis of her characterization and her epistemology.

There are two main elements to George Eliot's epistemology of interiority. The first is the repeated, multifaceted invitation to readers to "come inside"—the church, the farmhouse, the bedchamber, the mind of her characters. In a way, George Eliot is the great historian of human conscience and consciousness because of her profound sense of inner space, and of the difference between the outside and the inside, of surface and depth, which she represents as markers of egotism. One of many memorable moments that construct this sense of different spatial orientations is the "Bed-chambers" chapter in *Adam Bede,*[87] when Hetty's solipsistic and shallow gaze in the mirror is contrasted with Dinah's visionary gaze out the window and up to the sky.[88] (Taylor might call this reflection vs. reflexivity.) Related to this and also represented well in Hetty and Dinah is the kind of "feeling knowledge" that George Eliot celebrates: a knowing that is not only sympathetic or empathetic but personal and individual and costly. It is a knowing that is a kind of suffering because it requires that one enter in to the experience of the other.[89] As I've said, sympathetic imagination is the mark of George Eliot's religious and aesthetic code. As many have noted, she was fortunate to have George Henry Lewes as her first and her ideal reader; it was largely because her first reader was an intelligent man who loved her that she was able to love her characters into existence. And indeed, her letters record how making him cry was the sign that she had engaged his sympathetic imagination. If she could make this intellectual, critical, unchurched man cry about the sorrows of "an Evangelical curate and a woman with 'spiritual' weaknesses," as Lewes described the main characters of "Janet's Repentance,"[90] then, she believed, she had done something worth doing.[91]

George Eliot's understanding of interior being, like Kierkegaard's, is most often constructed in terms of an intimate relationship, not of romantic love, which she leaves to our imaginations, but of confession.[92] It is at this site of intimacy that her desire to "make others feel" what she feels[93] is most evident, just as Dinah's desire to make others believe what she believes is most powerful and effective not when she is preaching in public space but when she is fighting for the soul of Hetty in the richly symbolic prison cell. The confession scene in "Janet's Repentance" is the climax of a story that is based on a real-life situation from the time when George Eliot's "inward self" was developing in the Evangelical community. In one of her many stories of rescue, the abused, wayward Janet is saved by the intervention of the Evangelical minister, Mr. Tryan, another of George Eliot's admired clerics. This is the third of the clerical *Scenes*, and from the first page of the first one, when the reader is bid to "pass through the baize doors," she now arrives at the inner sanctum of intersubjectivity. George Eliot frames the narrative with pleas to the reader to recognize that "the only true knowledge of our fellow-man is that which enables us to feel with him"; that, whatever the followers of the "philosophic Deity" of abstraction might tell us, one lost sheep shows the "transcendent value of human pain"; that "analysis" must be "lit up by . . . love"; that "feelings of trust and resignation" must fill up the blanks of "the margin of ignorance which surrounds all our knowledge."[94] Mr. Tryan proves a worthy confessor when, accepting that necessary ignorance, he "enter[s] into the only half-expressed secrets of her spiritual weakness" and responds to Janet's need for confession with a confession of his own.[95] George Eliot makes clear that for Janet and Mr. Tryan this confession takes place in the inward space that Augustine and Kierkegaard posit, even seeming to invoke the latter when she writes that "confiding in human sympathy . . . prepared [Janet's] soul for that stronger leap by which faith grasps the idea of divine sympathy."[96] In explicitly differentiating on the last page of the story between Janet's sense of the "Divine love that had rescued her" and the "human love" that had mediated the rescue, George Eliot constructs the inward self as what Kierkegaard calls "a relation" to both the human and the divine other.[97]

What is remarkable, however, is George Eliot's intention to show that even the shallowest characters, notably Hetty, have a depth, an inside, which is far from evident on the surface; or that they have a possible depth, which can be learned or perhaps constructed, with the help of a loving community, by their response to suffering. Along with that of Hetty, George Eliot's exploration of Silas Marner's consciousness is a brilliant example, as I will discuss in chapter 5.[98] Hetty's failure is represented as a kind of childish but at the same time vicious egotism that manifests itself as a failure of empathy and a complete self-absorption, as if she is stuck in a Lacanian pre-linguistic mirror state. In fact she is nothing but a reflection. And the huge struggle in the prison cell, which Dinah sees as a spiritual battle to save Hetty's soul before she is executed, is at the same time an intense struggle to make Hetty see that there is something besides herself in the world, that there is an outside, and, conversely, an inside, to herself. Hetty's failure throughout the novel is not only a moral and emotional failure but fundamentally a failure of imagination, which to George Eliot is at the same time a failure of memory and of belief, which together constitute for her the basis of human fellowship and community and of individual identity.

George Eliot delves more deeply into the fraught relation between imagination, memory, and identity in her next works. Although many see George Eliot's early period as including *Silas Marner*, mainly because of its obvious affinity in setting and tone, I believe that in a psychological and religious sense this novel is written on the other side of a great divide, nicely symbolized by the bridge that the narrator leans on in chapter 1 of *The Mill on the Floss*, the novel that follows a year after *Adam Bede*. For *Silas Marner*, while it deals with the time of her early experience in the Midlands, is written from the perspective of the writer who has used earlier fictions to take her beyond that formative time.

Along with Wordsworth and Dickens, George Eliot helped create a more vivid evocation of childhood than readers had before seen. The importance of childhood to the shaping of consciousness and identity is most strongly represented in *The Mill on the Floss*, where its memory and imaginative reconstruction are represented, as in Wordsworth, as a religious shrine.[99] For George Eliot, our response to "the joy of childhood" is deeply akin to our response to religious experience, and her sense of the interrelation of memory, imagination, and faith is nicely captured in the midst of a description of Adam's faith in Hetty: though "much" of "the joy of childhood" has "vanish[ed] utterly from our memory" and "is gone forever from our imagination," she writes, "we can only *believe* in" it.[100] It is interesting that in *The Mill on the Floss*, which, rooted as it is in a working out of the trauma of familial and social rejection, is certainly the most autobiographical of her novels, George Eliot asks the reader to "believe in" Maggie's childhood joy while showing how much of the purported joy was a product of Maggie's imagination, mixing memory and desire, breeding lilacs out of the dead land.

The Mill on the Floss clearly puts a whole other spin on the idea of inwardness, first of all simply in taking George Eliot to a deeper inward place than any of her other works. Before looking further at the implications of this, I want to bring in to the discussion a short story, published between *Adam Bede* and *The Mill*, which served as a kind of doorkeeper to this other level of interiority. For my purposes the story bears the perfect title "The Lifted Veil," for it is densely figured with inwardness. The story is unique in George Eliot's opus in that it is a dark Gothic tale about a very unpleasant, self-centered, melancholy young man with unusual powers of insight. It comes at a crucial juncture following the revelation of George Eliot's real identity after she became fed up with being impersonated; and, given the associations of the veil with marriage and discretion, it seems to reflect anxieties of self-exposure, not only as an author but as a common-law wife who is daring, after all, to preach to her readers.[101] Two of George Eliot's most famous statements are relevant here. One (mentioned earlier) is her comment in a letter of this time with regard to Darwin's *Origin of Species*: "But to me the Development theory and all other explanations of processes by which things come to be, produce a feeble impression compared with the mystery that lies under the processes."[102] The other is the famous squirrel sentence from *Middlemarch*, commenting on the hidden tragedy that comprises ordinary experience: "If we had a keen vision and feeling of all ordinary human life, it would be like hearing the grass grow and the squirrel's heart beat, and we should die of that roar which lies on the other side of silence."[103] In "The Lifted Veil" it is as if Eliot lifts the veil and sees the unmediated pain underneath the surface. To me it is as if she is contemplating the horror of a kind of Nietzschean perception without sympathy, inwardness without religious consciousness.

In the end the story represents a kind of alter ego that George Eliot keeps at bay by her choice to believe in sympathy. But the movement toward the full development of her own authorial self is not complete until she purges her own childhood sorrows, killing off the heroine of her next novel (with so much crying in the process that Lewes feared for her health)[104] so that she herself might live. In this process she imagines a death of memory itself so that she can write outside of its shadow. For whereas earlier stories had drawn on memories that she had reshaped imaginatively, in *The Mill on the Floss* memory itself and the past from which it comes are the antagonists. This novel is the great culmination of George Eliot's early work and the enabler of what comes after, as she explicitly explores the implications of the "progress of the intellect" and of society, mainly by thematizing the education of a girl and boy and the growth of their consciousness in an oppressive provincial backwater. George Eliot explicitly structures the novel in biblical terms of a Paradise Lost, and the narrator explicitly identifies Maggie and Tom as "martyr[s]" of "historical advance."[105]

One could say that Maggie is Mary Anne Evans reincarnated: the precocious, affectionate child deeply in need of the love of her father and particularly her brother. Like Mary Anne, Maggie revels in the world of imagination and seeks safety and transcendence as a young woman in a strict religious otherworldliness that is actually a self-repression. Instead of making the break from her family that Mary Anne was able to do, Maggie binds herself to her past, living under the sway of a fierce god named Tom, who knows no forgiveness and no pity. Here, it seems to me, George Eliot allows her imagination to spell out some of the implications of her creed. In particular, the notion that feeling is a kind of knowing is a fatal one for Maggie, who invests her own identity in her brother's unforgiving care, believing that he must love her because he knows her so well. The narrator of *Adam Bede* had told us we must believe in those childhood joys; here, Maggie does believe, and it is this belief that kills her. When Tom says, after her elopement, "I can't believe in you anymore,"[106] we know, as does Maggie, that he has never believed in her. Her faith is completely one-sided, completely a construction of her imagination.

As she had *Adam Bede*, George Eliot interrupts the story of the Tullivers mid-way, this time to tell readers that tragedy is possible among these "vulgar" provincial types. She uses two European rivers, the Rhine and the Rhone, to set up the same kind of contrast she had created in the earlier novel between the woman peeling carrots and the angel, again affirming two different kinds of beauty. When tragedy does come, in the form of a river overflowing its banks, it is as if her art is rebelling against "the divine beauty of form" that allows her to keep from going mad with hearing the squirrel's heartbeat, as if the tears of sympathy are mocking their proponent. What, after all, she might be saying, is the value of art, of culture, of sympathy, when nature is always and everywhere the conqueror? Maggie's dramatic drowning with her nemesis brother Tom has been the subject of endless interpretations, almost all of them correct. Maggie does triumphantly kill Tom; she does allow social disrepute to destroy her; George Eliot does fantasize a death that is both revenge and defeat; it is a sacrifice, a martyrdom, a shame. That it is all of these things and more testifies to the glorious triumph of George Eliot's narrative imagination. Frank Kermode has written that the loss of "the sense of an ending" and of an authenticated beginning is responsible for a rich literary heritage. There is a direct correlation, he writes, between "the subtlety and variety in our fictions and remoteness and doubtfulness about ends and origins."[107] It is not just Maggie who dies at the end of George Eliot's novel, then, but the whole culture, the whole past that gave birth to her. For it is because of the death of that young self, because she has the courage to test the limits of faith and imagination, that we have novels of such "subtlety and variety" as these.

A Concluding Unscientific Postscript

The Word became flesh, says the author of the Gospel of John, and dwelt among us. The Word Incarnate spoke in parables and metaphors, inspiring faith by activating imagination and awakening an attitude of inwardness. This same interrelation of incarnation, inwardness, and imagination, I have been arguing, constitutes the basis of the aesthetic of George Eliot's early fiction. Maggie's death is the most important moment in George Eliot's career, for it is only by killing her young self that she creates her authorial self. This is crucial not only for George Eliot's career but in the larger scope of literary history, because it figures, not what Barthes famously called the death of the author that followed on the death of God, but instead what Foucault in response called "the coming into being of the notion of 'author' [that] constitutes the privileged moment of *individualization.*"[108] The italics are Foucault's, but they could be mine, both because George Eliot's conviction that the individual is the site of belief and value is crucial to her incarnational aesthetic and because Maggie's death heralds the birth in her creator of a new understanding of incarnation and its relation to narrative.

It is interesting that shortly after the publication of *The Mill on the Floss* George Eliot began what would become regular visits to Italy and traveled once to Spain, where she viewed sites and artworks of religious significance from the pre-Reformation world. This geographical and religious movement is the sign of an imaginative shift beyond the Evangelical religious terrain of her early inspiration; it is part of her quest "to know," as she says in a letter of this time, "if possible, the lasting meaning that lies in all religious doctrine from the beginning till now."[109] This continuing quest is the subject of the following chapters, but if readers experience in George Eliot's later, post-Evangelical fiction—as they surely do—what Richard Kearney calls the "redemptive power" of narrative imagination,[110] it is because she has herself learned of this mysterious, indeed mystical, power in the writing of these early stories.

Chapter 2

"Even Our Failures Are a Prophecy"

Toward a Post-Evangelical Aesthetic

> I was reading the sorrows of the aged Hecuba with great enjoyment. I wish an immortal drama could be got out of my sorrows, that people might be the better for them two thousand years hence. But fog, east wind, and headache are not great dramatic motives.
>
> —George Eliot, *Letters*, Haight edition, 4:139 (March 25, 1864)

Maggie's death inaugurates the second phase of George Eliot's career. The passage is marked in several interrelated ways: historical, geographical, aesthetic, psychological, and religious. While many critics note the change in tone and subject matter from early to middle works, the editors of George Eliot's journals, Margaret Harris and Judith Johnston, acknowledge the importance of the geographical element, judging the Italian journey of 1860 as the crucial turning point that marks "the shift from the working out of childhood memories to more studied work on the past in relation to the present, both reading the past in relation to the present, and writing it."[1] I would agree with this assessment but argue that what has been consistently overlooked is the way in which George Eliot's shift in religious perspective undergirds and helps to explain the meaning of the change in her approach.

As I argued in the last chapter, George Eliot wrestles with Maggie in a Hegelian life-and-death struggle that results in the death of the character and the birth of the author, such that one could say that the character is the mother of the author. The next phase—to pursue the Freudian model for a moment—is the adolescent testing of this new authorial life. What George Eliot does next will determine the meaning and value of Maggie's death and the very existence of the entity we have come to know as "George Eliot." We could see Maggie's sacrifice as the culmination of George Eliot's novelistic initiation, and in these terms one can understand the peculiar intensity that charges the writing of the next decade, with the shadow of futility and failure hovering over them. One could also say that Maggie dies a martyr to idealism in that her hopes and dreams can never be realized in the actual world of her experience. In this sense her struggle and defeat mark the next stage in George Eliot's lifelong effort to realize the ideal, to find a credible way to bring the ideal into her fiction and to model for readers the relation between the ideal and the actual in the world. While this could be said of any of George Eliot's works perhaps, this period is marked by a more deliberate exploration of the dark side of idealism.

This is the period of her two least-read novels, *Romola* and *Felix Holt, The Radical*, as well as her almost never-read long dramatic poem, *The Spanish Gypsy*. While scholars always find interest in these texts, they are typically judged as at best "transitional" works[2] and at worst and by most as works of relative failure. George Eliot's journals and letters of the time confirm this period to be her deepest slough of despond; never a stranger to discouragement, she struggles during this time with serious depression and even despair over the worth of her work. In other words, she not only explores the disappointments of idealism in her fiction but she experiences them herself. What most distinguishes George Eliot's work at this time, however, is the way she turns despair and disillusionment to account by making failure her theme. In this chapter I will explore some of the ways in which George Eliot's experience with failure informed the development of the incarnational aesthetic that shapes and grounds her religious imagination.

Geographical and Historical

This period begins a phase in which, having moved beyond the religious terrain of her youth, George Eliot is seeking a new kind of holy ground for her imagination; this quest took geographical and historical shape. Beginning with the death of her father, she had always traveled extensively, but in this period she travels farther and more frequently and ventures more deliberately to push geographical boundaries. We might see her using her body to mimic her internal adventures, with her travels reflecting her religious and personal journeying. As a young woman she had visited Switzerland and Germany, as if, following her intense engagement with Strauss and Feuerbach, she meant physically to go over the terrain of Protestantism that would soon be the ground of her fiction. The new stage begins in 1860 when, following the completion of *The Mill on the Floss*, she and Lewes embark upon their first Italian journey. This is the first of several visits to Italy, followed by a truly adventurous and highly significant journey to Spain, the nations which, along with France, are most associated with Roman Catholicism. Spatial journeying is matched then with temporal journeying when *Romola* takes her imagination to pre-Reformation Renaissance Italy, and *The Spanish Gypsy* takes her to medieval Spain, and thereby to religious worlds that predate both the Victorian crisis of faith and her own.

During her travels, she is gathering material and models for her post-Evangelical aesthetic, for these journeys mark a break out of the provincial environment that had suffocated Maggie. *The Mill on the Floss* has already suggested the need for such religious questing. Two of the most important references to religion in Maggie's life are her intense engagement with Thomas à Kempis and the futility of Dr. Kenn's attempt to help her in the face of the unloving Christian community. But I want to draw attention to a moment in Maggie's childhood when George Eliot points to a major flaw in the church. This occurs early in the novel when Mr. Stelling, Tom's tutor, famously crushes the precocious Maggie's spirit by granting her only the "superficial cleverness" of girls.[3] In talking about the education Tom is receiving, the narrator makes a long disquisition on the human dependence on metaphors, a dependence which prevents Tom's tutor from understanding the nature of his pupil's mind and teaching him accordingly. This critique of Mr. Stelling is part of a larger critique of an education system that uses language to close, instead of open, children's minds. But crucially this is also part of George Eliot's critique of religion, for Mr. Stelling is also a cleric, trying to eke out a living to supply his wife with fashionable clothes and furnishings. In this context the narrator writes of Mr. Stelling:

> He thought religion was a very excellent thing, and Aristotle a great authority, and deaneries and prebends useful institutions, and Great Britain the providential bulwark of Protestantism, and faith in the unseen a great support to afflicted minds: he believed in all these things, as a Swiss hotel-keeper believes in the beauty of the scenery around him, and in the pleasures it gives to artistic visitors.[4]

In the scathing image of England as a "providential bulwark of Protestantism," George Eliot points here to the narrow, provincial, self-satisfied attitude of a church that defines God and the universe in its own limited terms. Here too she alludes to the cleric's condescending attitude toward artists, who see more in the world around them than the hotel-keeper can imagine. And here too she points to the fundamental ingredient both of imagination and of religion: a faith in the unseen, which is guided by the senses and the reason but refuses to be limited by them.

One of the predominant tropes throughout George Eliot's fiction is the narrow vs. wide view, and here she gives it explicitly geographical shape in representing the smallness of English Protestantism. This is important in signaling the literal sense that grounds the imaginative journeying she is promoting; for it is significant that George Eliot had recently made a return visit to Switzerland, the destination of her first expedition away from England, and I don't think it is pushing the point too much to say that her analogy about the Swiss hotel-keeper gains imaginative power from its being based on actual experience. This analogy points vividly to a major idea that underlies her fiction: imagination is the vital ingredient of faith that is lacking in the religious institutions of her time, and religion must be vitally constituted of imagination. George Eliot's own experience manifested this need when she sought inspiration beyond the English Protestant "bulwark" in European countries of predominantly Roman Catholic cultural background.

George Eliot's letters of the 1860s contain several significant references that mark out the religious terrain she is traversing at this time. In response to two friends' interest in Roman Catholicism, she writes in December 1860 that while she adheres to the view that the "highest 'calling and election' is to *do without opium*," she does not begrudge anyone else the "comfort" to be found in the "forms and ceremonies" of churchgoing. She goes so far as to say, "sympathetically, I enjoy them myself. But I have faith in the working-out of higher possibilities than the Catholic or any other church has presented."[5] Earlier that month she had looked forward "with delight" to a performance of *Messiah*;[6] and two Decembers later, after another *Messiah*, she sees in Handel's "conception of the suffering Messiah" what must "surely" represent "the acme of poetry."[7] One of her strongest statements comes in a letter of a month earlier when she refutes any propensity on her part "to rob a man of his religious belief." She asserts:

> I have too profound a conviction of the efficacy that lies in sincere faith, and the spiritual blight that comes with No-faith, to have any negative propagandism in me. In fact, I have very little sympathy with Free-thinkers as a class, and have lost all interest in mere antagonism to religious doctrines. I care only to know, if possible, the lasting meaning that lies in all religious doctrine from the beginning till now.[8]

It is this quest for the meaning in religion that takes her, if not to "the beginning," at least far beyond her own space and time to Renaissance Italy and medieval Spain. Toward the end of the decade, in August 1868, having finished *The Spanish Gypsy*, she writes of her "yearning affection towards the great religions of the world which have reflected the struggles and needs of mankind, with a very different degree of completeness from the shifting compromise called 'philosophical theism.'"[9]

Aesthetic and Generic

As Harris and Johnston note, this period begins "a phase of experiment in GE's career,"[10] as this spatiotemporal movement provides the ground for a re-visioning in generic and aesthetic terms. This experimentation takes three related forms: a burgeoning interest in and use of other arts, particularly music and painting; the writing and publishing of her own poetical works, with *The Spanish Gypsy* being the most ambitious of these; and significant discursive wrestling with the question of novelistic form.

To consider the first of these, the attention to other arts, it is evident that while she had always demonstrated a penchant for *ekphrasis* by writing about other art forms, *Romola* and *The Spanish Gypsy* are particularly marked by an experimentation with the thematic power of visual art and architecture. Further, *The Gypsy* features a self-reflexive exploration of the power of poetry and music, not only in its generic form but also in the songs and dances within it. In short, rather than being just a phase of experiment, this period points to an unending spirit of experimentation, and this quest for new generic forms of artistic expression is integrally related to the quest for "higher possibilities" in religion, partly because much of her understanding of "the great religions of the world" comes at this time through art.

George Eliot's European journals are full of references to music and art. She and Lewes become personally acquainted with Liszt, dine with Mendelssohn, critique Wagner's operas, and hear Clara Schumann play. They tramp through the churches and galleries of Dresden, Florence, Venice, Rome, and Madrid, among others, absorbing and assessing and comparing works of art. While she makes the most direct use of her exposure to classical and religious visual art in *Middlemarch*, it is also the source of her inspiration for *The Spanish Gypsy* and informs the themes of *Romola*, as I will discuss. But George Eliot's passion for music is evident from her earliest work—in Caterina's singing in "Mr. Gilfil's Love Story" and in Maggie's piano-playing and her susceptibility to beautiful singing in *The Mill on the Floss*—to her last, in the female singers in *Daniel Deronda*.

The second form of generic experimentation to highlight is George Eliot's own poetry. George Eliot clearly showcases her interest in music in her fiction and uses it to explore themes such as passion and self-expression, but it is interesting that she writes several poems at this time that focus on musicians, thereby allowing herself to explore themes related to art and creativity outside of the constraints of novelistic realism. Her attention to music finds intriguing expression toward the end of this period in two substantial long dramatic poems, "The Legend of Jubal" and "Armgart" in 1870, and two slighter poems, "Arion" and "Stradivarius," in 1873. In all of these, music is represented as a high spiritual calling inevitably linked to misunderstanding and failure. Jubal is the creator of music, who is glorified at a distance but then mocked, beaten, and left to die, a prophet without honor in his own land. Arion is a great musician who dramatically leaps to his death at the moment the men who would rob and kill him realize the power and worth of his music. Antonio Stradivari dedicates his life to trying to make the perfect instrument, caring nothing for his obscurity and the philistine attitude of his fellow artist. And Armgart—a brilliant, proud, successful singer—is felled by an illness that destroys her voice and results in her becoming a dedicated teacher and a better person. These poems are vital to the process of developing George Eliot's incarnational aesthetic. For poetry offers space for more fanciful glimpses than she permits herself in her fiction, allowing her to indulge in Romantic, indeed tragic, celebrations of the glorious, painful calling of the artist and to speculate on ways to reframe apparent failure as a sign of true art and its sacred, perhaps immortal, value.

While any of these poems merits fuller discussion—and I will discuss "Armgart" and "Jubal" in chapter 3—I will focus here on another long poem from 1865, entitled variously "A Minor Prophet" or "My Vegetarian Friend."[11] This poem is not a Romantic piece about music or art but instead treats the broader question of idealism and related issues of perfection and failure with a more sardonic eye. The poem explores the idea of human progress that preoccupied Victorian thinking in the wake of Darwinism and other challenges to the traditional understanding of a universe in which God is overseeing humanity's advance toward an afterlife. It is framed as a playful debate between the titular Prophet and his friend the narrator. The Prophet, whose middle name is "Baptist," adheres to his ancestors' belief in a "Millennium"[12] in which haberdashery uniformity has been achieved, "casual talk" is "as good as sermons" ("A Minor Prophet," line 20), and the vegetarian diet has done away with any need for animals, with the result that human beings can fill up the whole "terraquaeous globe" (line 75). The Prophet looks forward to a time when

> All these rude products will have disappeared
> Along with every faulty human type.
> By dint of diet vegetarian
> All will be harmony of hue and line,
> Bodies and minds all perfect, limbs well-tuned,
> And talk quite free from aught erroneous.
>
> ("A Minor Prophet," lines 128–33)

In response to this doctrine of perfectibility, his friend the narrator defends his own penchant for "nature's blunders, evanescent types / Which sages banish from Utopia" ("A Minor Prophet," lines 175–76). Echoing the narrator from chapter 17 of *Adam Bede*, with his celebration of women peeling carrots standing alongside angels and madonnas, the narrator here assures his interlocutor that he worships "with the rest" in beauty's temple, but also that "by my hearth I keep a sacred nook" (lines 178–79) for "the dear imperfect things" (155), a practice which he calls his "piety" (182). Noting the "paradox" of his feelings (188), he expresses "pity" for "future men who will not know / A keen experience with pity blent" because perfection will have no need for "the pathos exquisite of lovely minds / Hid in harsh forms—" (189–92). In his perplexity the narrator expresses a paradox that pervades George Eliot's whole career: her love for beauty—along with her longing for a better world in which "order, justice, love" (287) prevail—is counterbalanced always by her conviction that it is the desire for good, dependent upon the existence of its opposite, that constitutes the best of human nature. While like this narrator she holds fast to the "high prophetic vision" that "beholds / The paths of beauteous order" (278–80), she too deplores a perfect future that leaves the sorry past behind.

While none of this is new to anyone familiar with George Eliot's novels, the sentiments expressed by the narrator of "A Minor Prophet" help explain the peculiar intensity of the energy that pervades her works of the 1860s. As suggested above, the narrator of the poem not only embraces George Eliot's religion of feeling but is self-conscious about its paradoxes. For he is aware of the pleasure he takes in the pathos prompted by pain and castigates himself for his "foolish" and even "wicked" unwillingness to witness the dawn of a perfect world ("A Minor Prophet," line 201). Also implied in his paradoxical attitude is the awareness that inspiring the sympathy that constitutes the best of human nature means that there must be people for whom we ought to feel the "pity" that spells "piety." In describing the "keen experience with pity blent" that reaches out to "ungainly forms" (lines 190, 183), he uses a telling analogy that illuminates George Eliot's understanding of a human-centered piety. Rather than "penetrating" these motley folks "like fire divine within a common bush / Which glows transfigured by the heavenly guest, / So that men put their shoes off," this pity enables one to be

> . . . engaged
> Like a sweet child within some thick-walled cell,
> Who leaps and fails to hold the window-bars,
> But having shown a little dimpled hand
> Is visited thenceforth by tender hearts
> Whose eyes keep watch about the prison walls.
> ("A Minor Prophet," lines 192–200)

This analogy vividly illustrates that the sympathy George Eliot promotes is not akin to a transfiguration—an encounter between human and divine as two alien beings—but is rather a purely human interaction between "a sweet child" who has somehow managed to get itself imprisoned and "tender hearts" who cannot free it but can at least "keep watch" over its safety. George Eliot is clearly not promoting the burning-bush piety of Moses but rather the merciful compassion of Jesus: "I was in prison and you visited me." Further, the image is ambiguous or fluid enough that it is impossible to keep the imprisoned child separate from the visitor, suggesting that all humans are sweet children imprisoned behind impenetrable walls—"lovely minds / Hid in harsh forms."

Another familiar saying of Jesus—the poor you will always have with you—comes to mind when the poem's narrator goes on to describe "the patched and plodding citizen" who exults "almost with a sob" in the coming of "some victorious world-hero" ("A Minor Prophet," lines 223–29) but then settles back into the "more easy fellowship" of his neighbors, acknowledging that "could he choose" he would turn time backwards, not forwards, in order to repeat the days of his hero-less childhood (lines 240, 256). But then, in a passage replete with George Eliot's characteristic "and yet" and "but," the narrator cries, "Yet no! the earth yields nothing more Divine / Than high prophetic vision—" (277–78). The poem resolves itself in a conclusion that accepts the paradox that the future must be the same but different: "Our finest hope is finest memory" (292).

The narrator further claims that "faith" is strengthened by the emotion that rises at the goodness evident in music, art, and "at noble and at gentle deeds" ("A Minor Prophet," lines 277, 303). He has earlier opined: "Bitterly / I feel that every change upon this earth / Is bought with sacrifice" (lines 144–46). But here, near the end of the poem, he confronts the more perplexing problem of a sacrifice that achieves no change:

> Even our failures are a prophecy,
> Even our yearnings and our bitter tears
> After that fair and true we cannot grasp;
> As patriots who seem to die in vain
> Make liberty more sacred by their pangs.
> ("A Minor Prophet," lines 311–15)

The poem beautifully illustrates the tension between the desire for perfection and the value of failure, and, while its focus is the question of human progress, the references to the value of art at the end also make explicit what is implicit throughout—George Eliot's doubts concerning her own progress and possible failure as a writer. While the poem's prophet is an ironic persona, George Eliot's own "high prophetic vision" inspires her whole creative effort, and this poem ends by articulating with a striking absence of irony the hope that even what appears to be failure may be recognized as a sacrifice that has a consecrating effect.

Here I must invoke Maggie in *The Mill on the Floss* again, whose death George Eliot accomplished, as reported by her husband, with more "bitter tears" than accompanied any other work.[13] Maggie's death is so very provocative because it gathers into itself many of the words we have for violent death—murder, suicide, sacrifice, and martyrdom—and affirms them all. Indeed, Maggie may be interpreted in terms of the paradox explored by the Prophet as a woman who is too in love with the past to have a future. Yet in these same terms hers is not a death that could be called "vain," for her death is also the birth of George Eliot, novelist. Had George Eliot stopped writing fiction at this point her novels would still be honored, but probably as pastoral, even nostalgic, accounts of the pre-industrial English Midlands. Instead, Maggie's death is a failure that is also a prophecy of George Eliot's commitment to writing novels that are "double mirrors, making still / An endless vista of fair things before / Repeating things behind" ("A Minor Prophet," lines 295–97). It is true of course that George Eliot had already achieved success before writing Maggie's fictional life and death, but I would argue that without Maggie, she would never have crossed the "bridge" figured so elegantly in the first chapter of that novel that took her from literary success to artistic phenomenon.

In the evolution of George Eliot's art that I am tracing, "A Minor Prophet" is itself a "double mirror" in the sense that it retrospectively illuminates Maggie's importance as the first in the series of heroes and heroines through whom George Eliot explores questions related to the problem of appearing to die in vain and the equally heroic but more quotidian problem of appearing to live in vain. She highlights her attention to the first of these questions in another important text, "Leaves from a Note-Book" (undated), when she quotes her own Fedalma, the Spanish Gypsy: "The grandest death! to die in vain—" in the "Note" entitled by the editor "'A Fine Excess.' Feeling Is Energy."[14] George Eliot reinforces her self-quote by saying, "I really believe and mean this—not as a rule of general action, but as a possible grand instance of determining energy in human sympathy, which even in particular cases, where it has only a magnificent futility, is more adorable, or as we say divine, than unpitying force, or than a prudent calculation of results."[15] While the self-sacrifice that achieves calculated results may indeed claim "the highest title to our veneration, and makes the supreme heroism," she concedes, "the generous leap of impulse is needed too to swell the flood of sympathy in us beholders."[16] Feeling, in other words—indeed an "excess" of feeling—cannot come from calculation and is necessary to provide the "energy" that fuels the struggle for goodness in the world. We "beholders" of heroic action are moved to good actions by acts of "magnificent futility" more than by results.

Also in this "Note" George Eliot castigates any who would use hopelessness as a reason for inaction, arguing ultimately, as in "A Minor Prophet," that apparently futile heroism energizes observers for good. To despair of the value of one's own actions towards a good end "comes from that sapless kind of reasoning which is falsely taken for a sign of supreme mental activity, but is really due to languor, or incapability of that mental grasp which makes objects strongly present, and to a lack of sympathetic emotion."[17] It is telling to read this kind of judgment from the pen of the woman whose self-doubt is legendary, whose journals are riddled with questions about the value of her work. Yet these judgments, as well as her frequent words of encouragement about the importance of even the smallest good work, hold all the more weight when we know that they are motivated by her sense of her own failings.[18] As I've said, this "Note" points to the major concerns that shape the themes and characters of the rest of her novels, but it is also important to recognize the metafictional element of such ideas. In this respect Maggie takes on further importance, as I suggested above, in that she might be seen as a martyr not only to the cause of women and to "historical advance"[19] but to the cause of George Eliot's writing. The "futility" of Maggie's death is "magnificent" indeed in its "fine excess" of feeling, which not only inspired generations of response but propelled George Eliot forward into a whole new stage of her career.[20]

This brings us to the third element in the aesthetic revisioning of this time, the question of the form of the novel. As discussed in the last chapter, this rethinking of religious and aesthetic possibilities had everything to do with rethinking the idea of incarnation. To recall A. S. Byatt's statement in her introduction to her edition of George Eliot's writings: "The long nineteenth-century debate about the precise meaning, or lack of meaning, of the Christian concept of the Incarnation . . . is inextricably connected, consciously and unconsciously, to the development of the form of the novel."[21] While the theological notion of the incarnation of Christ is a question separate from the incarnation of ideas in fictional form, George Eliot's intense attention at this time to the question of form, and specifically the problem of incarnating her ideas, certainly bears out Byatt's claim. Interestingly, Rosemary Ashton articulates the common criticism of George Eliot's works of this period in these very terms, stating that they "suffered from insufficient incarnation of ideas."[22] Indeed, though evidently quite different from each other, the three major works of this period have in common this manifestation of George Eliot's aesthetic experimentation with the question of, as she puts it in a letter of 1866, "how to make certain ideas thoroughly incarnate."[23] While George Eliot has written before about this question—notably in chapter 17 of *Adam Bede*—during this period she is unusually forthcoming about her struggles, partly because she is aware of embarking on untried ground.

This awareness of a new stage applies even to her writing of *Felix Holt*, despite its being set in familiar territory and based on a remembered incident. When she takes the unusual step of consulting an expert, lawyer Frederic Harrison, their correspondence following its publication illuminates the nature of George Eliot's aesthetic preoccupations at this time. Harrison, who has glimpsed in *Felix Holt* possibilities for a Positivist utopian novel, tries to persuade George Eliot that her "destiny" is "to produce a poem— . . . a drama," that gives form to the philosophy of Positivism.[24] Somewhat sympathetic to Positivist ideas and already engaged in writing *The Spanish Gypsy*, George Eliot expresses her mistrust of didactic utopias but tells him that she has "gone through again and again the severe effort of trying to make certain ideas thoroughly incarnate, as if they had revealed themselves to me in the flesh and not in the spirit." She makes clear that she is not interested in writing utopian fictions, because "they do not pretend to work on the emotions," which is always her primary goal. Imagine, she goes on, "the sort of agonizing labour to an English-fed imagination to make art a sufficiently real back-ground, for the desired picture, to get breathing, individual forms, and group them in the needful relations, so that the presentation will lay hold on the emotions as human experience." Relying on historical documents rather than primarily on personal memory for the writing of *Romola*, she tells him, cost her "unspeakable pains."[25] Such is the interrelation of the three texts that here we see her, while engaged in writing *The Spanish Gypsy*, using her experience with *Romola* to explain her ideas about aesthetic form to someone who has helped her with *Felix Holt*.

Psychological

The "unspeakable pains" George Eliot mentions are in fact literal—physical and psychological—and written of frequently in her journals. While her writing is always a painful process, this period, as mentioned above, is one of unprecedented suffering, and her journals are riddled with references to debilitating "headache and sickness" and "feebleness of head and body," frequently "producing terrible depression."[26] George Eliot's experience of suffering actually provides the crucial link between the incarnation as religious concept and incarnation as an aim of her fiction. For it is in experiencing the pain involved in investing her creations with life as "breathing, individual forms," I want to argue, that she experiences the power of incarnation as a divine force.

George Eliot goes so far as to use the term "incarnation" to describe her writing difficulties at this time, and the new problems she experiences in writing *The Spanish Gypsy* serve to articulate the issues involved. So troublesome was the writing of this text that her husband had prevailed upon her to "put aside" the work more than two years before "because," as she confides to Harrison, "it was in that stage of Creation or 'Werden,' in which the idea of the characters predominates over the incarnation." The drama—later to become, as a result of her struggles with form, a dramatic poem—presented a more serious challenge even than *Romola*: without the source of "a grand myth or an Italian novel" and instead writing only "under the inspiration of an idea," with her source "in the spirit," she feels "anything but omnipotent."[27] Six months later, still engrossed in this work, she confides to her publisher, John Blackwood, that she is writing "—prepare your fortitude—a poem," reiterating the distinction that "the plot was wrought out entirely as an incorporation of my own ideas."[28] In writing *The Spanish Gypsy*, then, George Eliot has the new experience of seeming to create out of nothing, a process that takes her to a deeper understanding of the incarnational nature of artistic creation.

Crucial to this process is her abiding but ever-deepening engagement with the topic of suffering, including her own. From the beginning, as no one familiar with her work needs to be reminded, George Eliot is convinced that her task as a writer is actually a vocation that charges her with an ethical responsibility to arouse sympathy in her readers for the sufferings and shortcomings of their fellow mortals. And from the beginning she takes as her model the suffering Christ. "No wonder [man] needs a suffering God," the narrator of *Adam Bede* had said,[29] and that whole novel is built on the struggle to believe in the transformative power of suffering and to show what it means to enter into the sorrows of others. In this context Maggie's death is also enormously significant in that it raises the question of the meaning of individual suffering. It is this question that energizes the works of the decade that follows, for in writing Maggie's death George Eliot's aesthetic undergoes a crucial change: from talking about the suffering of others in her fiction and talking about her own suffering to herself in her journal and to a few friends in letters, *The Mill on the Floss* has her integrating the two. For in this novel she participates in the sufferings of her characters, making them her own in a way that might be seen as masochistic or narcissistic—as we see in her intense grieving over Maggie's terrible and necessary death. But in this she is coming to a new understanding of the relation between writing and suffering.

This process takes her model of sympathy beyond the level of ethics and aesthetics so that, without being her own story, the text is constituted of her own suffering. The next stage is the one she works through in the terribly painful process of writing *Romola*, for, though the writing of the two works that follow it is also a painfully arduous process, she is in them coming gradually to a new state of awareness. By the end of this decade of sorrows, I believe, she has begun to understand, or more consciously to acknowledge, that rather than accomplishing her writing in spite of her suffering, she is suffering for her writing and writing out of her suffering. This is tricky ground because, as she herself is aware and as some critics have explored, there could be seen to be a morbid or superstitious element, carried over from her evangelical experience perhaps, whereby she is permitted to achieve success only by suffering, thereby paying for her happiness as all sinners must do. As Byatt notes, George Eliot passionately hated the "doctrine of Compensation," the cheap idea that one's sorrows will be compensated by future reward or an improvement of character.[30] She is aware of the danger that in seeming to preach about the redeeming power of suffering the writer risks minimizing the suffering and giving it a "meaning" that is insulting both to the sufferer and to any presumed god. This is such tricky ground in fact that except in occasional passing hints George Eliot defers conscious acknowledgment—some would say represses her knowledge—that her own suffering has served the purpose of shaping not only her writing but her very self, until she has finished with fiction. It is only in retrospect and in the form of a poem, "Self and Life," that she embraces this idea, and even then it is through a dialogue that separates her self from her life.[31] This elegant, little-known poem has Life schooling Self on the reason for all of its grief. Self learns that growth entails pain: the hard-won insight she achieves that "life is justified by love" requires accepting the truth that "half man's truth must hidden lie / If unlit by Sorrow's eye."[32]

This separation between self and life was an essential survival tactic throughout George Eliot's writing life. The obvious manifestation of this split is of course in her self-naming, primarily in her pseudonym but as well in the abundance of names she had for herself.[33] George Eliot's self-naming was a fructifying force for her writing, but it is also an element of the self-construction which Paul Ricoeur claims is vital to the "narrative identity" that all humans need to create for themselves.[34] Ricoeur argues that selfhood is a matter of "narrative interpretation," a practice which teaches us "the figural nature of the character by which the self, narratively interpreted, turns out to be a *figured* self—which imagines itself . . . in this or that way."[35] In these terms, we see Marian Evans Lewes engaged in constructing her writing self by creating fictional narratives and concurrently creating a "narrative identity" to write that self, or even by simply imagining herself as that writing self. This dual self-construction has been brilliantly analyzed by Harris and Johnston in their edition of George Eliot's journals, in which they show how she tried to keep a kind of textual division in her writing life by writing from both ends of her diary, often simultaneously, recording in the front mainly quotidian activities and concerns, and, in the back, events related to her writing and her travels. In fact then, this was a double doubleness, in that not only did she maintain two writing selves—one to write fiction, the other to write the diary—but the latter self was subdivided into two separate voices.

One of the early installments in the back of the "Journal," "How I came to write fiction," serves to illuminate the importance of the self-division to George Eliot's creativity. In this famous account, George Eliot writes of how, having long nurtured "a vague dream" of writing a novel, she was finally compelled to try when one morning she was "lying in bed . . . thinking" of what she might write, and her thoughts "merged . . . into a dreamy doze," until, she says, "I imagined myself writing a story of which the title was—'The Sad Fortunes of the Reverend Amos Barton.' "[36] This entry is intriguing in many respects: for one thing, dated December 6, 1857, it was written just over a year after she finished "Amos Barton" and when she is just two months into the writing of her first full novel. In other words, though she has only just started, she is already aware that she has begun what she calls "a new era in my life";[37] rather than gaining this sense of significance in retrospect, as we might expect, she already knows that this is the beginning of something significant enough to write about and essential to the construction of what Ricoeur would call her "narrative identity."

George Eliot's construction of this event is a prime instance of the narrative habit of mind that is signaled in her propensity to construct her own life in retrospect as a succession of narrative moments. As discussed above, her journal of the 1860s is a kind of litany of sorrows, and it is crucial to her writing life both that she constructs such a text and that she then rereads it, for it is in the process of interpretation that the sorrows become an energizing force. This returns us to "A Minor Prophet" and the "Note" on feeling, with their notion that an observer—in this case her self—is energized to work for good by the display of "a fine excess" of "feeling" represented in an act of "magnificent futility." In rereading her journal, George Eliot is frequently an observer, in that she encounters a suffering self that she has forgotten. In this regard it is interesting to note that despite her unconventional lifestyle, George Eliot's novels became a source of moral guidance and spiritual consolation to readers, some of whom—to add a further generic spin—were known to have "copied passages from [*Romola*] into their New Testaments."[38] This only happened because George Eliot modeled that behavior by rereading her journals in search of reassurance and consolation.

This practice continued even into the next decade, when she had emerged from the depths of the pit of despond (although she was still inhabiting its outskirts). In May 1870, for example, when she is beginning *Middlemarch*, George Eliot resumes writing in her diary after a lapse of seven months, and finds there references to earlier periods of "headache and depression" that reassure her that her present anguish "is not unprecedented." Later, with *Middlemarch* a huge success, she is similarly struggling over *Daniel Deronda* and is reassured in turn by references in her diary confirming "that I really was in worse health and suffered equal depression about Romola—and so far as I have recorded, the same thing seems to be true of Middlemarch."[39] Later, having recorded in her diary some heartening responses to *Deronda*, she writes: "I record these signs, that I may look back on them if they come to be confirmed."[40] This reconfiguring of her own words (and those of others) into "signs" reflects the crucial reinterpretation that established George Eliot's narrative identity. For, while her journals and letters are riddled with references to her own suffering, her understanding of the meaning of this suffering changes. Whereas she begins by seeing her ailments of body and mind primarily as inhibiting her writing, she later comes to see them as a sign of the value of her work and even as its substance. It is crucial to the power of this symbiosis, however, that the source of her energy remain hidden from herself: her suffering must retain the tenor of "futility" in order to produce the energy of excess. The quotation I use as my epigraph rather humorously captures this situation.

> Fog, east wind, and headache: there is my week's history. But this morning, when your letter came to me, I had got up well, and was reading the sorrows of the aged Hecuba with great enjoyment. I wish an immortal drama could be got out of *my* sorrows, that people might be the better for them two thousand years hence. But fog, east wind, and headache are not great dramatic motives.[41]

This first paragraph of a letter George Eliot wrote to Mrs. Peter Alfred Taylor in March 1864 exemplifies such a beautiful rhetorical flourish that it is difficult to believe that its writer is unconscious of the "enjoyment" future readers were to derive from her "dramatic motives." Nonetheless it is just this sort of blindness to self that facilitates her writing life.

George Eliot's journals and letters, particularly those of the young Mary Anne Evans, have always been subject to the charge of self-dramatization. Many have commented as well on the self-image she constructs in later letters: the suffering artist rescued from herself and a condemning world by the supportive spouse.[42] While this pattern may indeed smack of self-dramatization—as she herself came to suspect—it is vital to her narrative identity. And crucial to this pattern is the fact that the woeful accounts of her struggles and sufferings are alleviated by occasional glimpses of her sense of a special calling. In a letter of 1857 she writes of her hope that "the terrible pain I have gone through in the past years . . . has probably been for some special work";[43] and in a journal entry summing up that year she records her gratitude that "the long sad years of youth were worth living for the sake of middle age."[44] Notwithstanding this realization, however, this pain, as we have seen, is even more terrible with *Romola*, partly for the reasons mentioned above, and because she continues to be attracted to the Romantic aesthetic—that true art is the product of suffering—and to the Christian view that suffering is redemptive. In exulting in a letter to a friend over her triumph with *Adam Bede* and her happiness with Lewes, for example, George Eliot feels compelled to include her concurrent sadness over "the much work that remains," as if she is not allowed unalloyed happiness. But in a significant aside she acknowledges her "blessed" state in having "all this reason for being glad that I have lived, in spite of my sins and sorrows—or rather, by reason of my sins and sorrows."[45] This shift from "in spite of" to "by reason of" speaks volumes, not least because in refusing to appropriate it fully she keeps alive the tension that she almost superstitiously believes is essential to her narrative identity.

Ricoeur argues that "we never cease to interpret the narrative identity that constitutes us, in light of the narratives proposed to us by our culture."[46] For Marian Evans, the cultural narrative that deemed her a common-law wife living in sin with another woman's husband had to be urgently resisted by a counter-narrative, which she built upon the "figured self" of novelist.[47] Subverting the cultural codes, she claims "Marian Evans Lewes" as her true name, and the other self-naming, "George Eliot," actualizes that claim, reinscribing it with each novel.[48] Harris and Johnston have compared her pseudonym to a "second name, exactly like the one a religious assumes upon taking orders,"[49] an important gesture of self-anointing that proclaims the sense of vocation mentioned earlier.

It is tempting to say that George Eliot learned how to endure and at the same time to profit from her suffering by making Maggie a martyr for the cause of her writing. But *The Mill on the Floss* is more accurately seen as a kind of culminating and turning point: it is in writing this novel that George Eliot learns how to bring her life into her work without killing her self. Her earlier works had drawn heavily on memory, yet she was so unconscious of this dependence that she was genuinely surprised to find people identifying her characters with actual people. The ensuing battle over her identity and that of her characters is dramatic enough to have earned much critical attention, with the most interesting element being her telling silence when it becomes evident that she has been found out. Her own surprise is the most interesting aspect of this, in that it smacks of the astonishment that comes from having kept her knowledge even from herself. The anguish involved in having to fight for her authorial identity gives her a better understanding of the intimacy between her work and her life. And it is this that empowers her to write Maggie and to kill her, as she enacts the painfully paradoxical experience of embracing her past and separating herself from it forever. *The Mill on the Floss* thus represents a point of intersection between her self and her life, which she had until now determined to keep separate.

It is difficult to imagine a gesture more expressive of excess of feeling than Maggie's very literal "generous leap of impulse" into the raging Floss. Within the text it illustrates the futility that defines the magnificence of such gestures in that, had they waited, Maggie and Tom would have been rescued; outside of the confines of the text it also raises the question of futility in that the novel has sparked endless debate as to its success and meaning. In the context of my argument, this is interesting in that it focuses the discussion of suffering on George Eliot's experience of success and failure, whose terms are radically changed for her during this period of rethinking her aesthetic. It is certainly true, as discussed above, that she continued to agonize over her writing process and the value of her work, but I believe there is also a significant shift in her own sense of her work, a shift that is impelled by Maggie's death and then worked through in *Romola*. One of the reasons for this is the fact that with *Romola* she became financially secure. But equally material was the fact that in moving into new territory—geographically, historically, generically, emotionally, and professionally (in changing publishers for this one novel)—she frees herself, and in this way benefits from the heroic gesture of a martyr who has "[made] liberty more sacred by [her] pangs."

George Eliot's changing attitude to her work is signaled in two unusual responses: first, when she consults experts—a lawyer to help with the legal morass involved in *Felix Holt*, and an artist who is illustrating *Romola*—and, second, when she discusses the merits of her work in correspondence. As she did with the lawyer Frederic Harrison, as mentioned earlier, she engages in a kind of collaboration with the illustrator of *Romola*, Frederic Leighton, as part of the process of working out her ideas about aesthetic and generic form. Learning of the "impossibility of producing perfect correspondence between my intention and the illustrations," as she says in a letter in 1862,[50] is crucial to the way in which she wrestles with the meaning of incarnation for her work.

The second significant change relates to her opening herself to criticism in a new way in this period. Midway in the serial publication of *Romola* she replies to her friend Sara Sophia Hennell's interest by warning that the book is different from previous ones in not being "*intended*" to be popular (her emphasis). Her reference here to freedom is telling: "If one is to have freedom to write out one's own varying unfolding self, and not be a machine always grinding out the same material or spinning the same sort of web, one cannot always write for the same public." Since her publisher is in agreement with this idea, she says, she is "acquitted of all scruple or anxiety except the grand anxiety of doing my work worthily. Alas, I want to do something very much better than I ever *can* do it—if fasting and scourging oneself would make one a fit organ, there would be more positive comfort."[51]

Two more letters will help to further this point. After *Romola* has been published, George Eliot takes the unusual step of replying to Richard Holt Hutton's detailed and judicious critique, in which he says that this novel "will never be George Eliot's most popular book" but is in his view "the greatest she has yet produced."[52] George Eliot responds that she understands his "dissatisfaction with Romola herself," noting that "I have failed to bring out my conception with adequate fullness." She goes on to expand on the aesthetic problem, which to her is a religious one:

> With regard to that and to my whole book, my predominant feeling is—not that I have achieved anything, but—that great, great facts have struggled to find a voice through me, and have only been able to speak brokenly. That consciousness makes me cherish the more any proof that my work has been seen to have some true significance by minds prepared not simply by instruction, but by that religious and moral sympathy with the historical life of man which is the larger half of culture.[53]

In a similar vein a few weeks later, she affirms Sara Sophia Hennell's critique of Romola as "ideal" (rather than convincingly real) and similarly merges her explanation for this perceived flaw with an explanation of her religious aim: "I feel it acutely in the reproof my own soul is constantly getting from the image it has made. My own books scourge me."[54]

George Eliot's response to the reception of *The Spanish Gypsy* when it was finally published in 1868 reflects a similar insouciance about its popularity. She reports to a friend of being grateful for the public's "kindly" response to the work and describes herself as "serene, because I only expected the unfavourable."[55] While it would be easy enough to argue that this apparent acquiescence to these judgments constitutes a clever self-defense—and while it is certainly true that these positive responses are admixed with her usual consciousness of failure—I would argue rather that her responses are genuine. Perhaps her aversion to reading criticism of her earlier works had as much to do with her conviction that whatever anyone else said, she was only writing what she knew, whereas here she is making a whole new world. We would do better to take these comments as an index of her growing sense that she is engaged in a transition into another aesthetic realm, which is concurrently another religious realm, her interest in which develops out of that previously quoted "yearning affection towards the great religions of the world."[56] Central to all of this is the recognition that emerges in "A Minor Prophet" and her "Note" on feeling, cited above, that what is seen as failure is subject to interpretation and may from another perspective be seen as triumph.

Religious

The fact that Richard Holt Hutton was a Roman Catholic perhaps explains George Eliot's ability to articulate her feeling of being used as a kind of flawed vehicle through which ideas are being expressed. Here we may see a religious sense of herself as being chosen to convey, however imperfectly, what she calls in *Adam Bede* "the divine beauty of form." This experience and confession of failure to incarnate her ideas are essential to the development of her mature, post-Evangelical aesthetic. For, although the three main texts of this period feature a martyr or para-martyr figure, there is no longer a Maggie to die for George Eliot's art. What I believe happens here is that George Eliot's own aesthetic practice teaches her a deeper understanding of the Christian incarnation; in other words, while she is taking "unspeakable pains" to incarnate her ideas, she comes to see that the creative process is itself an incarnational activity by which something changes in her. While we might therefore see her labor pains as a sign of neurosis, we may equally see them as a sign of kenosis, the idea of self-emptying that underlies the Christian understanding of incarnation.

Romola: *The Failure of Art, the Art of Failure*

Central to the change I have been analyzing is a shift in George Eliot's understanding of the relation between the sacred and the secular. For while from the beginning of her fiction writing she had thought of her work as part of her religion, it is in this period that she is consciously working out the implications of this claim.[57] George Eliot continues to explore her favorite themes—the conflict between duty and passion, particularly for daughters, and the imperative of sympathetic suffering—but in *Romola* she formulates these themes in explicitly religious terms. The primary way in which she explores these ideas is through the figure of the martyr and the concomitant issues of sacrifice and belief. The letter quoted above contains what I have come to think of as George Eliot's definition of religion: "The contemplation of whatever is great is itself religion and lifts us out of our egotism."[58] *Romola* represents her most ambitious attempt to date to animate this idea. In it she dramatizes the contest during the Renaissance between secular humanism and institutional Roman Catholicism, embodying the former primarily in Romola's father and the latter mainly in Savonarola. But both these fathers are judged as wanting in George Eliot's religious terms by the extent to which their respective beliefs—in classical learning and in the Christian system—are tainted by their own egotism. And the novel's most fascinating character, Tito, is characterized as consumed by ego, a believer in nothing.

Like Maggie, Romola is subject to the will of several powerful men, all of them obsessed with their own desires and intent upon shaping hers to their own. Her father and brother, though ideological opposites, are similar in each being consumed by passion for a vision—for Dino, a vision of Christ's crucifixion, for Bardo, a vision of the classical wisdom of the past—that sets them apart from the world. Their allegiance to death blinds Romola to the falsity of the charming Tito's liveliness, and George Eliot uses his character to explore the possibility of a conscience-free egotism. One could imagine Tito's mocking response to Maggie's sacrifice, since he knows the meaning of sacrifice only insofar as he can sacrifice the needs and even the lives of others to his own desires. The narrator wonders, "could any philosophy prove to him that he was bound to care for another's suffering more than for his own?"[59] In the terms of George Eliot's religious philosophy, Tito's "contempt for the tales of priests"[60] is continuous with his contempt for social laws and duties. And she characterizes his lack of a "terror of the unseen" as a sign not of refreshing rationality but of his scorn for the "guardianship" such fear provides for "a moral law restraining desire."[61] In George Eliot's terms, Tito's lack of sympathetic feeling is a lack of morality. In a different way, Dino the monk also rejects the relation between human feeling and divine meaning. "What is this religion of yours," Romola asks him in exasperation, "that places visions before natural duties?"[62] Whereas Tito rejects all duty except that to his own pleasure, Dino, in his search for "wisdom," replaces human bonds with a religious one, not recognizing that in rejecting "human sympathies," as the narrator makes sure to tell us, he is rejecting "the very life and substance of our wisdom."[63]

Married to a man of no faith and yet unable to embrace the absolutism of her brother, Romola seeks to understand suffering in terms of the promise of transcendent meaning.

> What thought could reconcile that worn anguish in her brother's face—that straining after something invisible—with [Tito's] satisfied strength and beauty, and make it intelligible that they belonged to the same world? Or was there never any reconciling of them—but only a blind worship of clashing deities, first in mad joy and then in wailing?[64]

In a brilliant figure, George Eliot has Tito try to force Romola to accept art as the means to "reconcile" beauty and suffering by commissioning the painting of a triptych of the two of them posing as classical lovers and using it to cover Dino's crucifix. Tito's transparent effort to cover "sadness" with art (and artfulness) paradoxically reveals the power of art, in that the painting, instead of keeping sadness "hidden," becomes a mirror that reveals the truth of his deception and betrayal.[65] This is a fascinating image because rather than entertain the Romantic idea of art becoming a kind of religion, George Eliot makes her villain a man whose lack of belief extends along a continuous line that includes social duty, religious faith, and art, characterizing his egotism as a comprehensive failure of "imagination."[66]

As a young wife to a faithless husband, Romola is susceptible to the absolute faith claims of Savonarola, and what stirs her to the point of physical "sensation" and "thrill" when she hears him speak is his invocation of "martyrdom." Though a "transient emotion," she experiences the feeling as like "being possessed,"[67] and it is this idea of self-sacrifice, so foreign to her husband, that ultimately draws her to Savonarola, even though this call has the unwanted application of compelling her to return to her duty as a faithful wife. The narrator characterizes Romola's "tenderness and keen fellow-feeling for the near and loved" as her "religion"[68]; in Romola's recoil from Tito's anti-religiousness and Dino's anti-humanity George Eliot strives to represent her heroine as seeking to sanctify her religion of feeling. In this respect it is interesting that Savonarola identifies her calling as reconciling the claims of humanity and divinity in what Ashton calls "a kind of respiritualised secular humanism."[69]

George Eliot carefully delineates the process by which Romola chooses to leave her husband, having her don a religious habit to represent the holiness of her deliberation. Yet she makes clear too that her choice is a human one: "In those times, as now, there were human beings who never saw angels or heard perfectly clear messages. Such truth as came to them was brought confusedly in the voices and deeds of men not at all like the seraphs of unfailing wing and piercing vision."[70] Still, though George Eliot explicitly refuses to represent Romola's experience as supernatural, she also seems to want to cast a more than natural aura around the occasion. She describes the beauty of the dawn in which Romola "for the first time in her life" makes a free choice as casting a light that she feels "as a divine presence." This inspires "a certain awe," which Romola feels, not as something new, but as "a more conscious element in [her] feeling"[71] and a truer illuminator of her own path. Here George Eliot strives to create an image of the relation between the sacred and the secular, the human and the divine, as continuous, not oppositional. And in her effort to represent a human kind of sanctity George Eliot is careful not to mention faith; instead she offers her heroine a choice between "the path of reliance and action which is the path of life" and its opposite, the "loneliness and disbelief, which is no path, but the arrest of inaction and death."[72]

Decidedly human too is the stern monk Savonarola, who turns Romola back on this path through "nothing transcendent in [his] face"[73] but instead through his words, words that merely confirm what she already believes. Savonarola voices her own belief in the "fellowship with suffering"[74] as the highest calling and sanctifies her suffering by linking it with the suffering represented in "the religion of the cross."[75] He holds out the cross to her as a means whereby she can take "a share in the divine life which quenches the sense of suffering Self in the ardours of an ever-growing love."[76] In opposition to Tito's artful offer of art, then, Savonarola offers the cross, not to hide sadness but to reconcile and integrate Romola's own sadness with the universal sadness embodied in the sacrifice of Christ. And in the ultimate word of integration (and incarnation) he urges her not to go away in search of a holy calling but to return home: "Instead of taking a long exciting journey, she was to sit down in her usual place."[77]

George Eliot reiterates a central idea from *The Mill on the Floss* twice in *Romola*. After Maggie's elopement, the narrator had pontificated on the virtue of what we would call situational ethics:

> The great problem of the shifting relation between passion and duty is clear to no man who is capable of apprehending it: the question whether the moment has come in which a man has fallen below the possibility of a renunciation that will carry any efficacy, and must accept the sway of a passion against which he had struggled as a trespass, is one for which we have no master key to fit all cases.[78]

In *Romola* she is taking this great problem to another level by framing it in terms of a historical figure who suffered cruel torture and execution at the hands of the church: she sums it up as "the question where the duty of obedience ends, and the duty of resistance begins."[79] But more telling is the second iteration of this dilemma as a measure of Romola's growth of consciousness; for in deliberating on her decision to sever herself from her bigamist husband, Romola recognizes that she faces the same problem as her spiritual mentor—"the problem where the sacredness of obedience ended and where the sacredness of rebellion began."[80] This realization is crucial within the text and also in George Eliot's career. For Romola herself this awareness is a sign of maturity, as she realizes that despite her disillusionment with Savonarola, his "inspiring consciousness" that "had exalted even the minor details of obligation into religion" had been nonetheless genuine,[81] and that, further, she is herself capable of undergoing the same kind of spiritual struggle as her mentor.

For George Eliot's own work this statement is equally important in that she not only makes a point of rejecting the claim that Savonarola is a martyr, she also aims to humanize the meaning of his suffering and death by explicitly emphasizing the point that he did not see himself as a martyr. R. H. Hutton notes that she rejects the last words with which historians credit Savonarola—his declaration that he cannot be cast out of "the Church triumphant."[82] Instead, George Eliot wants to convince readers of the more complex point that seeing himself as a martyr in this way would actually detract from Savonarola's greater merit—the merit of doubting one's own worthiness and dying not in triumph but in "resignation."[83] Thus in refusing to accept Savonarola's official status as martyr, she attempts to enroll him in a more select group—heroes who have died in what seems "magnificent futility." Her aim is to make of him a human, flawed hero, rather than the purified saint of official church history. She then ends the novel—in what Hutton deplores as a "somewhat feeble and womanish chapter"[84]—by returning to Romola, thereby affirming as the last word in holiness the saintly blessedness of a woman who dedicates her life to the other wife and the children of her bigamist husband and enshrines the memory of the dubious martyr who has taught her the sanctity of duty.

This strategy has an ironic effect in that the novel, as mentioned above, is widely faulted, even by George Eliot herself, for the unbelievable goodness of its heroine, who is dubbed by Sara Sophia Hennell, for example, a saint rather than a woman. George Eliot seems to be unable to resist the compulsion to create an ideal woman, while at the same time insisting—to the point of emphatic italics—on the worthiness of a flawed hero, whose very worthiness lies in his sense of failure and unworthiness. The narrator claims that harder to bear than martyrdom is "the lowest depth of resignation . . . to be found when we have covered our heads in silence and felt, 'I am not worthy to be a martyr: the Truth shall prosper, but not by me.' "[85] Later George Eliot is more emphatic and even allows her narration to turn polemical: "There is no jot of worthy evidence that from the time of his imprisonment to the supreme moment, Savonarola spoke of himself as a martyr." This glorious idea had been succeeded by the inglorious one of "resignation," the narrator asserts. "*But therefore he may the more fitly be called a martyr by his fellow-men to all time.*"[86] Seemingly then, in trying to show the sanctity of ordinary life, George Eliot ends up merely transferring the halo from within the institutional church to another religious domain of her own construction where Saint Romola presides, thereby confirming the separation of secular and sacred instead of demonstrating their reconciliation in the human.

The Spanish Gypsy: *Annunciation as Renunciation*

George Eliot continues to tackle this problem of voicing "great, great facts" in human form in subsequent works. It proves so daunting in *The Spanish Gypsy* that she abandons the text, then comes at the problem from the opposite direction in *Felix Holt*, and afterwards returns to rework and complete the poetic piece. But it is vital in all of this that George Eliot is sufficiently self-critical that she can articulate her difficulties with *Romola* in terms of a failure to incarnate her ideas. As she says in her letter to Hennell quoted above, she is trying to do something better than she has done before, and such an effort entails failing. Shifting her expectations to this level of uncertainty by venturing into unknown territory means inviting failure; and yet, as with Savonarola, there is something glorious in being able to say "the Truth shall prosper, but not by me." It is just at this time that she sees in Italy what she will later identify as the inspiration for *The Spanish Gypsy*: a painting on the subject of the Annunciation, "said to be by Titian." As she later writes in her "Notes on *The Spanish Gypsy* and Tragedy," she saw in the idea of a young woman preparing for "ordinary womanhood" and learning "suddenly" that she is instead "chosen to fulfil a great destiny" the potential for a "great dramatic motive."[87]

It is not difficult to see why the woman who senses a destiny to incarnate ideas in a new way would be inspired by the story of the girl who is destined to be the vehicle of Christ's incarnation. Yet it is curious to see what she did with this inspiration: the young Jewish woman living under Roman rule becomes the model for a young Gypsy woman living as a Christian in a Christian realm in which Jews have been forced to convert, Moors are the enemy, and Gypsies are the most reviled of all. It is clear that the racial mix fascinates George Eliot and, as many commentators note, race is the lowest common denominator that determines Fedalma's choice and her lover Silva's "slow misery."[88] Commentators from the beginning have critiqued the implausibility of the heroine's choice and its implications, even calling it unethical for her to choose to follow a father and a racial group with whom she has no history and turn her back on the people with whom she has lived most of her life.[89] Readers all see in the heroine's dilemma a replaying of the dilemma of Maggie and of Romola, and the reiterated idea quoted above—"the great problem of the shifting relation between passion and duty"—suggests that George Eliot was quite aware of the vexatious nature of the question she was exploring.

In her "Notes on *The Spanish Gypsy* and Tragedy" George Eliot makes clear that what she aims to do in *The Gypsy* is to cast the heroine's dilemma in classically tragic terms. She speaks in these "Notes" of finding in each individual lot "the same story" involving "some grand collision . . . between the individual and the general."[90] While her whole career consists of illuminating the grand tragedies of ordinary human "renunciations,"[91] these works of the 1860s see her working out more consciously the meaning of the tragedy of renunciation by focusing more particularly on the figure of the martyr—here moving from the officially proclaimed Savonarola to the ordinary martyrdom of a young woman who "must walk an unslain sacrifice."[92] Her aim could not perhaps be made clearer than by her transformation of the story of the Annunciation into another tale of renunciation. In *The Spanish Gypsy* she translates the inspiration she receives from Titian's picture of the angel Gabriel appearing to Mary into a secular myth wherein the daughter Fedalma renounces her love for, as George Eliot puts it, "what we call duty."[93] Her aim, as these "Notes" suggest, is to translate what have traditionally been seen as divinely inspired acts into acts taking place within socially and naturally imposed structures wherein individuals make choices—choices that are constrained or even dictated by "the dire necessities of our lot, partly as to our natural constitution, partly as sharers of life with our fellow-beings"—that shape character and destiny.[94]

George Eliot's next move in this 1860s trajectory is to produce in Felix Holt a secular saint, the opposite of Savonarola in his lack of religious adherence but the famous martyr's equal, within his own provincial sphere, in charisma and influence. Felix Holt earns her the same charge as had Romola, in being too ideal for credulity, but George Eliot's ascription to him of the Miltonic (or perhaps more aptly Blakean) "human face divine"[95] points to her desire to exceed the limits of realism to outline a new kind of hero, the kind she points to in her "Note" on feeling, who inspires others by his very failure.

The Martyrdom of Ordinary Life

As noted above, no one is more aware than George Eliot herself of her failure at this time to "incarnate" her ideas. Neither is anyone more capable of articulating her own difficulties or of articulating her way out of those difficulties in and through her own works. In her "Notes on *The Spanish Gypsy* and Tragedy" she reminds readers that "rational reflection" will not allow anyone to make their peace with "inherited misfortunes." "Happily," she goes on, "we are not left to that.

> Love, pity, constituting sympathy, and generous joy with regard to the lot of our fellowmen comes in—has been growing since the beginning—enormously enhanced by wider visions of results—by an imagination actively interested in the lot of mankind generally; and these feelings become piety—*i.e.*, loving, willing submission, and heroic Promethean effort towards high possibilities, which may result from our individual life.[96]

This statement could serve as a fine summation of George Eliot's aesthetic, and I want to pay particular attention to the understanding of imagination she expresses here. This imagination "enormously enhance[s]" feelings of love by finding grounds for hope for the future, by extending these feelings beyond ourselves to humankind in general, and by at the same time giving us models of "heroic" action that demonstrate the value of "individual life." By this process, the imagination turns feelings into piety. It is this kind of religious imagination that George Eliot does demonstrate in her greatest works, and she makes her way to the most masterful of them, *Middlemarch*, by working out her incarnational aesthetic during this period.

An important element of the experiments she was conducting at this time consisted in an exploration of the nature of religion in different contexts. First she has Romola conduct her own experiment in institutional religion, from which she emerges with a sense that her personal, noninstitutional kind of religion is holy. Then George Eliot considers religion in the cultural context of medieval Granada, in which Silva's uncle and Fedalma's father construct race as religion, promoting a faith in one's own people. In this context she lingers over the possibility of no religion, both in the Gypsies and in her Christian hero. When he abandons his own culture, Silva has the uncomfortable sense of being naked without a creed: unlike the Gypsies, "He could not grasp / Night's black blank mystery / And wear it for a spiritual garb / Creed-proof."[97] In contrast, Zarca claims that "the Zincali exult in having no god,"[98] that theirs "is a faith / Taught by no priest, but by their beating hearts: / Faith to each other"; the Gypsies "call our Holy Place / The hearth that binds us in one family."[99] Still, Zarca's claim seems romantic and egotistical in that he goes so far as to credit himself with bearing "the power divine that chooses them and saves."[100] In the end both Zarca and Silva seem doomed, however, with Silva ending his days as a pilgrim doing eternal penance and seeking forgiveness from the pope, and the Gypsies aiming in vain to construct a nation based on Zarca's inspiration and memory. After working in this medieval melting pot of religious and cultural difference, George Eliot experiments further in *Felix Holt* with the idea of a religion-less hero as she moves back home to the England of her youth and to a secular hero, who makes a religion out of his devotion to the oppressed workers of his community.

In the terms of my discussion, we might think of this period of the 1860s as the beginning of George Eliot's own return to the fraught landscape of her youth, equipped with a sense of the wider range of imaginative and religious possibilities that she has gleaned from her excursions into foreign spheres. She emerges from this experience of the art in which saints, angels, and madonnas abound with a sense, not of a god who is dead, but of what Richard Kearney calls "a God who may be." Kearney's understanding of the poetic imagination helps to explain this development; he speaks of its threefold ethical powers—the utopian, the testimonial, and the empathic[101]—in a way that resonates with George Eliot's practice. Among the aspects of imagination that Kearney identifies and George Eliot explores are "a priority of moral testament over moral theory,"[102] "the imaginative power of sympathy" as "a *sine qua non* of all ethics,"[103] and the "redemptive power" of imagination.[104] To recall George Eliot's "Notes" on tragedy, she speaks there of how her own love and joy in her fellow humans have been "growing since the beginning—enormously enhanced by wider visions of results—by an imagination actively interested in the lot of mankind generally." And she has deepened her understanding of the "piety" that is grounded in "loving, willing submission" and "heroic . . . effort towards high possibilities, which may result from individual life."

One can only imagine what Tito's son could be thinking of Romola's response to his statement that he would like to grow up to be "great" and "happy," and have "a good deal of pleasure." His "Mamma Romola" replies:

> We can only have the highest happiness, such as goes along with being a great man, by having wide thoughts, and much feeling for the rest of the world, as well as ourselves; and this sort of happiness often brings so much pain with it, that we can only tell it from pain by its being what we would choose before everything else, because our souls see it is good.[105]

George Eliot defines here, in this goal of a happiness that is only morally distinguishable from pain, a kind of martyrdom of ordinary life. While the statement may easily be seen as sanctimonious and morbid, it is also inspiring because it is spoken in the voice of a woman who has learned in much sorrow the lesson she is passing on: "If you mean to act nobly and seek to know the best things God has put within reach of men, you must learn to fix your mind on that end, and not on what will happen to you because of it."[106] It seems to me that George Eliot experiences, in trying to incarnate her ideas in this period, the pains and failures that lend credibility to the sufferings of the ordinary martyr.

Again it is one of her poems, "O May I Join the Choir Invisible," written a year before *The Spanish Gypsy* was finally published, that most poignantly expresses the consolation she derives from this experience.[107] The editors of the *Standard Edition of George Eliot's Essays and Poems,* published in New York (n.d.), strategically situate this poem at the end of their text, while at the same time noting that it was originally published a year before *The Spanish Gypsy*, which is situated as the first poem in this American edition. Perhaps the editors seek a kind of closure in the poet's prayer to join the invisible choir of "immortal dead who live again" in others who live better than she herself has been able to do. She calls such a membership "heaven," in its legacy of "that sweet purity / For which we struggled, failed, and agonized / With widening retrospect that bred despair." While the poet does not call herself a martyr, she does find consolation in the hope that "martyred men" give for a future life after the end of "human Time." And she expresses a wish or prayer to be, like them, the inspirational "cup of strength" for others who follow her.[108] My aim in this chapter has been to show George Eliot's triumph in failure and to demonstrate the necessarily religious tenor of this paradox. In these works of the 1860s she learns what she could not have learned through obvious successes, and the works that follow will show how fruitful this experience would be.

Chapter 3

✦

Religion in a Secular World

Middlemarch and the Mysticism of the Everyday

> . . . for the soul can grow,
> As embryos, that live and move but blindly,
> Burst from the dark, emerge regenerate
> And lead a life of vision and of choice.
>
> —George Eliot, *Felix Holt*, "Epigraph," chap. 41

By any measure, *Middlemarch* is an extraordinary book. It brings to the reader the world of mid-nineteenth-century Britain, while conjuring a sense of the most intimate experience of individual lives. The novel is all the more remarkable for creating this profound sense of intimacy while maintaining strict discretion: readers are not invited into the bedrooms of its characters, but into their hearts and minds, as well as, I would argue, their souls. For while *Middlemarch* is less overtly concerned with religion than is *Romola* or *Adam Bede*, it is a radically more religious novel than either because with it George Eliot aims to redefine the notion and practice of religion for a society in which, as she says in the novel's "Prelude," there is "no coherent social faith and order."[1] She does this in large part by reminding readers, in a rather Kierkegaardian fashion, that they have souls.

There are three main vehicles for religious ideas in the novel: Dorothea herself, whose changing understanding of religion the reader is invited to monitor; the actual clerics: Casaubon, Cadwallader, and Farebrother, along with the latter's rival, Tyke, and Casaubon's curate, Mr. Tucker; and the hypocritically religious Bulstrode. In all three of these strands of the novel's narrative web religion is less a designated theme than a means of developing an exploration of the idea of personal integrity. But just here is where we find George Eliot's important statement about religion: rather than its being a force that stands outside of and apart from ordinary human life, religion must be seen as integral. Religious concerns must be seen as integrated with personal and social concerns and bound up with the pursuit of integrity.

The Vocation of the Artist: "The Legend of Jubal" and "Armgart"

George Eliot's key imaginative way of expressing the complexity of these ideas is through the metaphor of the web that pervades the novel, and her awareness that this complexity is reflexive—that she herself is caught in this web—is evident in two poems that herald its writing, "The Legend of Jubal" and "Armgart." These poems offer insight into George Eliot's self-understanding as an artist, and in doing so they provide a means of self-expression that both allows her to disentangle some of the knots of her own life's web and prevents these personal strands from becoming enmeshed in the novel's narrative web. Indeed, this process of what I would call self-integration depends on a triangular relation among the novel-in-process, the poems, and her own lived experience. *Middlemarch* has such profound integrity in a formal and in a thematic sense because while it is a realistic account of mid-century life and emerges out of George Eliot's own experience—or, more accurately that of Marian Evans Lewes—this realism is made authentic and more than merely personal by the mediation of the idealizing, Romantic perspective of the poems. The poems represent the mysterious transmuting power of art in that, by allowing George Eliot a more nakedly personal exploration of the nature of art and the role of the artist, they afford—in the sense made famous by that other Eliot—an impersonality that frees her to write this novel.

The wrestling with form that occupied George Eliot's imagination through the 1860s continues into the following decade with an intense period of poetic activity, starting in 1869 with two rather whimsical pieces, "Agatha" and "How Lisa Loved the King," followed in that same year by the highly personal series of sonnets on her childhood, which came to be called "Brother and Sister." By this time she is already meditating characters for a new novel she is calling *Middlemarch*, which she first mentions in her journal on the first day of 1869 and begins in August. Between October 1869 and January 1870 she writes "The Legend of Jubal," and then "Armgart" in August and September 1870. At the beginning of December that year she mentions working on a story she is calling "Miss Brooke"; two days later she has changed her plans, having decided to combine "Middlemarch" (which had focused on Lydgate) and the story of Dorothea into one novel.[2] When we contemplate this process, particularly in light of the poetic activity that punctuated it, we might see George Eliot's artistry as seeking to give shape to the "coherent social faith and order" that she notes as lacking for her heroine. Intriguing as well is the fact that the theme of integration that emerges as central in the story of the Middlemarchers is given form in *Middlemarch* itself. For, originating as it does from two separate ideas, the novel is nonetheless, as Joan Bennett remarks, "a single organism" that "gives a remarkable impression of unity" founded upon "singleness of vision."[3]

With apparent singleness of purpose then, George Eliot dedicates herself to this work until its completion at the end of 1872. But while one might sense the novel relentlessly taking shape during this period, the debilitating illness and self-doubt discussed in the last chapter continue to plague her. She is physically more seriously ill for longer than ever before, and she expresses in her journal her fear of never again being able to write a novel as good as *Felix Holt*. In this state of psychological dis-ease the poems serve a number of useful purposes. For one thing, they may be seen to be "priming the creative pump," as she is able to produce shorter works that stimulate her imagination and gird up her confidence. And "Jubal" and "Armgart," in taking the artist figure as their main character, explore the nature of art in a more direct, more daring, and more Romantic way than she allows herself to do in her novels. In these two poems George Eliot allows herself to voice her fears, her feelings, and her fantasies about being an artist.

Both these poems deal with the art of music. Born on the feast day of Saint Cecilia, the patron saint of music, George Eliot had a keen interest in music and was a skilled pianist and a regular concert- and operagoer. Maggie Tulliver's passion for music reflects her own, but she avoided constructing a novel around the artist figure, coming nearest to this focus with singers, Caterina, from her second story in *Scenes of Clerical Life*, "Mr. Gilfil's Love Story"; and Mirah and Alcharisi, as well as the artist and teacher Klesmer from her last novel, *Daniel Deronda*. She pays some attention to painters as well, in Will's friend Naumann in *Middlemarch*, and Daniel's friend Hans in *Daniel Deronda*. It is thus significant that only in poems does she give artists, Jubal and Armgart, center stage.

George Eliot builds her long poem "The Legend of Jubal" from the single reference in Genesis to one of the sons of the exiled Cain, who was "the father of all such as handle harp and organ" (Genesis 4.21), following a medieval tradition and references by Chaucer and Dryden.[4] George Eliot's poem is fascinating firstly in the way that she spins a myth of cultural origin out of the legend of Jubal.[5] The poem begins with Cain, banished by Jehovah for murdering his brother, seeking a land ruled by "wild joyous gods, who winked at faults and folly / And could be pitiful and melancholy." The narrator goes on to note that Cain never doubted the existence of such gods since "he looked within, and saw them mirrored there."[6] Cain's people live in a kind of Paradise, where "time was but leisure" and love reigns, because no one but Cain knows of Death.[7] When an accidental death occurs, everything changes. With this Fall, "Death was now lord of Life," Content became marred by Haste, "Work grew eager, and Device was born"; but, as if in compensation, everything in the world takes on a "new dearness" from its vulnerability to death. Then, with the new sense of "dread" of loss comes "Memory,"[8] which gives Jubal, who had already begun "the pastoral life" by extending the "ties that bind the family" to include animals,[9] the idea to "fashion acts that are to be / When we shall lie in darkness silently."[10]

Thus, "in that home of Cain the Arts began."[11] The poem traces Jubal's inspiration to construct the first musical instrument and then create the first song as he begins to find music around him, first in his half-brother Tubal's pounding of metal, then in the birds, then in human voices and animal sounds, "Till thought self-luminous flamed from memory, / And in creative vision wandered free." George Eliot strains to represent the source and process of inspiration as metaphysical:

> It was his thought he saw: the presence fair
> Of unachieved achievement, the high task,
> The struggling unborn spirit that doth ask
> With irresistible cry for blood and breath,
> Till feeding its great life we sink in death.[12]

The narrator thus foretells Jubal's fate as, after his music becomes so popular that all he hears is his own songs, he leaves his homeland in search of fresh melodies. When he returns after many years, his own people fail to recognize him; instead they scorn and mock the old man while enthusiastically singing the praises of the now-mythic Jubal. In a final apotheosis, death does not after all have the last word: instead, Jubal is taken up into heaven by a "face" who identifies herself as "thy loved Past, / The soul that makes thee one from first to last."[13]

Indeed, a prophet has no honor in his own country, but George Eliot makes the parallel to Christ explicit when "the face" asks whether anyone could ask more "from any god / Whether with gleaming feet on earth he trod / Or thundered through the skies" than to bear the pain involved in binding himself to the solitary task of providing music to accompany the "sweet unrest" of humanity. The face goes on to explain:

> Thy fate
> Was human music's self incorporate
> Thy senses' keenness and thy passionate strife
> Were flesh of *her* flesh and her womb of life.[14]

Jubal, then, gave birth to and died for human music—he incarnated it—and must "atone" with his final suffering at the hands of these same humans for the offense of having "too much" to give.[15]

Clearly, this poem tells of a legend and a myth, but it is also an allegory about the role of the artist. Most fascinating is the fact that with this poem George Eliot reintroduces the martyr figure, here as an artist. Thus in the figure of Jubal she incarnates the notion of art as religion, laying explicit claim to the high calling of the artist that she has articulated otherwise only in letters and personal writings. Familiar here from her earlier fiction, however, is George Eliot's preoccupation with the high price of any sense of special calling and the worthiness that must be proven by suffering.

"Armgart" pursues similar themes in a very different way. This is a dramatic poem in five short scenes, taking the titular character from glorious triumph as a successful classical singer, whose performances show her to be not simply a singer and performer but an artist, to an illness that damages her throat so that she is driven to leave the stage and languishes in despair before deciding to become a teacher. On one hand, this is a tale of hubris being humbled as Armgart moves from her proud scorn of being anything but the best and of jeopardizing her greatness by becoming a wife to a recognition of the aspirations and talents of those around her—whom she has heretofore seen only as the supporting characters in the drama of her life—and an acceptance of her own ordinariness. In a way, George Eliot is subtly confronting here the contradiction inherent in the notion that it takes a special person to recognize and explain the value of the ordinary. As a writer who takes as her life's work the celebration of the significance of ordinary life, she must practice a kind of doublethink whereby she forgets that her own work requires a special gift. It is for this reason, in part, that she speaks of her writing as both a high calling and as merely the work that she, like anyone else, does in the best way she can and with just as much labor, heartache, and pain.[16]

Like Jubal, Armgart must suffer a kind of death, but first George Eliot indulges a fantastic vision of a powerful, supremely gifted female artist whose narcissistic egoism and perfectionist, all-or-nothing expectations for herself are sustained by her companions and teacher and buoyed up by the applause of an adoring public. But she is a more complex figure than this would at first suggest. A true descendant of Maggie Tulliver, she is aware of a "rage" within that would wreak havoc on the world if she did not have her singing voice to "channel" it.[17] Moreover, though her lover admires her talent, he sees it as reflecting an "ambition" in conflict with her womanhood,[18] and Armgart is right to judge that as his wife she would not be free to pursue her career. Likewise she knows that the audience would turn on her and condemn her for impropriety if they were not swept away by her singing. Further, though she exudes such confidence, she is at the same time embroiled in a conflict between the demands of pure artistry and the appeal of performing virtuosic trills that imitate the birds but alarm her teacher (and are perhaps the reason for her eventual throat damage).

All these struggles over ambition, propriety, love vs. career, and art vs. popularity seem but surface ripples, however, compared to the depths of Armgart's artistic passion. For, while she may give the impression of vanity, George Eliot wants us to believe that Armgart, like Jubal, is a god of music. Her performance of Gluck's Orpheus, her teacher says, makes pleasure indistinguishable from pain; it does away with the music's writer and the singer's teacher: "Orpheus was Armgart, Armgart, Orpheus."[19] Returning to the stage after her performance, she is like a shy bride, says Leo, and Armgart concurs:

"I *was* a bride / As nuns are at their espousals."[20] Armgart agrees that her ambition includes adulation—even what might be seen as the blasphemous "gifts, / Gold, incense, myrrh"[21]—but affirms something other than "mean vanity" in her enjoyment. Not a prima donna, she says,

> No, but a happy spiritual star
> Such as old Dante saw, wrought in a rose
> Of light in Paradise, whose only self
> Was consciousness of glory wide-diffused,
> Music, life, power—I moving in the midst
> With a sublime necessity of good.[22]

George Eliot affirms Armgart's sense that she was born an artist with a spiritual calling. Like Elizabeth Barrett Browning's Aurora Leigh, Armgart rejects her suitor's proposal because she knows that she cannot be both a wife and an artist; she sees in her art a "supreme vocation" that affirms womanhood but precludes the "wife's renunciation."[23]

But the similarity stops there. Barrett Browning permits her heroine to reform and then to marry a chastened Romney, but George Eliot has her heroine reject the marital renunciation only to choose a more difficult one. Here, it is another woman who teaches the heroine her true calling. Armgart's teacher is her devoted cousin, Walpurga, whose limp makes physical and seemingly reasonable her role of helpmate to the gifted artist. When Armgart, having lost her sublime voice, acts out her new chosen role of tragic heroine, Walpurga shows her the puerility of the melodrama and the shamefulness of her egoism. And when Armgart despises her new role as voice teacher, giving it the sarcastic title "The Woman's Lot: a Tale of Everyday,"[24] Walpurga turns on her, berating Armgart for her narcissistic arrogance—always the speaker, never the listener; always the star, never the friend. She is fierce about the depths of "ruthless Nature's charry average" to which Armgart scorns to sink and where Walpurga has always had to live.[25] Walpurga calls her to recognize her own moral lameness, to call this change not a defeat but a "new birth—birth from that monstrous Self."[26] And in the end Armgart acknowledges her blindness toward others and graciously accepts her new "humble work" as teacher.[27]

In this poem George Eliot allows herself to air some of her deepest fears and anxieties, which, rather than being dispelled by her undeniable success, simply adapt themselves to this new stage and mutate to reveal the dark side of fame and success. As she begins *Middlemarch*, she wonders if her popularity actually means that she has succumbed to the temptation to a kind of a virtuosic trilling that has destroyed her true voice. She wonders how she can reconcile her respect for the "everyday" with her contempt for mediocrity, and how she can avoid mediocrity in her writing without obsessing about perfection. In Armgart's explosion of grief over her lost talent, George Eliot expresses her own fear that she might be asked to exchange the pain of suffering as a gifted artist in the pursuit of her "one high function"—which comes with the consolation of knowing that she has been set apart—for the more ordinary pain of an unremarkable calling, which comes with the more acute pain of living without that sense of special purpose. And yet, again, how can her need for such a sense be other than hypocritical in one whose calling is to celebrate the everyday?

The answer to these doubts takes what George Eliot would call a religious form. For while Armgart will no longer perform as an artist, she is determined not to contribute to the fund of "mediocrity" by "doing great tasks ill"; instead she chooses to "take humble work and do it well."[28] In other words, George Eliot reaffirms Armgart's sense of integrity in her changed role, the same sense that had sustained her sense of purpose as an artist. As she has told Walpurga, her "joy" as an artist was not in being separate from the world.

> All my good
> Was that I touched the world and made a part
> In the world's dower of beauty, strength, and bliss;
> It was the glimpse of consciousness divine
> Which pours out day and sees the day is good.[29]

This implied comparison of her own creative work to that of the God of Genesis might be seen as arrogant but must also be seen as the source of the sense of meaning and purpose that undergirds George Eliot's own sense of calling.

These two poems prepare George Eliot psychologically for the work of *Middlemarch* by allowing her to celebrate and affirm the purpose and joy of art and her sense of herself as an artist, while at the same time expressing all of the doubts and fears attached to that sense of herself as an artist and the equally strong doubts and fears that she might not, after all, be a true artist. Importantly, this includes the bold affirmation of the role of the artist as a holy calling, a religious activity, which is for George Eliot an utterly necessary conviction. The profundity of the psychological exploration that she achieves in *Middlemarch* is rooted in the depths of her own psychological struggles and self-analysis, and these poems provide her with an outlet for that self-attention, which the novel can use to tell a story that both is and is not her own. Important as well is her understanding that mediocrity does not consist in doing something ordinary, or in her case writing of the ordinary, but in doing badly whatever one is doing. Conversely, doing the ordinary well and with the intention of contributing one's own "good" to the general good offers what Armgart calls a "glimpse of consciousness divine."

Social Order and Professional Integrity

One way of looking at Armgart's dilemma is to say that she is challenged to reframe her sense of integrity in terms of integration—to sacrifice her sense of a special calling for the sake of performing a duty to and in the everyday, by integrating her own good into the web of social good. The theme that we found in earlier works is here again in new form: renunciation. It is this call to reframe one's own desires and interests for the good of the whole that is the burden of the key players in *Middlemarch*. "Armgart" helps us to see that for George Eliot this theme is profoundly religious, reflecting both her personal project of integration as professional writer, artist, and woman and her exploration of the place of religion in her world.

In *Middlemarch* her challenge is to explore the place of religion in public and private life in a world that lacks a "coherent social faith and order." But it is interesting, that, unlike Trollope in his *Barchester Chronicles*, George Eliot does not focus on the politics of the religious structures of the day (although we certainly learn something about this), but continues instead to write of clerics as human beings and as citizens of the human community and of their work as part of the whole work of that community. For, while she acknowledges that clerics are still traditionally considered to have a special role, she is concerned to show their influence in the everyday. For example, early in the novel she shows us that Mrs. Cadwallader, though she is more renowned for her intrusiveness and stinginess than for her piety, is primarily a good neighbor, whose foibles and eccentricities give more pleasure than grief to her husband's parishioners and tenants.

This notion of tenants introduces a key issue that comes into focus for George Eliot at this period. For in this middle period of her career, which culminates in her writing of *Middlemarch*, with its focus on the agitation surrounding the passing of the First Reform Bill in 1832, she turns her attention to the issue that has just resulted—in 1867—in the passing of the Second Reform Bill: the issue of class. In terms of my argument, this means that this novel's exploration of the question of integrity revolves around the treatment of the lower classes by their social superiors and the problem of mistaking rank for merit; and the movement toward reform, in these terms, is a movement away from hierarchy and segregation toward a more integrated structuring of society. Central to George Eliot's interrogation of these themes is the question of whether a religious response could have a bearing on these contemporary debates and what forms it might take.

George Eliot's move to looking at the construction of contemporary society shapes the narrative arc that extends from *Felix Holt* through *Middlemarch* and becomes a meditation on the notion of order and its role in forging the link between public and private life. Turning her attention for the first time to contemporary sociopolitical matters, she explores in these two novels the pressing questions of personal integrity and the vulnerability of the individual in the context of public unrest. For while she is always the author of personal lives, she makes explicit here the principle that informs her approach when the narrator of *Felix Holt* notes that "there is no private life which has not been determined by a wider public life,"[30] a statement broadened and deepened by the narrator of *Middlemarch* to become: "there is no creature whose inward being is so strong that it is not greatly determined by what lies outside of it."[31]

George Eliot addresses the question of social order in *Felix Holt* directly by embroiling her peace-loving hero in a situation of violent disorder, which results in a killing for which he is inadvertently responsible. But, interestingly, she examines the question of the relation between private life and public order primarily as an issue of gender, as she entangles her naive heroine, Esther, in a legal morass that almost results in a marriage of Gothic dimensions. Here we see how George Eliot demonstrates the social reality that women are social beings only through marriage, an idea whose implications she will confront more directly still in her last two novels. And it is fascinating that, in her own state of unwedded, technically adulterous bliss, George Eliot passionately believes in marriage, to the point that she goes so far as to articulate Esther's awakening to the possible felicities of marrying Felix with explicitly religious language. Although Esther is believed to be the beloved daughter of a devoutly religious minister, she is indifferent toward religion. And while Felix is a deliberately nonreligious man, George Eliot gives his selfless passion for justice a holy fervor, describing his countenance as he addresses the workingmen, for example, as "worthy to be called 'the human face divine.' "[32] Further, George Eliot describes Esther's turn from the Byronic "Childe Harold" to Felix as a conversion that entails "the first religious experience of her life—the first self-questioning, the first voluntary subjection, the first longing to acquire the strength of greater motives and obey the more strenuous rule." While the man's primary interest is in the sociopolitical order, then, the woman's is in obedience to the good man's "law" and adoption of the "rule" of his order.[33]

George Eliot's explicit designation of the man's influence for good and the woman's submission to a good man as religious is reinforced in "Address to Working Men, by Felix Holt," which was hoped by her publisher, John Blackwood, to have a moderating influence on workers agitating for reform in 1867. This piece merges the rhetoric used by Felix in the novel to promote orderly change through education with the rhetoric used by the novel's narrator to promote what is called the order of wedlock: in his address Felix advocates patience, "obedience," and adherence to the "rules of fellowship" as a kind of "religion" that will produce a harmonious and indeed sacred social order.[34]

Written as it is in the period surrounding the Second Reform Bill and dealing as it does with the period leading up to the First Reform Bill, it is not surprising that this question of order is a major preoccupation of

Middlemarch. But George Eliot shares with Percy Shelley's *Defence of Poetry* the view that there is a deep human longing for order that goes beyond politics. As the epigraph for chapter 9, Book I, of *Middlemarch* has it, "human souls" have always been the theater for "the struggle" for "order and the perfect rule." Of the many meanings of "order" in the *Oxford English Dictionary*, number 17 outlines the idea that is a starting point for both these novels, with *Middlemarch* teetering on the brink between traditional society and the imminent reforms that will irrevocably change the inflection of the definition: "The state in which the laws or rules regulating the relationship of individuals to the community, and the public conduct of members within a community, are maintained and observed and authority is obeyed; the rule of law or constituted authority; social cohesion; absence of riot, anarchy, or violent crime."

Having set *Felix Holt* in the period immediately following the passage of the 1832 Bill, when order has given way to riot and violence, George Eliot moves backwards in *Middlemarch* to the time leading up to the bill's passing and to a world in which the "social cohesion" included in definition number 17 is giving way. Here her concern is to probe more deeply the meaning—and the meanings—of order. The society of *Middlemarch* offers a cross-section of the burgeoning, diverse middle class of the mid-century English Midlands. As such it is a world preoccupied with the *Oxford English Dictionary*'s seventh meaning of "order," which is defined by "social class" and "specific rank." While it can be said that the most admirable people in the novel avoid this obsession and accept their own rank, several of the best of them are compromised by their inability to recognize the extent to which their superior social rank constitutes a privilege and, in being taken for granted, becomes a hindrance to self-understanding and growth. Others less fortunate (because of less fortune) see nothing but their own lower status and are desperate to leave it behind for what the narrator calls "that middle-class heaven, rank."[35]

This comment slyly alludes to the supreme power of rank, which is so seductive that it becomes a satisfactory replacement for religion, generating an almost metaphysical aura that readily blurs the concept of "order" into meanings 14—"the condition in which everything has its correct or appropriate place, and performs its proper functions; the force for harmony and regularity in the universe"—and 15: "the fixed arrangement found in the existing state of things; a natural, moral, spiritual, or social system in which things proceed according to definite, established, or constituted laws." This facility to project onto order, as manifest in rank, a "natural," "moral," or even "spiritual" good that is seen to be reflected in and sanctioned by the cosmic order underlies the preoccupation in this middle-class world with the great guarantor of heavenly bliss—and the source of so much calamity in the novel—marriage. It is this facility to blur meanings that turns marriage into an ultimate good that is necessary not only for social but also for cosmic order and turns this constructed order and the ranking system that upholds it into religion. And it is the religious power of such language that insidiously defines the "correct or appropriate place" and the "proper functions" of women in terms of their domestic relations with men.

I think it is clear that order was supremely seductive for George Eliot herself, and this is why she writes of its abuses, excesses, and mystifications with such compassion and subtlety. What the narrator says of her heroine, Dorothea, could be said of George Eliot herself: "Permanent rebellion, the disorder of a life without some loving reverent resolve, was not possible to her."[36]

In this her most ambitious novel to date, George Eliot takes on the whole social order of mid-century Britain, sustained as it still is by the money and power of the landed gentry and flirting or threatened with reform on almost every side. The issue of medical reform is a main thematic focus, and George Eliot represents Lydgate's work as bound up with his quest for one kind of order and his corresponding ignorance of another. His passionate longing is "to demonstrate the more intimate relations of living structure, and help define men's thought more accurately after the true order."[37] Ironically, however, Lydgate's study of "certain primary webs or tissues"[38] has blinded him to his own enmeshment in a social and sexual web spun out of female wiles and middle-class and professional envy. Like a fish that can't recognize its own dependence on the water it swims in, Lydgate is oblivious to his entrenchment in a particular place in the social order that controls his actions and even his feelings. His egoism blinds him, to the point that he ends up trapped in a marital structure that is devoid of true "intimate relations" and leaves the doctor virtually taking orders from an anatomically perfect but perfectly shallow, vain, materialistic wife. There is a certain poetic justice in Lydgate's hen-pecked, soul-destroying fate in that his foolish sense of his own power has included a deep scorn for women as persons. Nonetheless, readers are left to mourn him as an almost classical hero, because George Eliot makes clear that he was indeed of a different order and surely deserved a less cruel fate.

Social Order and Holy Orders

Despite Lydgate's romanticism and misogyny, George Eliot encourages readers to admire his pursuit of "the true order" and to sympathize with his quixotic self-image as a knight of the order of physicians. For George Eliot, this sense of professional integrity, shared as well by Caleb Garth in relation to "business," does amount to membership in a kind of sacred order.[39] Indeed, the men in the novel whose profession is "holy orders" in the traditional sense are held to the same standard. In this respect we can say that George Eliot treats clerics in the novel as part of the social order and asks the reader to assess them in terms of their integrity with respect to their calling, which notably does not include a distinguishable sense of a spiritual life.

In other words, George Eliot represents the novel's clerics as members of a particular profession, like medicine and business, rather than as set apart for religious life.

While George Eliot did not dedicate her career to an extended series of "Scenes of Clerical Life," she did include such scenes in almost all of her fiction, and *Middlemarch* represents a culmination of these representations. It will be useful at this point to sketch some of the major shifts that occurred in the role and function of the church of her day and its clergy.

The church historian R. A. Solway tells us that Anglican clergymen were "an integral part of the traditionally landed social and political establishment that governed the country throughout the eighteenth and much of the nineteenth century."[40] This mutual establishment of Church and State was completely entrenched in class, of course, as Trollope has illustrated so memorably, with ecclesiastical appointments having more to do with "whom one knew and whom one was related to" than standards of "merit and virtue."[41] Party and family alliance extended to university education as well. Nonetheless, while patronage told much of the story, the climate of reform helped encourage a higher standard in university education in general and in theological training in particular, such that there was some overall improvement over this period in the intellectual quality, and sometimes the sense of spiritual vocation, of clergy.[42]

The period leading up to and immediately following the passage of the First Reform Bill saw crucial changes in the role and function of the clergy. As W. M. Jacob puts it,

> Until about 1835 the parish was the critical unit of government in people's lives. . . . The parish was the backbone of the State. The key figure in a parish, exercising both a civil and ecclesiastical function, was the parish priest, the rector, vicar, or perpetual curate. Clergy and local elites were closely involved together in the civil and ecclesiastical government of a parish where there was little distinction between what was later distinguished as religious and secular.[43]

After the 1830s, Jacob goes on, the increasing separation of church and state brought about by reform meant that the role of clergy gradually became "spiritualized."[44] He points out that later centuries interpret the clerics' close integration in their society as secularizing and their withdrawal as spiritualizing, with the ironic effect being the loss of the bonds of understanding they once had. Another factor in these changes was urbanization and the concentration of working people in towns, a situation that contributed to the increasing politicization of the working class and sealed their disaffection from the established church.

George Eliot's fiction serves as a record of the changing function and role of the church, as embodied in each of the clergymen she depicts. From the first *Scenes* to *Middlemarch* she portrays a range of clerics, all of whom work in parishes as they were in the pre-1835 period described by the historians above, when the vicar "still enjoyed a great deal of prestige and influence."[45] In her earliest works of fiction—the three *Scenes* and *Adam Bede*—George Eliot represents clerics from the time of her youth, and from stories she heard as a youth. Mr. Gilfil, from her second story, set in the 1780s, might be seen to exemplify what J. R. H. Moorman calls the "typical" parish priest of this period: "He lived the comfortable life of a small country squire, took the necessary services on Sundays, visited where there was sickness, and spent his evenings playing cards or dining with his neighbours."[46] In the traditional fashion, Mr. Gilfil's clerical life is centered around his role as chaplain to the gentry, for whom he conducts family prayers. What is distinctive about George Eliot's depiction of Mr. Gilfil, of course, is her desire to show the heartache that has shaped his life and belies his apparent ease.

From the 1830s of Mary Anne Evans's youth, we have the hapless Amos Barton, who might fit Moorman's profile of one of "a large number of simple men who carried out their modest duties with reasonable efficiency," and the self-sacrificing Mr. Tryan from "Janet's Repentance," one of the "few really devoted parish priests,"[47] in this case one who, in this crucial time of social change, is extending his work to the poor in the towns. In *Adam Bede*, we see this picture developed, in the context of a glimpse at the comparative work of the established church and one of its dissenting brethren in the first decade of the century, as Dinah works among the urban poor while Mr. Irwine devotes himself to the rural parish and lives closely (albeit in relative poverty) with the landed gentry. Mr. Irwine is typical of the pre-1835 period in serving a multifaceted social role entailing officiating at or giving assistance to parishioners in legal, financial, and medical matters, as described by W. M. Jacob.[48] Mr. Irwine and Amos Barton also instantiate nicely another aspect of the shift occurring around this time: the classics-steeped Irwine represents the cleric more typical of the earlier age, who, according to Jacob, was often "in the forefront of intellectual life,"[49] while Amos is more typical of the curate whose origins in the lower class means in part that he serves his parishioners without notable intellectual gifts or theological training. Mr. Irwine also shares with Dr. Kenn, from *The Mill on the Floss*, the qualities of compassion and wisdom that make the local clergyman the person to whom Adam (in the first decade of the 1800s) and Maggie (a decade or so later) turn in their trouble.

The relationship between established churchman and Dissenter that we find in *Adam Bede* is given another turn in *Felix Holt*, set at the very moment of Reform in 1832. Like Dinah, the devout Mr. Lyon is well versed in the Bible and is dedicated to the poor and working folk, but he is at the same time a man of his political time, working for changes that will benefit the working class. His ecclesiastical adversary, the Reverend Augustus Debarry, as a member of the ruling family (as "always"),[50] is what the narrator calls a "fine specimen of the old-fashioned aristocratic clergyman."[51] The ironic voice of the narrator makes clear that such a specimen does not demonstrate theological knowledge or much pastoral care, but this doesn't matter in any case since the farmers' presence at church, where there is room for Debarry tombs but not for parishioners, is at best "exceptional."[52] Debarry thus embodies the incumbents that, according to Solway, were still most prevalent in the 1840s: "ambitious, pleasure-seeking, mediocre party-men who owed their advancement to family and friends."[53] Despite the fact that Mr. Lyon's earnest spirituality and absent-mindedness make him a laughingstock to many, George Eliot leaves the reader in no doubt about her own respect for such men as he and about the fact that it is the Reverend Debarry who has more to answer for with respect to the decline of religious observance.[54]

In *Middlemarch* it is as if George Eliot brings these various clerical figures together to take up familiar roles on this larger stage. But while most of them played central roles in their previous appearances, here they are all, except for the miserable Rev. Casaubon, just part of the social web—significant players, one or two quite important, and all of them worthy of interest, but none a major focus of narrative attention. Certainly George Eliot's main object from the start has been to show clergy as men like other men, but here she sharpens her attention to the fact that each of them is no more important than any other person. This might be George Eliot's strongest statement about the parish clergy of 1832: the idea that, whether they know it or not, they are becoming less and less important, less and less influential. Still, she represents them with the deepest respect and evenhanded tolerance.

One might think that she has a soft spot for poor clergymen, and perhaps she does, but in fact, as Solway notes, the church of this period was served by "thousands of curates eking out a bare subsistence serving several parishes for pluralistic non-residents, many of whom were themselves holding additional cures to obtain an adequate income."[55] As George Eliot's ironic narrator puts it in introducing Amos Barton, curate at Shepperton Church, and his rather large family: "Those were days when a man could hold three small livings, starve a curate a-piece on two of them, and live badly himself on the third."[56] In *Middlemarch* all the clerics except the miserable Casaubon are poor. George Eliot's favorite among them, Farebrother, is like Reverend Irwine in being prevented from marrying because all of his meager income goes to support his mother and unmarried sister and aunt. Farebrother is also similar to his ecclesiastical forebear from *Adam Bede* in being an intellectual, but times have changed in that, while Irwine's intellectual passion was classical literature and language, Farebrother's is science. Similar as well is their pastoral ability; Irwine's, as we saw in chapter 1, is of a practical, wise kind without much regard for doctrinal purity or theological rigor. Farebrother demonstrates a similar pastoral skill and care for his flock and is like Irwine too in not being drawn into doctrinal debates and in delivering sermons that, according to Lydgate and others, are worth listening to.

But in the later novel George Eliot is interested in constructing a more complicated clerical figure. For Farebrother takes the neighborly card-playing mentioned above to another level in being driven by his poor financial state to gambling. Also unlike with Irwine, we get a glimpse of his internal state when he struggles with and finally resists the temptation to compete for the affection of the woman he can finally afford to marry, and when he admits, at least in private, that he is pursuing the wrong calling and would rather have been a man of science than a man of the cloth.

Another churchman in *Middlemarch* whose calling we might wonder about is the Reverend Cadwallader, rector of Freshitt and Tipton, who nonetheless shares with Irwine and Farebrother the ability to preach well. He too is a poor man but has been luckier than the other two in being able to marry the woman he loved, a "high-born" woman[57] who romantically defied her family by marrying a destitute clergyman, and who not only loves him and keeps his household with a stringent attention to their modest pocketbook but tolerates his lackadaisical ways and even enjoys his sermons. Cadwallader's professional abilities remain otherwise obscure to the reader since, though he is a good-natured man, he avoids getting involved in the lives of his parishioners and giving unsought opinions on any subject other than fishing, his true passion. Though we hear the irony, the narrator seems to resemble Cadwallader himself in her response, not seeming to see any reason to pass judgment on a harmless man "who take[s] life easily,"[58] the most severe adjective that is used against him being his wife's epithet, "charitable."[59]

George Eliot uses Farebrother to bring to light another feature of clerical life, when he competes with clerical colleagues for vacant ecclesiastical positions. Where once a clergyman depended on family and friends for advancement, the new social structures mean that they now depend more on business and professional people of the middle classes. In this respect clergymen are in a position very similar to members of other professions, with medical men being George Eliot's particular focus in *Middlemarch*. While there is no reason other than his good will, common sense, and high intellectual standards—rather than any religious sense that we are made aware of—to credit Lydgate's opinion on these matters, George Eliot's narrator takes his admiration of Farebrother's sermons and character as enough to ground Dorothea's willingness to consider him for the living at Lowick. Lydgate calls Farebrother's the best preaching he has heard, full of "plain, easy eloquence" in the style of Hugh Latimer.[60] Neither he nor Dorothea can see any use in the "apostolic" style of his rival, Tyke, or the latter's propensity to preach on obscure doctrinal matters.[61]

This brings us to the cleric whose vacant living Farebrother will fill, Mr. Casaubon. Although we are never made privy to the subjects or quality of his sermons, his scholarly bent suggests that they would involve a lot of etymology and historical documentation, rather than attempting to provide the "wider blessing" Dorothea is hoping for in the sermons of his successor.[62]

As mentioned, Casaubon is the only clergyman in *Middlemarch* who is not poor, and his wealth allows him to employ a curate to do the parish work, as is standard practice, leaving him free from clerical duties other than Sunday sermons. By the time the reader visits Lowick, in chapter 9 of Book I, everyone except Dorothea already knows that Casaubon has no room in his tiny consciousness for the people of his parish. Instead, Mr. Tucker, like Amos in being blessed with many children and noted by the ironic narrator as "one of the 'inferior clergy,'" is "able to answer all [Dorothea's] questions about the villagers and the other parishioners."[63] And we are not surprised at Casaubon's ignorance in these parochial matters, since we have already learned from Mr. Brooke that Casaubon is "a little too buried in books" to get involved with working for the reform of laws whereby sheep-stealers are hanged.[64]

Only someone as insistently blind as Dorothea could fail to see that Casaubon is not concerned with goodness, in other than a strictly moralistic sense, nor with anything to do with the well-being of others, except as a Christian duty, nor with any matters that might be called spiritual, except in the most church-bound sense. As such Casaubon serves as almost a caricature through which George Eliot can exemplify the deplorable state of the Christian clerical system. In going through the motions of religious service, Casaubon can be seen to represent a type of clergyman that Solway claims is typical, whose generosity was "often a matter of role obligation essentially split off from any genuine emotional involvement with the suffering poor."[65] And in Casaubon's case, of course, he is split off from involvement with the suffering of anyone except himself.

Nonclerical Religious Life

Dorothea's unique blindness concerning this "dried bookworm towards fifty"[66] is fascinating and indeed almost unbelievable, a fact that leads attentive readers to the conclusion that George Eliot has particular cause for making her heroine unlike anyone else. Her sister, the knowing Celia, knows that Dorothea "always sees what nobody else sees" and misses what everyone else sees.[67] In this respect Dorothea is a true seer in the tradition of Tiresias, of the nineteen-year-old, female, nineteenth-century variety. She shares with Lydgate the social blindness that is the corollary of a deep insight into a high, true order—in his case an order of science, in hers of religion—that others fail to see. And while Casaubon is almost a caricature and Dorothea is almost an ideal, together they make a thoroughly believable unhappy marriage. One of the reasons Dorothea mis-sees him is her intense idealism, which includes a desire for goodness and truth that is so palpable that it takes on substance for her in the form of the first person in her small world who appears, like herself, not to belong in the social order of Middlemarch described above.

Casaubon is devoted to something different than are the usual male suspects of her acquaintance, and her desire easily reconstructs his obsession with his studies as a passion for an ideal of truth and goodness that is beyond the ordinary world of her experience.

As mentioned, George Eliot herself knew the seductions of the pursuit of order, including one that would explain the universe.[68] In *Middlemarch* we find her replaying Maggie's relationship with Thomas à Kempis, whose voice, speaking across time as if alive in his *Imitation of Christ*, promises "a secret of life that would enable her to renounce all other secrets," the "key" to happiness.[69] Her successor in this quest, Dorothea is attracted to a living man who is in pursuit of the "Key to all Mythologies," but the narrator makes clear that his quest is so blighted by his "morbid consciousness" and "melancholy absence of passion" as to be a pursuit of death.[70] According to the principles of George Eliot's own religious code, Casaubon is the worst of sinners in being, not just obsessed with his work and blind to his own failings—as most of us are—but in being ruled by loveless ego to the point of seeking absolute power over his wife, not only in his lifetime but after his death. Sir James is correct to call their marriage "horrible": Casaubon is indeed, as the jealous suitor says, "a mummy"[71] but also proves a veritable Gothic villain, whose desire is to control his wife even after she has become his widow.

Perhaps Dorothea is duped partly because Casaubon's duplicity is so deep-seated that he himself mistakes it for integrity. And in this we find George Eliot's subtle commentary on the worst flaws of the clerical system, in that while she herself in creating a realistic picture must represent clergy as just another profession, there is still a sense in which this profession is meant to be different. This is why Casaubon's failure, like that of the church he serves, has such dire consequences. Because he is a priest (something readers might be forgiven for forgetting) his obsessiveness becomes all the darker—more Gothic and more deplorable—for his way of turning his profession of holy orders into a cover for what Walpurga called "monstrous Self."

Casaubon's profession must be seen as crucial to the naive Dorothea's attraction to him. George Eliot makes clear that her intensely religious nature puts her at odds with the predominantly secular world in which she lives. But it is important that Dorothea does conform in the matter of the key expectation for a young woman: to be in need of a husband. Somewhat oddly to many readers, the novel is prefaced by a "Prelude" in which George Eliot explains why a nineteenth-century woman may not imitate the sixteenth-century Saint Theresa, who "found her epos in the reform of a religious order" rather than marry. Perhaps George Eliot feels the need to explain why she makes marriage the central event of her heroine's life. She ranks her heroine among many unfulfilled Theresas, whose "ardour alternated between a vague ideal and the common yearning of womanhood"[72] and then casts Dorothea's fate as ultimately determined by the latter. Given that, George Eliot constructs Dorothea as a woman who, since she must marry, will seek a religious man. And in Casaubon she believes she has found "a living Bossuet, whose work would reconcile complete knowledge with devoted piety . . . a modern Augustine who united the glories of doctor and saint."[73]

Dorothea's desire for a holy husband follows from her devout nature: her beauty has the appeal of "the Blessed Virgin," and her style of dress "gave her the impressiveness of a fine quotation from the Bible."[74] In marriage she is "yearning" for a context in which to practice "her own rule of conduct." Filled with a sense of her own uselessness, she longs for "the submergence of self in communion with Divine perfection"[75] and mistakes Casaubon's seriousness for the wisdom that will facilitate it. If it were not so tragic, her quixotic determination to see the dried-up old scholar, not as a knight in shining armor but as "a modern Augustine" mixed with Pascal, would be laughable. From the silly vanity of the more ordinary Esther we have moved to the almost pathological self-loathing of the beautiful young girl who looks to this grotesque "union" to "deliver her from her own girlish subjection to her own ignorance, and give her the freedom of voluntary submission to a guide who would take her along the grandest path."[76]

For although Dorothea is full of illusions about her future husband, she has no illusions about her dependency as a woman. Though she is different from most women—and the virtual opposite of Esther—in combining an "intensity of religious disposition" with a "passionate desire to know and to think" and an equally passionate concern for "doing good,"[77] at the age of nineteen she has already learned the limits of gender. Her large, ardent nature feels "hemmed in" by "a labyrinth of petty courses, a walled-in maze of small paths" that require her to follow "rules which were never acted upon." She wishes to exchange a rule of life that she sees as petty and meaningless for one that is "grand" and purposeful: the rule of married life.[78] Her "faith" fatally transforms Casaubon's "frigid rhetoric" of courtship into an invitation to the purposeful, shared life of her imaginings,[79] such that she sees in his work the "Key" to her finally discovering "a binding theory which could bring her own life and doctrine into strict connexion with that amazing past, and give the remotest sources of knowledge some bearing on her actions."[80]

More than a husband, the narrator says, Dorothea wants "a sort of father"[81] and teacher, a wise older man to conduct her, via Latin and Greek and perhaps even a smattering of Hebrew, to those revered "provinces of masculine knowledge" that "seemed to her a standing-ground from which all truth could be seen more truly."[82] She believes that knowledge must be the means to wisdom, goodness, and the power of action, and, having perhaps learned from Maggie to moderate her desire, accepts that she will attain such knowledge through her husband. In this way she hopes to "arrive at the core of things, and judge soundly on the social duties of the Christian."[83] Although the narrator notes that Dorothea would be content to be a humble "lamp-holder" for her husband's explorations,[84] she also observes that the young woman "had not reached that point of renunciation at which she would have been satisfied with having a wise husband: she wished, poor child, to be wise herself."[85]

At the same time though, it is not merely intellectual improvement Dorothea longs for.

> She did not want to deck herself with knowledge—to wear it loose from the nerves and blood that fed her action; and if she had written a book she must have done it as Saint Theresa did, under the command of an authority that constrained her conscience. But something she yearned for by which her life might be filled with action at once rational and ardent; and since the time was gone by for guiding visions and spiritual directors, since prayer heightened yearning but not instruction, what lamp was there but knowledge? Surely learned men kept the only oil; and who more learned than Mr. Casaubon?[86]

While she does hope to get to "the core of things," then, Dorothea more urgently seeks to engage her whole being, to become part of a greater order. As the novel's "Prelude" informs us, this heroine is no Saint Theresa, but she is nonetheless on a spiritual quest, yearning with her whole being for "something" that will connect knowledge and action, mind and body, reason and passion. Dorothea believes that marriage to a good and learned man is her ticket to that "something"—the necessary conduit to link the woman to the world and give sanction and legitimacy to her action. Sadly, of course, she is even less able to act once she is married. Bound by "the gentlewoman's oppressive liberty," she finds herself after her marriage "in a moral imprisonment" in which "her religious faith was a solitary cry" and her hope for a purposeful life is sustained only by an "inward vision."[87]

In Dorothea's plight George Eliot replays the comedy of a blind, romantic girl falling for a man devoted to his cause to the point of farce and then tragedy. We are thrust from Jane Austen to William Blake here however, as the innocent, "childlike" Dorothea[88]—God's gift—is forced by her marriage to chant the dirge of experience. The reason for this has everything to do with order, in that, like Lydgate, Dorothea overlooks the everyday power of social and conventional order and is at the same time duped by a belief that in marriage she is submitting to the rule of a holy order that will sanctify and bless her submission by turning it into good action. And indeed this is just what does happen for Esther, so that with the triangulation of these three texts—*Middlemarch, Felix Holt*, and Felix's "Address to the Working Man"—we catch a glimpse of the complexity of George Eliot's response to the question of order. For what Felix is exhorting the workingmen to adopt is modeled by the "voluntary submission" of Esther and Dorothea, and the religious resonance of his language suggests that adopting such "rules of fellowship"[89] will produce a harmonious, and indeed sacred, social order.

But for the heroine of *Middlemarch* the situation is more complicated. At crucial moments in the novel, George Eliot compares Dorothea to Saint Theresa, whose "passionate, ideal nature demanded an epic life," but she does so, as mentioned above, in order to make clear that such a life is forbidden to her nineteenth-century heroine. This is because of the contemporary requirement of marriage for a woman and Dorothea's misguided choice of husband, along with the fact that in her society religion has been replaced by secular values to the point where there is "no coherent social faith and vision" to help her.[90]

It is interesting, however, that both *Felix Holt* and *Middlemarch* in the end represent the same vision of marital joy: two young people deep in love and conversation. For Dorothea, who had "looked up gratefully" to the Reverend Mr. Casaubon believing he could "understand the higher inward life" and join with her in "some spiritual communion,"[91] finds a true lover and soul mate in Will Ladislaw, a young man with whom she can talk and even laugh. When Casaubon is disposed of, Dorothea's friends continue to believe that another "husband is the best thing to keep her in order,"[92] and her second marriage might on the outside look as if it is satisfying this convention, for Ladislaw does become "an ardent public man" and she, a mother and dutiful wife whose life seems to "have been absorbed into the life of another."[93] But George Eliot carefully designs Ladislaw as a husband who, being what Middlemarchers call a "gypsy" who belongs to "no class,"[94] will not perpetuate the existing social or marital order. Instead, George Eliot makes clear that their private life, "hidden" from the eye of the world and from the reader, is a relationship of the highest order that two human beings can achieve.[95] She thus seems to confirm the pronouncement of Philip Wakem's father: "We don't ask what a woman does—we ask whom she belongs to."[96] But she puts forward the idea, first in a rather bald way in *Felix Holt* and then in a fuller way in *Middlemarch*, that wedlock may actually be the holy order of a contemporary religion. In a "Finale" that answers the "Prelude," George Eliot suggests that her heroine's apparent insignificance as the wife of Will Ladislaw and the mother of his children is representative of all—even ourselves and the author herself—whose vital influence for good is both "unhistoric" and endlessly fruitful.[97]

Dorothea and the Mysticism of Everyday Life

George Eliot's invocation of Saint Theresa reminds us that though she scorned the various forms of spiritualism that were gaining prominence in the later years of her life, this period also marked the beginnings of her renewed interest in ancient traditions of mysticism. In *Middlemarch*, we see George Eliot tentatively but certainly engaging with religious mysticism in a way that anticipates the great modernist thinkers on mysticism, Evelyn Underhill and William James. In Dorothea, George Eliot creates a neo-Theresa, whose "hidden life" as the unheralded influence for "growing good" provides a model for the reader.[98] Dorothea follows George Eliot's Renaissance heroine, Romola, in finding a new way for faith after her disillusionment with clerical, institutional Christianity; and the religious practice she develops could be understood in terms of Karl Rahner's description of a mysticism of everyday faith.

Dorothea's spiritual odyssey and its significance for George Eliot's religious imagination may also be understood in the context of some recent ideas of the philosopher Richard Kearney, including his consideration of how various mystical traditions have responded to disillusionment with the familiar idea of God.[99] In his 2010 book *Anatheism* Kearney asks: what happens "for those who—after ridding themselves of 'God'—still seek God?"[100] Crucial to Kearney's purpose here is to challenge the post-Enlightenment claim that societies and individuals "grow up" and grow out of faith, replacing religious belief with rationality; in response, Kearney is arguing that we grow indeed—not necessarily away from God, however, but from one kind of God to another.

Kearney's subtitle is *Returning to God after God*, and he eloquently encapsulates his idea of a return to theism with the prefix "ana," which in its compound meaning—"up, back, again"—conjures the notion of a constant movement towards, away from, back to, and around the divine in a kind of cosmic and intimate dance. Kearney explores many forms of this return in our post-religious, post-secular age, and it is key that it is a return of what was once known, a retrieval of what has been—a recognition, rather than a discovery of something new. Religion, in one of its meanings, is about links and bonds, and Kearney's conception here is of a link to something outside oneself—not simply a subjective sense—that is already known and thus recognized. Important too, and resonant with the Christian terms of the resurrection story, is the necessity for a departure that will afford a recognition and a revelation of meaning that couldn't be known by continued presence. It is necessary, in other words, that there be a withdrawal, a detachment, in order for there to be the new perspective that allows for true belief by awakening passive reception to active engagement. And sometimes, says Kearney, we need to hear stories of the death of God and experience the absence of God—just as Jesus did on the cross—in order to find out about and enact God's living presence.

All of Kearney's ideas pertain to cultural as well as personal development, and, indeed, the micro and macro levels of religious experience mutually inhere in and facilitate each other. At both levels the return he is heralding is marked by two essential shifts in religious understanding that resonate with George Eliot's thinking to the extent that we can see her as anticipating Kearney's anatheistic approach. These are the shift in understanding from the sovereign God to the suffering God, and the concurrent shift from "my God" and "our God" to the God of all. The first of these is taking shape, as I will outline here, from the beginning of George Eliot's fiction; from this follows her exploration of the second of these shifts in her final novel, *Daniel Deronda*. This process demonstrates a crucial idea that George Eliot shares with Kearney—that religious understanding evolves and indeed must evolve if any faith is to claim to be alive, an idea that I will develop more fully in chapter 5.

Kearney argues that all religions hold a view of both a sovereign and a suffering version of God and that they have emphasized the former at the expense of the latter. Christianity holds to a "God of power and might" (as the Anglican tradition celebrates in its liturgy) because we need to believe in a God who is powerful; and while we also believe in a suffering God—manifest primarily in the person of Christ—we underplay this vulnerable aspect because of the dominant culture of fear. In simple terms, one could say that a culture must "grow up"—leaving behind the god who demands blood sacrifice and provides inspiration and strength and warrant for war and other forms of cultural dominance—and instead model the god who suffers and dies for others. Along with this, a culture must surrender the notion of a god whose interests are identified with one's own and embrace instead a god who is there for everyone, even one's enemies.

In George Eliot's early work we can see an exploration of the divine in terms of a dialectic of sovereignty and suffering. Particularly in several of her early essays we see a positively vitriolic response to the narrow, smug claim to a god who rewards me and my religious fellows while punishing all others unmercifully. Typically for George Eliot, the vitriol is poured out as much because of the intellectual as the moral and spiritual stupidity of this mind-set, which sees salvation as the end, rather than the beginning, of a movement toward holiness and the unfolding of God's will.[101] George Eliot's early works of fiction all re-create her experience as a young Christian in a far more positive light than do these essays, and the sympathy she evidently feels and encourages from her reader is taken by most critics as what one calls "a piety about the past";[102] that is, a kind of pious memorializing of religious piety. Most readers recognize in *Adam Bede*, for example, a reframing of biblical images and parables that works to either sacralize the ordinary or naturalize the sacred (or both). And the narrator also takes great pains to make early Methodism comprehensible to the sophisticated, urban, even unchurched contemporary reader. While for many readers Dinah never loses her ultra-pious and thus unrealistic and unsympathetic quality, Adam's and the narrator's love for her almost succeeds in bringing her down to earth. And while Dinah's preaching may grate on us, her prayerful, visionary sensibility is more readily acceptable for the ease with which it can be reframed in nonreligious terms as a superior kind of intuition. As if knowing how unpalatable all of this is to a modern day reader, the narrator intervenes with a double-edged injunction, asking readers both to understand that things were different back then and to recognize that their own perspective is not as rationally unimpeachable as they might like to think.

As has often been discussed, the germ of *Adam Bede* is the story told to Mary Anne Evans as a girl by her Methodist aunt, and the novel that results is redolent with re-created memories of her girlhood. For the purposes of my argument here, it is interesting to think of this childhood origin as a kind of metonymy for the idea of a progressive cultural consciousness; George Eliot is here telling a story of her own religious origins as well as those of her culture. In a way she is saying, "Don't you see how valuable and important and rare this traditional religious view was?" And, conversely, "Now I'm grown up, I'm rational and sophisticated, just like you." Of course it is not an either/or for George Eliot, and the point is more to say, "I experienced and believed in this religious consciousness, and now along with my rationality and intelligence I have a deep sense of something more." In other words, I think we can say that at this point in George Eliot's career and life, she endorsed the post-Enlightenment rationalist view and realized that she had grown out of faith. Importantly, however, her fictional work belied the simplicity of this shift and revealed instead that there was still something more to be said. We find clues throughout her first novel, but the real truth-teller comes in another narratorial interlude when she is speaking of Hetty's lost-sheep wanderings and refers to the image of the crucified Christ, which she says is never to be found along the lanes of her enlightened English Protestant countryside but only in Europe. It is as if the narrator is pulled up short in her own wanderings here as she exclaims, "No wonder man's religion has much suffering in it: no wonder he needs a suffering God."[103] It seems to me that it is her knowledge of the truth of suffering that makes the post-Enlightenment claim that persons and cultures grow out of faith implausible for George Eliot.

Another key signpost on this journey is the struggle that the heroine of *The Mill on the Floss* undergoes. Here we see George Eliot, as discussed in previous chapters, leaving her childhood past behind; as we know, instead of growing up Maggie drowns, but her death is the crucial sacrifice that allows her creator not only to live and to write but also to move beyond childhood territory and avoid the compulsion to return. In Maggie we see a childish need to be loved by and to please the sovereign father, and her best efforts to overcome this need to submit are thwarted again and again by the insidious guilt-producing introjections that prevent her acting in her own best interests and according to her own feelings. Here too we witness an intuitive understanding that suffering is the true touchstone, but Maggie is trapped in a kind of double stereotype—of gender and of extreme religion—that makes her see herself as the one who must suffer.

George Eliot's other heroines, notably Romola and Fedalma, work out her trademark tragedy of renunciation in less tragic though still deeply costly ways, but it is in Dorothea that we see George Eliot arriving at what I will call a mystical solution. Like Maggie, Dorothea is seduced by the idea of sovereign authority, which she thinks she finds in Casaubon, who is obviously more of a father figure and teacher than a lover or companion. Like Maggie too, Dorothea is convinced of her need to be taught; she has a pressing need to find a way to be of use in the world, and it is her enforced acquiescence to the cultural view that women find usefulness through their husbands that leads to her severe humbling and then her maturity. Like Maggie too, she is almost betrayed into voluntarily walking into "a virtual tomb"[104] by the insidious allure of guilt and pity. The danger of this belief in sovereign power and the complicity of social forces to ensure its reign even into the future are given ghoulish weight when Casaubon tries to control his wife from beyond the grave, through his will.

But Dorothea is not Maggie; neither is she Dinah. Like Dinah, however, Dorothea is unusually pious, but it is the suffering caused by her marriage that reveals an otherwise unsuspected depth of inwardness, which she experiences in her disillusionment as "spiritual emptiness and discontent."[105] When we first find the newly married Dorothea in tears, the narrator claims that we cannot be expected to regard the young bride's marital misery as "tragic" despite its sublime Roman background. But she nonetheless convinces us that it is tragic—could we bear to recognize it—because of "the very fact of frequency." It is indeed Dorothea's tragic destiny to learn just how painful unseen tragedy can be: in short, it is Dorothea's destiny to grow up, to leave behind the belief in a husband who will be a benevolent, powerful guide. But, the narrator hastens to tell us, it is not in Dorothea's nature to rebel: "Permanent rebellion, the disorder of a life without some loving reverent resolve, was not possible to her."[106] And so at this point and in this way she is like Maggie, but George Eliot does not leave her here, for she is now ready to develop the next stage in this progression of religious experience.

Eighteen months or so into Dorothea's miserable marriage, after her husband has repeatedly rebuffed any overtures of intimacy, we witness another deep inward crisis. Now however, Dorothea experiences "a rebellious anger" which forbids tears in favor of words (to herself) of self-defense. The sound of her own words shocks her into acknowledging the destruction of "her young hope" and the abandonment of "her best soul in prison, [where she could pay it] only hidden visits." It is fascinating here to see Dorothea taking another huge step toward maturity when she recognizes in herself the desire for vindication by a sovereign god: "Her anger said, as anger is apt to say, that God was with her—that all heaven, though it were crowded with spirits watching them, must be on her side."[107] The wording here suggests the childishness of this perspective, however human for us all and however permanent it might remain for many of us. This is a dark night of the soul for Dorothea, and "the struggle changed continually" through that night, until her anger is transmuted to pity, subdued by the "shadowy monitor" that her husband still embodies. "It cost her a litany of pictured sorrows and of silent cries that she might be the mercy for [his] sorrows—but the resolved submission did come . . ."[108]—to the disappointment of most readers perhaps, but true to the nature of this heroine.

But her creator isn't finished with her yet. Whether by means of a deus ex machina or poetic justice or a sovereign but merciful author, Dorothea is rescued from this miserable fate because there are better things in store for her. For the next step in her process of maturing is through the independence afforded by a wealthy widowhood that allows her to experience and model a different kind of power. Every reader is familiar with the eulogy to the insignificant with which the novel ends, but I want to focus on one of Dorothea's life-changing yet "unhistoric acts." After her husband's death, one responsibility she has is to bequeath the clerical living at Lowick. In a beautiful touch, George Eliot allows Lydgate, the physician who is himself inwardly ailing, to diagnose Dorothea's deepest need: "She wants perfect freedom," he says, "more than any other prescription."[109] Lydgate is right, because Dorothea has moved beyond the need for sovereign power, and she must start experiencing in grown-up fashion the conundrum that Lydgate too is confronting. Dorothea's innocent question concerning Farebrother, "Why has he not done more?" casts a glaring light on Lydgate's own failings, but he replies simply, "It's uncommonly difficult to make the right thing work: there are so many strings pulling at once."[110]

When it comes to her decision about the living, Dorothea experiences the same difficulty but in nicely (for my purposes) ecclesiastical terms: "She was wishing it were possible to restore the times of primitive zeal," the narrator notes, "and yet . . ."[111] This "and yet" tells it all, because Dorothea has learned by now that she is living in a new era when she must take responsibility for trying "to make the right thing work" as best she can. She also knows that Mr. Tyke's so-called "apostolic" affiliation[112] represents a dead kind of traditionalism that is more focused on claiming a link to the past than developing a connection with his parishioners. Instead of doctrinal pronouncements, Dorothea states a preference for Farebrother's way of teaching Christianity, which "makes it a wider blessing than any other . . .—I mean that which takes in the most good of all kinds, and brings in the most people as sharers in it."[113] Even her difficulty in expressing this desire signals a shift to a more complex and mature attitude that witnesses her discovery of an indescribable depth in ordinary religious practice.[114]

In this small scene between Dorothea and Lydgate we see a number of important things: the friendship between two people, a man and a woman, who recognize in each other a will to do good in a way that brings them together and has far-reaching effects. In part, each has been brought to this understanding and mutual respect by marital disappointment; each has learned something that helps create a bond between them and allows them to intervene to improve a worthy clergyman's life and the lives of the people who will be his parishioners. For Lydgate, the painful education in the power of a woman has meant a new understanding of this woman's grace. For Dorothea, the religious idealism of her youth remains, but she is now prepared to put aside those ideals in favor of a visible and practical good. Still, she is granted the power to "rescue" Farebrother,[115] and later is able to help Lydgate in a way that enforces the sense of a new religious order, sustained by a desire for the good that is not bound by doctrinal definition.

Although George Eliot allows her heroine only a temporary period as husbandless disposer of her own life, here we see her giving Dorothea an opportunity to act under her own power. In this, George Eliot is expanding an idea she introduced in *The Mill on the Floss*, when Maggie recognized in Dr. Kenn's face a sympathetic response. The narrator pauses then to reflect on the importance of such a connection:

> The middle-aged, who have lived through their strongest emotions, but are yet in the time when memory is still half-passionate and not merely contemplative, should surely be a sort of natural priesthood, whom life has disciplined and consecrated to be the refuge and rescue of early stumblers and victims of self-despair. Most of us, at some moment in our young lives, would have welcomed a priest of that natural order in any sort of canonicals or uncanonicals, but had to scramble upwards into all the difficulties of nineteen entirely without aid, as Maggie did.[116]

Here George Eliot gestures toward a new religious order—"natural" yet "disciplined" and "consecrated"—consisting of one human being helping another. And it is important that Dorothea is a member of this order, her gender and her relative youth notwithstanding.

Dorothea's growth away from a sovereign, private god enshrined in a doctrinal code toward a Christianity that is focused on addressing the suffering of all through love accords with Kearney's ideas on "anatheism." It also, I think, further defines George Eliot's rejection of a theologically based understanding of faith in favor of something akin to what Evelyn Underhill called "practical mysticism." Relevant here too is Karl Rahner's understanding of "the mystical way in everyday life." Rahner's idea of "the experience of God" as "the experience of grace in everyday life"[117] could describe Dorothea's influence—herself "the gift of God" to those with whom she lives. And Rahner's identification of this everyday mysticism as a "wintry spirituality," which is "'closely allied with the torments of atheists' and modern rationalism"[118] accords with Kearney's ideas concerning a middle ground between theism and atheism.

There are three main elements of mysticism, at least as Underhill and Rahner propose it, which could be seen to resonate with George Eliot's religious position. First, there is the combination of idealism and pragmatism. George Eliot rejected various forms of spiritualism because they did not represent what she called "a practical religion"; conversely, as Rosemary Ashton says, "George Eliot was not at all [impatient] with the beliefs of those who strove after some genuine but ideal object."[119] Second, as Kearney demonstrates, there is the common ground shared by various mystical traditions that speak of a widening scope not only within but beyond their own tradition. We see George Eliot's further exploration of this common ground in her next novel. Third, and perhaps most deeply appealing to George Eliot, would be the commingling in mysticism of knowledge and feeling; that is, a way of knowing that is not discursive but almost indistinguishable from feeling. As Adam Bede has said to Dinah, "feeling's a sort o' knowledge,"[120] and George Eliot continues to demonstrate her own agreement with him throughout her career until she is explicitly proposing the idea of "emotional intellect" in her final novel.[121]

As the narrator of *Middlemarch* says of its heroine, she was incapable of "permanent rebellion"; and I would propose the same for her creator. Indeed, among the beautifully subtle hints of the constantly evolving religious feeling in this novel is George Eliot's gifting to Dorothea—an earnest, naive, idealistic young woman—not only the name "gift of God" but the gifting of a clerical living; that is, the ordaining, in practical terms, of the clergyman to serve her community. According to Kearney, "Theresa of Avila argued that true mystical experience testifies to the sacramental movement from mystical meditation back to the ordinary universe."[122] Dorothea's radical yet relatively "hidden" and "unhistoric" gift to Farebrother, I would argue, is an expression of just such a mystical movement.[123]

Chapter 4

✦

"The Religion of the Future"

Daniel Deronda and the Mystical Imagination

> Could there be a slenderer, more insignificant thread in human history than this consciousness of a girl, busy with her small inferences of the way in which she could make her life pleasant?—in a time . . . when the soul of man was waking to pulses which had for centuries been beating in him unfelt, until their full sum made a new life of terror or of joy.
>
> —George Eliot, *Daniel Deronda*, 2:11 124

Daniel Deronda enacts a tremendous shift in the scope of George Eliot's religious imagination, but it also represents a culmination of all of the themes and concerns that have shaped and informed the religious imagining of her previous novels. What George Eliot means by religion in this novel is something new, and its meaning is inflected throughout with a radical understanding of imagination. Religion and imagination converge in this novel in George Eliot's continuing exploration of mysticism.

All readers recognize *Daniel Deronda* as distinctive in George Eliot's canon for being deeply rooted in contemporary English life and culture. In a sense, she has written her way to the present, tracing a clear route from her own childhood past in the novels and tales up to and including *Silas Marner*, then widening the circle to include the distant historical European past in *Romola* and *The Spanish Gypsy*, then approaching a more recent and less personalized past in *Felix Holt* and *Middlemarch*. All four of the latter end with a sense that the protagonists and their cultures are poised to enter the future, on the brink of a new beginning. *Daniel Deronda* plunges into the present but problematizes the notion of contemporaneity by invoking at the same time a radical sense of atemporality. The much-discussed epigraph to the first chapter of the novel reflects fittingly on the constructedness of all beginnings, in science as much as in poetry, and claims to presuppose everything. This novel takes up the issue of time itself—as a philosophical and religious question—and though it is all about the present it is also charged with the past and aimed explicitly toward the future. Further, the novel's orientation is to no merely temporal past or future but to an eternal, ongoing dimension that is perhaps indeed best described as presupposing everything.[1]

George Eliot insists in this novel on forcing a collision—a favorite word of hers—between two worlds that could hardly be more different: the ordinary London world of Jews, including that of a Zionist seeking the promised land, on the one hand, and, on the other, the blatantly secular world of a jaded English middle class. Deronda himself is the link between the two worlds and largely bears the burden—for most readers with mixed success—of making the otherworldly realm credible, both to his own contemporaries within the text and to George Eliot's readers. She employs the age-old device of student and teacher in order to instruct the reader while Mordecai is instructing Daniel, who in turn is instructing Gwendolyn.

Religion in *Daniel Deronda* has little to do with Christianity. Through the desperate plight of her heroine, Gwendolyn, George Eliot discloses, as if on second thought, the inadequacy of the Christian Church. Gwendolyn attends the church of which her uncle is the pragmatic and well-meaning though spiritually obtuse rector as she does any other social function. Further, through Deronda's silence on the subject of Christianity, as he searches for a way to identify and pursue a vocation, George Eliot suggests the church's downright irrelevance. Deronda's fascination with Judaism is of course explained by his eventual discovery of his own heritage, but it is significant that he never identifies the heritage in which he has grown up as "Christian" but rather as "English," a point that serves to denigrate religious affiliation in favor of racial and national allegiances. For all its deliberate bracketing of the Christian Church as irrelevant, however, this novel that has least of all George Eliot's fiction to do with Christianity is the one that is most explicit of them all about the need for faith. Its most obvious engagement with religious questions is of course Daniel's fascination with Judaism, but equally important is George Eliot's thorough engagement with the religious climate of the time.

Daniel Deronda and the Contemporary Religious Climate

We can identify in very simple terms two sets of related issues that pervade English religious discourse during the decade in which *Daniel Deronda* is produced. The first is the cluster of theological questions that have been in the air from the beginning of George Eliot's career—questions about the existence of God, the nature of Jesus, and the status of the Bible. The second is the cluster of questions about human nature and destiny that follow from a move away from certainty on the first set of questions—questions about the existence of the human soul, the nature of human individuality, and life after death. And following from these latter questions for most thoughtful Victorians is the existential question of the meaning of life in the absence of certainty concerning a God and an afterlife as traditionally understood. One can say that while the first set of questions is still very much alive in contemporary religious circles, "religious circles" have become quite a bit smaller by this time. George Eliot is deliberately turning her attention in *Daniel Deronda* to the second set of questions, which she believes to be the pressing ones for the present and future.

In a letter of this time, George Eliot is explicit in stating that this shift in perspective does not mark a change in her point of view. In answer to a correspondent who laments the evidence of a loss of faith in her later works, she claims that

> there has been no change in the point of view from which I regard our life since I wrote my first fiction—the "Scenes of Clerical Life." Any apparent change of spirit must be due to something of which I am unconscious. The principles which are at the root of my effort to paint Dinah Morris are equally at the root of my effort to paint Mordecai.[2]

This correspondent's mistake can be identified as a literary rather than a theological or religious one, in that she mistakes George Eliot's stories as embodiments of their author's belief rather than as what she calls, in another much-quoted letter, "a set of experiments in life."[3] Even if we accept her statement about the consistency of her views, however, a shift in perspective is evident. And to suggest the way in which George Eliot's own response to religious questions has developed, I would like briefly to situate her responses in relation to those of two contemporaries: her friend Sara Sophia Hennell, sister-in-law of Charles Bray and writer on theological and religious matters, and the poet and cultural critic Matthew Arnold.

Hennell and Marian Evans Lewes maintain a correspondence throughout their lives whose original focus, aside from personal friendship, consists of theological discussions. But once George Eliot emerges and begins writing fiction, Hennell's friend Marian Evans is no longer interested in tackling theological questions. Though they continue to correspond and Marian even maintains her pet name Polly or Pollian in writing to Hennell, it is as if the latter continues along the same track, writing about "the Development principle" in religion while Polly abandons talk of principles and simply develops into George Eliot. Hennell continues painstakingly to thrash out a theological position in hopes of showing that the new understanding of God and religion is but a development of the old. One can see in *Present Religion as a Faith Owning Fellowship with Thought*, published in 1865, for example, Hennell's turn on Feuerbach's ideas of God. In response to his idea that God and religion are in effect a creation of humans, Hennell states that, though she no longer sees God in the traditional way "as a Being apart from man," she now sees God, not as a creation of man's imagination and need, but "as the universal spring of human action"[4]—the source of any human thinking on

God and religion. Hennell's thinking is sophisticated enough to acknowledge that "God" is a symbol, as is all human knowledge that language attempts to conceptualize.[5] Hennell continues to consult her friend, now George Eliot, on matters of style and titles, and Marian/Polly responds with what could be described as polite, generous interest and tries to be helpful, enlisting Lewes's aid in practical and stylistic matters. But her response to such theological questions is now found in her fiction, articulated according to her incarnational aesthetic.

Almost a decade later in 1873 in *Literature and Dogma*, Matthew Arnold is writing in a similar though far more fluid and less anxious way than Hennell of a god whom he defines as "*The enduring power, not ourselves, that makes for righteousness*"[6] and championing the Bible as a necessary source for faith but only to be understood in terms of literary, rather than dogmatic ideas. The following year he begins *God and the Bible: A Review of Objections to "Literature and Dogma"* by defending this new theology against charges of heresy, comparing his own situation with that of Polycarp, in his own time seen as a heretic of the Greek religion and later recognized as a Christian martyr. It is interesting that Lewes, who does not show interest in religion and is what one could call unchurched, notes in response to Arnold's *God and the Bible* an enormous shift in the cultural climate: "What a singular spectacle is presented by the contrast of the general tone of men's minds on this subject of Religion at the present day and that of some twenty years ago! And the progress rushes on, it does not simply move."[7] George Eliot's claim that her view has not changed, then, begs to be inserted into this context in which everything has changed.

Also interesting is Lewes's statement in the same letter that "we"—he and his spouse—agree with much of what Arnold says. Lewes comments that he "profoundly agree[s]" that "righteousness is salvation" but that "I, myself" don't see what the Bible has to do with it. He then reiterates a rejection of the idea of a personal God in favor of a human manifestation of goodness.[8] To me it is interesting here that he at first claims an agreement of "we" and then seems to distinguish an individual opinion on the Bible. Though one could debate George Eliot's position on all of this, it is certainly true that she does seem to see what the Bible has to do with it: while she has withdrawn from theological discussions, she continues to produce biblical echoes and quotations throughout her fiction and in her letters; and as late as 1876 she is asking to borrow Hennell's copy of the apocryphal gospels.[9] A further shift is evident in this period around the time of the writing of *Daniel Deronda*, for she now seems ready at least selectively to rejoin the religious conversation although, as I suggested above, her attention is on the human, rather than the theological questions.

Several reasons may be suggested for this change, one being her position as a respected woman of letters and wise counselor who has gathered around her a coterie of like-minded correspondents, some of whom seek answers from her to troubling religious questions. The major issues we see George Eliot discussing with correspondents and visitors in this period belong to what I referred to above as the second set of questions, having to do with human destiny and the meaning of life and the consequent threat of fatalism. In her letters she takes up the challenge of fatalism in two main situations: firstly, because of the problems that death raises, particularly when the idea of personal immortality is no longer taken for granted; and, secondly, in the dilemma of an apparently purposeless life.

The letters of this period certainly reveal a greater attention to death, partly owing to her and Lewes's age and their more serious and unrelenting physical ailments. But she marks its inevitable approach with equanimity, as noteworthy for example in her dedication to Lewes of the 1874 edition of her collected poems, which includes this quotation:

> 'And the last parting now began to send
> Diffusive dread through love and wedded bliss,
> Thrilling them into finer tenderness.'

Her sanguine attitude toward death can be accounted for partly by the fact that—even though she is still prone to depression verging on despair over the writing of her novel and feels threatened by the "too much" that can "almost nullify one's own small individual effort"[10]—she now has two strong bulwarks against hopelessness: her conviction of the contribution that she has made through her work, and the value of her relationship with Lewes and their mutual love.

The question of life after death is pressing for many contemporaries who have abandoned traditional religion, and George Eliot's own stand on this issue is not to take a stand. In comforting Mrs. W. H. Smith, a friend who does not believe in immortality, on the death of her beloved husband, she writes of the "blessed reunion, if it may come,"[11] and suggests that in doing good to others Mrs. Smith may keep the presence of her husband alive. To Mrs. Henry Ponsonby, who in moving from an ardent faith to atheism has lost her sense of purpose, George Eliot preaches against what she seems to see as the most pernicious foe of this time, "hideous fatalism." She rails against allowing the lack of belief in a supernatural power to excuse any moral lapse, arguing

> that the fellowship between man and man which has been the principle of development, social and moral, is not dependent on conceptions of what is not man: and that the idea of God, so far as it has been a spiritual influence, is the ideal of a goodness entirely human (i.e., an exaltation of the human).

She goes on to counsel that our job is to keep doing what we can since "the progress of the world—which you say can only come at the right time—can certainly never come at all save by the modified action of the individual beings who compose the world."[12] This conviction—the belief in progress and in the idea that it can come only through the purposeful action of human beings—is fundamental to her religious mind-set at this time.

The notion of the significance of individual action is not new for George Eliot, but in letters of the time and in *Daniel Deronda* we see a new urgency prompted by her concern over this "hideous fatalism." In *Daniel Deronda* she focuses on the problem of a pervasive attitude of almost existential meaninglessness, embodied primarily in the monstrous Grandcourt and symbolized in gambling and the motif of chance. George Eliot's concern over a widespread sense of purposelessness is evident in a letter of September 1876 in which Emily Davies reports to her friend Annie Crow on a conversation she had with Mrs. and Mr. Lewes on the topic of education and the question of teaching morals to children.

> [Mrs. Lewes] was anxious that my friend [a prospective teacher] should impress upon them the wide, far-reaching consequences of every action, as a corrective of the common feeling that it does not signify what we do—and on the other hand how society reacts upon us, and how much we owe to it. People are always asking, *Why* should I do what is good for society? What is society to me? The answer is that if it were not for the accumulated result of social effort, we should be in the state of wild beasts.[13]

According to Miss Davies, Mrs. Lewes also expressed scorn for the attitude of "stupid scepticism" that claims life is not worth living.[14] Two months later, in the reflective mood of their shared birthdays, she writes to Sara Sophia Hennell that she would indeed "scold" young people who claim "that life is not worth having" were it not for her remembrance of her own "young discontent."[15] But while the current sense of purposelessness may remind George Eliot of her own youthful despair, Emily Davies notes that Mrs. Lewes asks in the conversation reported above: "was there not a great deal among girls of wanting to do some great thing and thinking it not worth while to do anything because they cannot do that?"[16] To this Miss Davies can only reply in the negative, thus distinguishing George Eliot's own youthful sense of thwarted purpose from the widespread ennui of the present generation.

Another theme that returns at this time is George Eliot's scorn for "consolation" as the vapid doctrine that compels people who suffer or simply contemplate death to find their hope in a world beyond. Again we may note an unchanged principle but a changed attitude based on the pressing issues of the day. Refusing to hum the refrain of consolation, she focuses her religious understanding on action and experience in the present, along with an openness based on a willingness to accept her lack of knowledge. In an oft-cited letter from this time to Dr. Joseph Frank Payne, a self-confessed freethinker who worries about the fate of his loved ones after death, she notes traditional religion's inadequacy in being "chiefly precious as a source of consolation" and hopes for something more from "the religion of the future."[17] In this letter she clearly wishes to reject a religion based on false hope and refuses to offer any clear-cut answer. Instead she gives Payne the true consolation of sharing his concerns and offers her fictional works, not as answers to his questions but only as "experiments in life."

It is worth quoting at length from this important letter since it points to several more ideas I will pursue here:

> Your letter will have associated you with questions which are the most frequently in my thoughts—questions which are my chief prompters to write anything at all. But my writing is simply a set of experiments in life—an endeavour to see what our thought and emotion may be capable of—what stores of motive, actual or hinted as possible, give promise of a better after which we may strive—what gains from past revelations and discipline we must strive to keep hold of as something more sure than shifting theory. I become more and more timid—with less daring to adopt any formula which does not get itself clothed for me in some human figure and individual experience, and perhaps that is a sign that if I help others to see at all it must be through that medium of art.[18]

This notion of "experiments" is fascinating in that there is a sense in which science, particularly as she witnessed and participated in her husband's physiological and psychological explorations, had caught up with her long-standing belief in the essential power of feeling, linked here with thought as the source of human endeavor. As she writes in another letter of this time, "the most thorough experientialists admit intuition—i.e., direct impression of sensibility underlying all proof—as necessary starting-points for thought."[19]

Her claim here to the importance of these fictional experiments in showing the way to a firmer foundation than "shifting theory" is echoed in another letter to Mrs. Ponsonby in which she expresses a mistrust of a physicist "or other 'ist' " if he "strands us on results that seem to stultify the most ardent, massive experience of mankind, and hem up the best part of our feelings in stagnation."[20] Throughout these letters there resounds a confidence in feeling and experience as the basis for knowledge. This echoes the findings of Lewes as well, who notes in a letter at this time, "my doctrine, all doctrine is primarily emotion."[21] In George Eliot's early letters we heard her upholding feeling, particularly in terms of her sense of a duty to teach readers to feel, as the basis for her writing; here we see her standing on the same ground of feeling and intuition, living out Adam Bede's confidence that "feeling's a sort o' knowledge"[22] as she gestures toward "the religion of the future."

The letter to Payne shows George Eliot responding to questions of ultimate meaning through a combination of knowledge—based on feeling and intuition—and hope in what humans "might be capable of." This emphasis on capability, possibility, the "promise of a better" points to the striving after an ideal which, while applicable to all of her works, is framed in new ways in *Daniel Deronda*. And the final sentence of the quotation above, in which she articulates her need to clothe ideas in human figures, identifies the key to that novel and to the whole of George Eliot's approach—the incarnational aesthetic that underlies her religious imagination. While we may accept George Eliot's claim that her "point of view" on religious matters has not changed since her first work of fiction, she would not say that she was simply repeating herself in each work; in fact she made frequent claims for the distinct purpose of each and said that she could not repeat herself. For, though her position may not have changed, her ways of expressing it and even of understanding it are constantly evolving. As we saw in chapter 1, she knows that the "treatment" of an idea is inseparable from the idea itself and that the idea is impossible to distinguish from its treatment. So, while her "principles" and "point of view" may be consistent, the changes in her mode of representation suggest that her correspondent was correct to detect a "change of spirit." This change is manifest in *Daniel Deronda* in a powerful new expression of her incarnational aesthetic, articulated by means of a veritable concert of arts.

By setting Daniel's idealistic quest in the context of a comprehensive exploration of the power of art, George Eliot aims to address the contemporary religious problem of a demoralizing disdain for feeling that leads to a lack of hope. She creates two characters, Daniel and Gwendolyn, who, in very different ways and for different reasons, are seeking purpose and meaning. Gwendolyn moves according to a familiar George Eliot pattern from a state of narcissistic egoism in which her only purpose is to please herself to an awareness of others and of her humble place in a larger world.[23] Daniel, in contrast, thinks and feels for others—partly because of a sensibility that has been finely tuned by the mystery and sometime dread surrounding his uncertain origins—and is driven by an almost uncanny sense of wanting something more, shaped by a conviction that achieving his own identity and purpose will involve taking responsibility for others. This novel is both unique and related to previous novels, and here one may note a link to *Middlemarch*. As unlike Dorothea and as like Rosamond as she is, Gwendolyn nonetheless eventually learns an attitude of self-denying attentiveness to others that includes a new appreciation of the value of life in all its "unhistoric" ordinariness. Daniel, on the other hand, experiences and facilitates an interpretation of life that evolves from Will Ladislaw's somewhat undeveloped Shelleyan perspective to encompass a vast and deep form of neo-Romanticism.

In their own ways, both individually and together, Gwendolyn and Daniel learn the meaning of faith, and through them George Eliot demonstrates the mystical notion that faith allows one to see poetry in the everyday. The novel explores the possibilities for mysticism in contemporary life in three major ways, and while I must discuss them separately, their necessary interrelation is crucial to George Eliot's conception. The simplest of the three is most evident in Daniel's schooling of Gwendolyn in a practice that will be formulated in the next century in terms of the mysticism of everyday life. For reasons which are never explicit, Daniel, at the age of twenty-five, is an expert in this practice: his blatantly secular middle-class lifestyle has been the proving ground of a disciplined practice that allows him to discern a deep value and significance in everyday things. This attitude emerges as, and merges with, a preparedness for the second, more ethereal and more obviously religious form of mysticism that he will be schooled in by Mordecai. Yet Daniel and Mordecai are both steeped in the third form of mysticism, which is the mysticism of imagination—an attitude that is interfused with the other two in its power to elevate the commonest sights and experiences to heights of romantic and religious grandeur.

Gwendolyn Harleth and the Mysticism of the Everyday

As I suggested in the last chapter, we can understand Dorothea as modeling a practice that will come to be known as the mysticism of everyday life. In *Daniel Deronda* George Eliot develops this motif, this time by having her very un-Theresa-like heroine be deliberately instructed by her hero in this practice. She conducts this instruction mainly through a complex series of encounters; increasingly they are private, but they are intense even in a crowd or in the midst of a mundane social gathering. The meetings between Daniel and Gwendolyn are part of what by this time has become a great George Eliot tradition of one-to-one encounters, each serving as a metonymy for the powerful influence one person can have on another. From Mr. Tryan and Janet, to Dinah and Hetty, to Dorothea and Rosamond, these encounters exceed mere intimacy to achieve the status of a kind of entity unto themselves in which time and space are transcended in the experience of eternal immediacy and presence.

Each meeting between Daniel and Gwendolyn is more intense and serious than the last, and George Eliot carefully develops the significance of these encounters so that we come to understand their relationship as religious. Gwendolyn invests Daniel with power from the first, when she interprets his aloofness from gambling and his intervention over the necklace as disapproval—as indeed it is—and casts him in the "unique" role of a "superior," the only man she has ever known who is immune to her charms; by his "standard" she measures her "littleness."[24] George Eliot chooses not to be subtle about the religious tenor of Deronda's influence: after Gwendolyn betrays

Lydia Glasher, Deronda observes an intriguing change in her, which the narrator describes in deliberately religious language: "a conscious error had wakened something like a new soul";[25] later we learn that "he was *becoming* part of her conscience."[26] Without need for words, Daniel sees "confession" in her look[27] as she continues to invest him with the power of a confessor. As if writing a spiritual biography, George Eliot notes Gwendolyn's consciousness, in the misery of her fear and humiliation, "of an uneasy, transforming process."[28] By the end of this chapter the narrator is describing the process as "conversion," with Daniel cast by the young woman in the role of "priest."[29] The narrator is explicit about the suitability of the term "conversion" for "that change of mental poise" that occurs only when "some personality touches [another's] with a peculiar influence," until which point "neither heaven nor hell has any revelation."[30] The narrator notes that Gwendolyn sees Daniel as a priest "without the aid of sacred ceremony or costume"; but when Gwendolyn says, "I wish he could know everything about me without my telling him,"[31] her words seem to echo those of the Samaritan woman, who said about the provoker of her own conversion—also not robed as a priest of her time—"He told me everything I have ever done."

The rest of the novel traces Gwendolyn's arduous transformation, for which she seeks out Deronda's guidance. One of the clearest markers of her growth is the gradual movement from a habitual desire and compulsion to do what she likes to a commitment to doing what she ought to do.[32] Like a recalcitrant child or a criminal trying to turn over a new leaf she repeatedly pleads, "tell me what to think and what to do . . . Tell me again what I should do."[33] And again, after her husband's death, "I wanted you to tell me what I ought to do . . . I want to be good . . . What ought I to do?"[34] The extremity of her dependence on Deronda is intentional on George Eliot's part, as she tries to demonstrate the enormity of the "change" required to effect "the subsidence of self-assertion."[35] In marrying Grandcourt, Gwendolyn had encountered a person even more intent upon pleasing himself than she is, but George Eliot decides to allow this shallow girl redemption. Her irrational fears and her almost infantile need for her mother, along with her resistance to sexual overtures and her claim that she is unable to love, all suggest not only a troubled psyche that Freud would love to analyze but a spiritual depth waiting to be detected. Like a composite of physician and priest—again, like a Jesus figure—Deronda guides and ministers to her.

Their initial conversations resemble that between Jesus and the Samaritan woman in their tension and her testy defensiveness as Gwendolyn presumes that his sympathy must be reserved for women unlike her who are always doing right. She scorns the lost sheep metaphor and then looks up at him "like a wounded animal" when he says that some people need a "shock" in order to grow.[36] In response to her facetious question of why she should care to do anything other than what she likes, he tells her to look outside of herself, to "try to care" about other lives and other things besides herself. "Try to care for what is best in thought and action," he advises, echoing Matthew Arnold. With this, "a change came over her face."[37] Next she is asking, "What is the good of trying to know more, unless life were worth more?" and one can imagine George Eliot's "indignant severity" coming through in Deronda's as he tells her that it is in her power to give life meaning by pursuing "some real knowledge." Gwendolyn's response again is dramatic as she is "startled and thrilled as by an electric shock." Again echoing the conversation reported in Emily Davies's letter, Deronda asks, "What sort of earth or heaven would hold any spiritual wealth in it for souls pauperized by inaction?" He charges that "our own inanity" is "necessarily impious, without faith or fellowship" and again enforces an explicitly religious message:

> "The refuge you are needing from personal trouble is the higher, the religious life, which holds an enthusiasm for something more than our own appetites and vanities. The few may find themselves in it simply by an elevation of feeling; but for us who have to struggle for our wisdom, the higher life must be a region in which the affections are clad with knowledge."[38]

This is a highly charged moment of encounter, and its power shakes them both such that they feel "as if some third person had arrested them." Daniel could be speaking to himself when he urges: "Try to take hold of your sensibility, and use it as if it were a faculty, like vision."[39] He advises her to turn her suffering into a source of light and her fear into a safeguard; he is struck by a sense of her need of "rescuing," seeing her as if "drowning while her limbs were bound."[40] She leaves this scene with strengthened resolve: "I will try . . . It may be—it shall be better with me because I have known you."[41]

As her marriage becomes more bitter and her suspicions concerning Daniel's relationship with Mirah take hold, Gwendolyn needs further reassurance. More desperate, she holds to her need for his "believing in me" and her "faith" in him;[42] and later, more desperate still, as she struggles with thoughts of murder or suicide, she pleads, "I want not to get worse."[43] The intensity of her struggle is writ large in spiritual terms, particularly through the abundance of references to Dante's *Divine Comedy*, and after Grandcourt's death she again seeks absolution from Deronda. Again she gains strength from his faith in her: "I believe you may become worthier," he tells her. Gwendolyn claims, "You have saved me,"[44] and the narrator affirms the claim, calling Deronda her "outer conscience" and stating explicitly: "our brother may be in the stead of God to us." The rhetoric mounts in operatic intensity: "You can, you will . . . be among the best of women." His is "like a touch of a miraculous hand"; his presence is "her spiritual breath."[45] It is "as if flames had been mounting around her, and she had flung herself into his opened arms and clung about his neck that he might carry her into safety. She identified him with the struggling regenerative process in her which had begun with his action."[46] The narrator makes clear that it is not romantic love that Gwendolyn is experiencing, but rather the Love that effects essential change and undergirds all others:

> Mighty Love had laid his hand upon her; but what had he demanded of her? Acceptance of rebuke—the hard task of self-change—confession—endurance. If she cried towards him, what then? She cried as the child cries whose little feet have fallen backward—cried to be taken by the hand, lest she should lose herself.[47]

Later, as we approach Deronda's departure and their last meeting we find a transformed Gwendolyn, chastened and elevated by her ordeal. She is "experiencing some of that peaceful melancholy which comes from the renunciation of demands of self" and relishing "the ordinary good of existence, and especially kindness, even from a dog, as a gift above expectation." The narrator tells us that we can look at life itself as "an escape, . . . as a salvation"; that "self-knowledge" may bring an understanding of "this habitual feeling of rescue."[48] Here we have George Eliot's amazing transfiguration of the romantic, sensational, operatic motif of rescue into the wonder of the everyday. And even more to inscribe its significance, she is not finished with Gwendolyn yet. For even now she is totally self-absorbed and can only weep hysterically in saying her farewell to Daniel Deronda. Here we move from the woman at the well to the woman at the tomb perhaps as Daniel assures her, "We shall never quite be parted . . . I shall be more with you than I used to be."[49] In response Gwendolyn again cries like a lost child but then resolves, "I shall live. I mean to live . . . I shall live. I shall be better."[50]

We know nothing of Daniel's lasting effect on Gwendolyn, but the main indication of her change of heart is in her sense of having been rescued into the life with her family that she once took for granted and could not wait to be rescued *from*. Her kindness to her mother and sisters is that small sign of immense transformation that consists of "the subsidence of self-assertion" and the corresponding assertion of love.[51] For readers of George Eliot, it is striking to see her using the handsome young Daniel Deronda as the fictional means by which she suggests the possibility that a character who is like Rosamond could be redeemed to become a character more like Dorothea. For as far as Gwendolyn is from Dorothea, we find her at the end of the novel arriving at the place where she is beginning to see unhistoric acts as life-giving and herself as something other than the "rose of the world." Particularly in light of her predecessor Dorothea's revival of the mystical way of Theresa, we can see Gwendolyn's arduous, contrary journey as a kind of modern-day mysticism as she arrives at the place of origin and knows it for the first time. In these terms and in the context of the pervasive Dantean echoes, Daniel's role is likened to that of Virgil. But in George Eliot's universe the guide too needs a guide, and Daniel has Mordecai.

Mordecai's Mysticism: "An Inherited Yearning"

"Receptiveness"[52] has everything to do with both Mordecai's and Daniel's visionary callings. What George Eliot aims for in the reader is modeled in her hero: an attitude of receptiveness to the notion of the convergence between the human and the divine, the seen and the unseen. For this reason George Eliot painstakingly lays the groundwork that explains the nature of their unique callings and the connection between the two men. While she does not represent Daniel as a messianic figure, it is clear that he is a special person and the disciple that Mordecai has been waiting for. While I do not wish to encourage any view of Daniel as a Jesus-figure, we have already added his name to the list of characters George Eliot invests with a special power of influence. It is significant that, while Gwendolyn joins the ranks of other women consigned to living out a newly embraced spiritual discipline in her own domestic sphere—Janet, Dinah, Romola, Dorothea—Daniel himself, instead of either reintegrating himself into his own sphere or dying, in the way of other influential men—Mr. Tryan and Savonarola—is set upon a visionary, far from everyday mission. And while he is not a Jesus-figure, Daniel saves Gwendolyn by instructing her in a new way of seeing herself and the world, a new outlook that could be identified with the mystical way that Dorothea discovered by her hard experience and some unspecified action of grace. But it is somewhat more difficult to understand how Daniel comes to be schooled in this way of thinking and what draws him to find in Mordecai's teachings the affirmation of his own calling.

We can see Daniel as another in—and perhaps the epitome of—a long line of George Eliot characters whose heroic status is based on their selfless ability to sympathize with others. In the case of Deronda, we are told that his is an almost debilitating ability to empathize, something that costs him success in any conventional career. He is almost dangerously egoless, it seems. In part at least this attitude could be accounted for by his uncertain origin, which causes him to sympathize with the vulnerable and the outcast, to the point where he almost forgets himself. But it also contributes to his unusual sense of having a purpose beyond or other than what is set out in conventional social terms. One could say he is in the world—in all his strikingly handsome elegance—but not of it. He is always looking through and over what is happening to see what it all means. The world is offering a story to him, but he has yet to find the code by which to read it. Meanwhile he goes about being kind—with Hans Meyrick, Mirah, and Gwendolyn (along with his own adopted family) his main benefactors. If readers find him odd and difficult to believe in, it must be said that most people, other than those who were directly touched by Jesus, also found him odd and impossible to believe in. Again, I am not suggesting that Daniel is meant to be a Jesus-figure but only that George Eliot might want us to imagine the reception a prophet can expect in his own country. Like Jesus, but also like the young Marian Evans herself, Daniel knows he is different and believes he is set apart for a special calling. And this helps prepare him to hear Mordecai's call when it comes.

The perplexing question of Daniel's calling is intrinsic to the unusual nature of this novel. George Eliot sets up the plot of his story in a way that can readily be faulted for improbability; the web of coincidences is too dense to be convincing in any strictly realistic sense. But, as Terence Cave points out in his edition of the novel, she has readied herself for that charge by framing the whole tale with references that range from Aristotle on probability to Jeremy Taylor on the "something more" than "mere learning" that is required for "divine knowledge," and by actively embracing elements of myth and romance.[53] As Cave notes, this novel "challenges and disrupts the canon at every level—social, ideological and formal"[54]—and does something recognizably new by recovering ancient fictional modes. Cave identifies many key references that comprise a "network of reverberations" that link this tale to a wealth of cultural moments across time and place.[55] One biblical text he does not mention comes from the Apocrypha: the book of Tobit tells a romantic tale of two lovers brought together by an angel; but even more romantic is the convergence of the story of young love with that of the vindication and healing of a devout old blind man. Key to the structure of the story is the narrator's phrasing, "It chanced on the same day . . ." (Tobit 3:7). It is this kind of understanding of the working of providence, or fate, or destiny, or coincidence, or serendipity that has always underlain the telling of tales and, George Eliot wants to suggest, the stories of lives. Indeed, she opens chapter 38, which tells of Mordecai's uncanny expectation of Daniel, with a blatant "apology for inevitable kinship" as she waves the "flag" of "second-sight."[56]

Further to complicate this generic web, George Eliot suggests throughout the novel—and not just for Gwendolyn—that it is possible to see life itself in terms of the age-old romance trope of rescue. When Daniel happens to be on site to rescue Mirah, they are both in fact rescued into another way of living. She and others see him as an angel, but he knows that he too is drowning and in need of his own rescue, which comes through Mirah as she becomes his conduit to Mordecai and to what both men recognize as Daniel's calling, a recognition that in turn rescues Mordecai. While in the Tobit tale Raphael is the angelic agent of convergence and rescue, here Daniel plays a dual role as rescuer and rescued. One can broaden this application to include Gwendolyn as well, since there is in the relation between her story and Daniel's the quality represented in that "It chanced on the same day . . ." motif. This is only most notable when, as he was for Mirah, he is there to rescue Gwendolyn when she emerges from the water in Genoa. Convincing readers of the credibility and indeed the necessity of faith in such coincidences is fundamental to George Eliot's method in this novel.[57]

A marvelous scene of convergence that can serve to illustrate the new thing George Eliot is doing with this novel and this hero occurs almost exactly midway in the text when Sir Hugo, accompanied by Daniel, is showing his guests the renovations that have been undertaken at the Abbey. Sir Hugo is proud of "the mixture of undisguised modern with the antique," being in favor of preserving the old insofar as we can inhabit and enjoy it by joining it with the new, rather than either "reproducing the old" or destroying it.[58] To him, the modern surroundings that support the ancient remnant make the historical value of the latter all the more evident, such that the effect enhances the beauty of both old and new. To reproduce the structure to suit ancient usage makes little sense, he argues, or "You may as well ask me to wear out the stones with kneeling." In other words, since kneeling is out of fashion, we need not reproduce the spaces in which our ancestors knelt. Grandcourt predictably not only agrees but mocks the idea of "wanting to howl litanies," and Daniel equally predictably rejects the cynicism of this response: "I think that way of arguing against a course because it may be ridden down to an absurdity would soon bring life to a standstill."[59] He goes on to speak of keeping up "affection" for old things.[60] This affection extends to a deeper feeling when they enter a choir turned stable, complete with hay, a few horses, and dogs. Here, Gwendolyn's response—"Oh, this is glorious!"—gives words to Daniel's equally spontaneous response of doffing his hat.[61]

When Daniel leads the group to the exquisitely preserved cloister, George Eliot has him pose a question that leads the reader from the discussion of the relation between the ancient and the modern to the postmodern: "I wonder whether one oftener learns to love real objects through their representations, or the representations through the real objects."[62] Though his concern here is the relation between nature and art, the setting encourages the reader to apply the speculation to religious questions such as those George Eliot translated Feuerbach as asking: What is the source of our religious feeling? Do we seek in our sacred spaces to represent something we believe to be real though unrepresentable; or to create something real that we can invest with meaning despite its representing nothing but our own idea or feeling? Indeed, when Daniel tells his guests that he does not need the specific place of his home at all but "carr[ies] it with [him],"[63] she is taking us beyond the aesthetic and the cultural to the realm where both intersect with the personal and the religious. For while Daniel's attitude is entirely secular, it is also an attitude that is reverent enough to sanctify the secular—in short, a mystical attitude.

This scene occurs just three chapters after Daniel has visited a synagogue in Frankfurt and experienced his first Jewish liturgy. In both of these scenes, Daniel experiences the living presence of the past and the almost uncanny intermingling that makes "decay" and "faint beginnings" difficult to distinguish from one another.[64] George Eliot seems to foreshadow in this insight the indeterminate relation between "real objects" and "representations" that he will draw attention to in the cloister. The synagogue scene vividly brings forth Deronda's divided spirit, "wandering between two worlds," as Matthew Arnold puts it in his poem "Grande Chartreuse." Daniel's feelings are equally intense for apparent opposites—for democracy and conservatism;

and for "speculations on government and religion" and the treasuring of "long-sanctioned forms"—to the point of near paralysis.[65] It is in this habitual frame of mind—yet newly focused after having discovered through Mirah "that Judaism was something still throbbing in human lives"[66]—that he enters the synagogue, "like a yearning disembodied spirit" seeking "fixed local habitation to render fellowship real."[67] While the service is powerfully moving, however, Daniel still holds himself an observer, and he is insulted when asked if he is Jewish. But his continued resistance to his Jewish heritage allows George Eliot to suggest the complexity of his attraction to Mordecai's vision. This is partly because, even after he embraces his Jewish identity, Daniel will resist its religious implications.

While we are privy to a few specifics of Mordecai's vision for a united Israel, readers agree with Daniel that it is "nebulous in detail."[68] In fact, its vagueness is intentional since George Eliot does not want to suggest that Daniel would find any specific vision compelling. Rather, he is compelled by the scope of the vision itself and the faith of the visionary, which includes a faith in him. For just as Gwendolyn develops a faith in Daniel's faith, Daniel develops a faith in Mordecai's. Mordecai makes clear that the Gentiles have been mistaken in accusing Judaism of enforcing an inflexible law; instead "our Masters" were ever "enlarging and illuminating [the law] with fresh-fed interpretation."[69] In other words, what Mordecai holds out to Daniel is not a fixed belief system but the possibility of belonging to a community of interpreters, a long line of questers. Mordecai's passionate "yearning for transmission"[70] meets Daniel's equally passionate "yearning . . . after the obligation of avowed filial and social ties."[71] And Mordecai's belief that visionaries sustain human life, preventing its decline into "the narrow tenacity of insects," inspires Daniel, pained as he is by the sight of a life like Gwendolyn's that "dwindle[s] and shrivel[s] without vision."[72]

Daniel is eager to receive the transmission, first from Mordecai and later from his own grandfather. And this connection with his mother's estranged father suggests the depth of another mutual need that Mordecai and Daniel's relationship satisfies: "for the sense of spiritual perpetuation in another resembles that maternal transference of self."[73] It is important to note that Mordecai does not give Daniel what he yearns for; rather, Mordecai "give[s] shape" to what Daniel comes to recognizes as "an inherited yearning."[74] His yearning will continue but will now gain purpose and direction by being joined to the yearning of others. And just as the visionary is impotent without a disciple, Daniel's "receptiveness," which has been so far an impediment to action, can now finally achieve its "rare and massive power."[75] The power their relationship generates is not in anything they have but in something that they yearn for and, equally, in the fact of their yearning, their desire for "something more."

What makes Mordecai not just a visionary but a mystic is his adherence to the teachings of Cabbala. He believes that the soul of a medieval believer was "born again" within him, carrying with it memories of the sorrows of Israel throughout the centuries.[76] He sees Daniel as next in line in this rebirthing process by which imperfection is gradually removed and "the Messianic time" is prepared for, in a long process whereby "a soul liberated from a worn-out body [joins] the fellow-soul that needs it."[77] When Daniel finally discovers his Jewish heritage it is indeed as if he proves the truth of this doctrine: the narrator notes that Daniel is "speaking from Mordecai's mind as much as from his own" when he declares, "Our souls have the same vocation. We shall not be separated by life or by death."[78] Such statements as these explain the narrator's frequent need to concede that Daniel is "romantic," not only in matters of the heart where Mirah is concerned but in these more spiritual realms where he meets Mordecai. And the emotional tenor of their conversations makes clear that, notwithstanding all their brooding over textual matters, Mordecai and Daniel's is not only a meeting of minds but of hearts and spirits. Indeed, George Eliot suggests the arbitrariness of such a distinction when she has Daniel muse upon the equal value of "emotional" and "unemotional intellect."[79] And it is the recognition that "the lines of what may be called their emotional theory touched"[80] that leads to the third mode of mysticism, that of imagination.

The Mysticism of Imagination

This third form of mysticism infuses and completes the other two by showing how the everyday is made sacred by the working of imagination. Indeed, throughout the novel George Eliot is intent to show how faith and poetry meet in the ordinary world around us. This idea emerges in her richly nuanced attention to art in this novel. For while *Daniel Deronda* continues George Eliot's celebration of the arts—most obviously in the singing of Alcharisi and Mirah and the painting of Hans Meyrick—her more interesting statement has to do with the incorporation of art in everyday life. Continuing the story of the female singer represented in Armgart, she depicts Alcharisi's choice of a professional singing career as ultimately misguided (though complex in its harsh depiction of the patriarchal father and its sympathetic depiction of her need to pursue her art); likewise she gives Mirah the kind of voice that is unsuited to the public stage and instead finds its best venue in the private drawing room. Though one might see in this theme of the dangers of public performance for women a conventional bias, we may also note George Eliot affirming the possibilities for performing art in the everyday.

At the same time, George Eliot upholds the sublime value of true art when Gwendolyn learns through Klesmer how rare and uniquely important art is and how much dedication and sheer effort it requires. George Eliot pursues this theme of the ultimate significance of art in her representation of the

Meyrick family. As well as recognizing Mirah's talent, the Meyrick women sacrifice their own comfort for the sake of their son and brother's artistic career (a choice we might find sadly patriarchal). But, more importantly, their home is clearly proposed as a model for true culture. "Outside, the house looked very narrow and shabby," but this poverty only serves to highlight "a culture the more spotlessly free from vulgarity."[81] The narrative dwells on this small house, where "there was space and apparatus for a wide-glancing, nicely select life, open to the highest things in music, painting, and poetry."[82] The same scene makes good on this claim to the wide scope of art and culture in the small domestic space by including references to the reading they are constantly engaged in—here a popular French historical novel about a rescue that prepares them to receive the rescued Mirah into their midst, a text which Mab compares to a chapter in Revelations and to Schiller, thereby further blurring the line between realism and romance, popular and high culture, and secular and sacred text. Here too the description of their beautiful embroidery further extends the definition of culture by suggesting that the typical domestic work might be considered art. This understanding of culture—wide and open yet select—provides an obvious contrast to the more materialistic attitude of the wealthy characters.

Later the expanse of the Meyricks' cultural range is made literal when they "make space for Kate's drawing, as well as a great length of embroidery."[83] In this scene, Mirah is reading aloud Charles Lamb's essay "The Praise of Chimney-Sweeps," another literary reference that sharpens the cultural theme. For, while a great friend of Wordsworth's, Lamb famously scorned the early Romantic's devotion to nature, celebrating instead the glories of the city. In this way George Eliot is not only affirming the Romantic elevation of art but also entrenching it ever more deeply in everyday contemporary life. For example, she takes great pains to catalog the range of small engravings of famous paintings, which, together with the sunlight on the nearby river, turns the small parlor into a "temple."[84] The Meyricks' home is not a temple for the worship of art, however, but rather a cultural environment in which the valuing of art is integrated into the valuing of everyday lives, domestic relations, and natural surroundings. The little parlor is a temple, then, in the sense that every space may house the sacred.

Throughout *Daniel Deronda* George Eliot makes explicit the notion that has been made current in the generation before hers by Romantic poets and thinkers—that we see the world that we believe in, that our imagination constructs our world. She intermingles poetic imagination with matters of religious faith in a way that vindicates the Romantic and the believing sensibility, showing in various ways that one must be receptive to finding romance and meaning in the world—to finding a "temple" in Chelsea. The link between imagination and faith is suggested, for example, when Daniel, on a self-confessed romantic quest for Mirah's parent, finds Ezra Cohen decidedly too "unpoetic" to qualify[85] but then is moved to think Ezra "not utterly prosaic" when he is attired for the Sabbath ceremony.[86] Daniel too has made the ultimate importance of one's own subjective response clear to Gwendolyn when he has rebuffed Grandcourt's cynical dismissal of sacred gestures, as we saw above. Earlier in the same chapter he has told Gwendolyn that whatever lack of meaning we find in the world is due to our own perception: "I think what we call the dulness of things is a disease in ourselves."[87] George Eliot builds up a strong case throughout the novel on the side of imaginative sensibility and correspondent belief, rebuffing cynics in her own right: when Daniel is emotionally stirred by the discovery of his heritage, the narrator proclaims: "Impossible for men of duller fibre—men whose affection is not ready to diffuse itself through the wide travel of imagination, to comprehend, perhaps even to credit this sensibility of Deronda's, but it subsisted, like their own dulness, notwithstanding their lack of belief in it."[88]

Another manifestation of the power of perception, the dependence of the world on interpretation, and the intermingling of imaginative sensibility and religious sensibility, comes as well in the central synagogue scene, when the narrator reminds us of Daniel's "fervour which made him easily feel the presence of poetry in everyday events." Here, the Jewish quarter "rous[es]" in him "the sense of union with what is remote," and "set[s] him musing on two elements of our historic life which that sense raises into the same region of poetry:—the faint beginnings of faiths and institutions, and their obscure lingering decay."[89] This is an exquisite evocation of the ineffable influence of the past as well as a comment on the power of perception, in that it is in the eye of the percipient to decide whether this liminal, transitional space is the site of new birth or of death. And it is indeed the percipient whose sense of meaningful life is either awakening or decaying. To further underline the relation between imagination and faith, the narrator here explicitly places musings on matters of faith in "the same region of poetry."

It is indeed up to the mind that views the world to make space (as the Meyricks do) for "movements of awe and tenderness" and for "fellowship which thrills from the near to the distant, and back again," so that "all the apparatus of heaven and earth" may "make poetry" for it.[90] This mind-set, both poetic and religious, constitutes the kind of mysticism that George Eliot is promoting here, and its most forceful representation comes in the context of but also transcends Daniel's encounter with Judaism. The philosophy that underlies her approach here is a development on the artistic credo articulated in the famous chapter 17 of *Adam Bede*, in which the narrator argues that the aesthetic merit of a painting of a woman peeling carrots in her kitchen may be equal to that of a painting of angels and madonnas. In her last novel, the narrator pushes these ideas to a new level when she describes Daniel's excursions into the gritty, shabby Jewish quarter of London, noting that searching for a fair maiden's relatives in beautiful ancient Cordoba or witnessing "a glorious martyrdom" far more readily evokes a sympathetic response than does the sight of

> commonplace, perhaps half-repulsive objects which are really the beloved ideas made flesh. Here undoubtedly lies the chief poetic energy:—in the force of imagination that pierces or exalts the solid fact, instead of floating among the cloud-pictures. To glory in a prophetic vision of knowledge covering the earth, is an easier exercise of believing imagination than to see its beginning in newspaper placards, . . . ; and it might well happen to most of us dainty people that we were in the thick of the battle of Armageddon without being aware of anything more than the annoyance of a little explosive smoke and struggling on the ground immediately about us.[91]

It is striking here to see George Eliot—even ironically—suggesting that most of us do not have the eyes to see the spiritual battle that might be waging around us. And the explicitly incarnational aesthetic in her reference to "the beloved ideas in flesh" that are "really" incarnated in "half-repulsive objects" of ordinary life begs the question of whose ideas they are after all—not simply those of the novel's author, surely. It is clear that the "believing imagination" has a greater challenge than simply enjoying "a prophetic vision"; rather, it must believe that the most unpromising and unexceptional beings are worthy of love and conscious attention.

George Eliot clearly endows her hero with what she calls here "the chief poetic energy" that allows him to discern the value and significance and beauty in this unlikely location. But she adds a surprising additional layer when she represents Mordecai as not only a prophet and visionary but as himself a person whose religious sensibility is inseparable from his poetic sensibility. This comes out explicitly in his poetry, of course, but it is interesting to see George Eliot making the prophet also an artist whose vision of his disciple is of a beautiful creature modeled after an ideal he seeks to find represented in the National Gallery. Even more, his poetic nature comes out in a sensitivity to the beauty of his city that Charles Lamb would approve. That he is "keenly alive to some poetic aspects of London" means that he shares the "poetic energy" mentioned above and brings together a poetic and religious sensibility to suggest a transfiguring mystical vision. Sunset or sunrise amidst the busy commercial activity on the river affects Mordecai in the same way that "a fine symphony to which we can hardly be said to listen makes a medium that bears up our spiritual wings."[92] George Eliot's insistence on Mordecai's poetic mind-set serves to ensure that readers do not set him up as some kind of stereotypical religious extremist; rather, her framing of his poetic nature brings to mind not only the Jewish poet Judah Halevi[93] but the ever-urban, ever-mystical William Blake. And when we read of Mordecai's love for London's river and his "poet's yearning for the wide sky, the far-reaching vista of bridges, the tender and fluctuating lights on the water which seems to breathe with a life that can shiver and mourn, be comforted and rejoice,"[94] we may think of the boldly progressive and contemporary yet almost mystical art of J. M. W. Turner. I mention these associations to emphasize how deeply the religious themes of this novel are interwoven into a rich artistic tapestry to produce this sense of a modern mysticism.

Daniel Deronda and "the Religion of the Future"

Like all of George Eliot's works, *Daniel Deronda* promotes an attitude toward life; we can see the Gwendolyn-Deronda plotline as working out a mandate for action represented by ideas having to do with sympathy, duty, self-denial, and the good of humanity that hearkens back to earlier works. However, while Daniel's story is grounded through Gwendolyn's in a mission of present action in the world, it also goes beyond that in a way only hinted at in some other works, notably *Romola* and *The Spanish Gypsy* and several of the poems. What comes to the fore here is a belief in progress—both in a personal and a cultural sense—that adumbrates a belief in or at least speculations about what may be called the evolution of consciousness (an idea to be discussed more fully in the next chapter). This energy toward the future is driven by George Eliot's attention at this time to death and to questions such as what lies beyond death and what to make of life in the face of death. And whereas earlier works aim to provoke sympathy as the grounding for what has been called her religion of humanity, this novel goes beyond that in aiming to produce or re-create religious feeling. In a letter to Harriet Beecher Stowe at this time, George Eliot proposes that "there is one comprehensive Church whose fellowship consists in the desire to purify and ennoble human life," a desire that transcends differences between "all narrower churches."[95] And it does not seem to be going too far to suggest that she constructs the relations between Daniel and Mordecai on the basis of a shared "yearning" that echoes this "desire."

My contention in this chapter has been that in representing three interrelated modes of mysticism, George Eliot renders in her last novel the mysterious way and truth and life of a religious attitude that grounds its contemporary relevance in a constant opening to the future. She does this by producing characters who understand the religious life in terms of what she calls in a letter of this period the vital "inward light of poetry—that is, of emotion blending with thought."[96] George Eliot's defiance of generic categories, suggested above, goes so far as to produce a novel that is also more than a novel; not only does she push her fiction into the realm of religious manifesto, but she also pushes her prose, as we see particularly when she tries to render Mordecai's mystical consciousness, into the realm of poetry. But her defiance of genre is also a defiance of the strictures of rational, institutional, and ideological thought. In the same letter to Beecher Stowe, we find, in the context of a discussion of Goethe, a definition of mysticism that can be applied not only to Mordecai's religious attitude but to that of much of the novel: "the delighted bathing of the soul in emotions which overpass the outlines of definite thought."[97] This blurring of boundaries also applies to the boundary between life and death we find represented in various ideas and images in the novel. For example, Mordecai clearly understands the Cabbala to be pointing to apparent death as the means of birth, with the death of one person only making way for the birth of another; and Gwendolyn's battling with her brutal husband is framed by references to Dante that suggest the struggle with forces of death that can help bring forth new life out of purgatory and even hell. While this motif of life-out-of-death is a familiar literary trope, George Eliot invests it here with ultimate significance, requiring the reader, like Daniel in the Jewish quarter, to decide whether the ruins of religious thought and feeling are remnants of something dead or signs of new growth.

Chapter 5

✦

Evolutionary Spirituality and the Theopoetical Imagination

George Eliot and Teilhard de Chardin

> I am a pilgrim of the future on my way back from a journey made entirely in the past.
>
> —Teilhard de Chardin, *Letters from a Traveler*

> But no story is the same to us after a lapse of time; or rather, we who read it are no longer the same interpreters.
>
> —George Eliot, *Adam Bede*, 6:54, 472

As I mentioned in the "Introduction" and have aimed to demonstrate throughout, George Eliot's view of her work was deeply evolutionary, in the sense that she wrote from a strong conviction that her ideas were constantly developing. Each new work reveals new insights and emphases and purposes. If she had stopped writing novels with *Middlemarch*, readers would have been left with a sense of a worldview grounded in the ethics of human community, fostering hope on the basis of empathetic action and a sincere adherence to social duties, with what I have called the mysticism of everyday life offering a way to sanctification that is manifest in love. Indeed, in keeping with the evolutionary model I am proposing, her next novel includes and develops these ideas, refusing to abrogate this everyday mysticism but instead adding to it the forms of poetic and ethereal mysticism that I described in the last chapter. With *Daniel Deronda* she reaches beyond ordinary human experience and beyond human time as we know it, moving back into an old way of being—not in historical terms but in the sense that she reveals the past alive and active in the present in religious belief—and gesturing forward toward a time and place beyond the reaches of England and Europe and even of her own imagining. In this way George Eliot's last novel shows her embracing the idea that evolution is a comprehensive force that encompasses her work and herself and continues beyond contemporary knowledge.

This conviction of evolution as a comprehensive and fundamental power is evident throughout her work, and in a letter to Harriet Beecher Stowe in 1869 aiming to clarify her "religious point of view," she is emphatic:

> I believe that religion too has modified—"developed," according to the dominant phrase—and that a religion more perfect than any yet prevalent must express less care for personal consolation, and a more deeply-awing sense of responsibility to man, springing from sympathy with that which of all things is most certainly known to us, the difficulty of the human lot.[1]

The challenge to Christianity that emerged in the nineteenth century could be summed up in the discovery of evolution, and throughout George Eliot's work we see her embracing the evolutionary religious perspective she expresses in this letter. But thoughtful Christians struggled throughout this period to reconcile the new findings regarding the nature of the earth and the universe with biblical accounts of creation and miracles as traditionally understood, and it wasn't until the twentieth century that evolution was satisfactorily reconciled with faith. This understanding was achieved in the work of the Jesuit priest and paleontologist Pierre Teilhard de Chardin, who is considered by many, notes scholar Louis M. Savary, as "the first to integrate evolutionary science and Christian theology."[2] Teilhard (as he is usually called) was born in 1881, the year after George Eliot died. It is virtually certain that he never read her novels, and yet, I will argue, his work follows upon hers, and her ideas anticipated his in the deeply evolutionary way in which an embryo contains the future unfolding of a plant or animal.

The Religion of the Future

Teilhard met the challenge of evolution by formulating an evolutionary faith, which he proposed as the most faithful response to our knowledge of God and creation. Rather than being cowed by evolutionary ideas, Teilhard exulted in them, proclaiming, as Savary puts it: "that God from the beginning created an evolving universe is a pivotal fact of divine revelation."[3] In his classic work *The Phenomenon of Man*, Teilhard traces the development of life and the emergence of consciousness in evolutionary terms, and notes that it was only in the middle of the nineteenth century—George Eliot's lifetime—that a crucial threshold was crossed. Finally by then humans had begun to see themselves as part of the evolutionary process and to recognize that evolution is not just another system or theory but "a light illuminating all facts, a curve that all lines must follow."[4] George Eliot would have delighted in Teilhard's key terminology and metaphors as he argues that it is in her time that people began to understand the "*irreversible convergence* of all that exists" and the interrelation of every part of life, such that even "the least molecule" is "knit into the web of life."[5]

Coincidentally (shall we say), Teilhard and George Eliot both use the phrase "religion of the future"; this notion illuminates a core element of their respective beliefs and, as such, a profound connection between them. For a key reason why George Eliot was unable to embrace conventional Christianity was its entrenchment in the past and in outworn doctrines and its adherence to the view that the task of the church was primarily to carry on an existing tradition rather than actively engage with a living, ever-changing faith.[6] Suggesting a fundamentally evolutionary attitude toward religion, she "urge[s]" her friend Mrs. Ponsonby "to consider your early religious experience as a portion of valid knowledge, and to cherish its emotional results in relation to objects and ideas which are either substitutes or metamorphoses of the earlier."[7] George Eliot adheres to a "religion of the future" in other senses as well: as we see in *Daniel Deronda*, for example, she conceives of true religion as yet to be known, sending Daniel off to an unknown fate and Gwendolyn to what Daniel calls a "religious life" that will take shape as she lives it out.

At the same time, however, a "religion of the future" suggests an understanding that has nothing to do with temporal measurement, in the sense that it is a kind of religion that has always had some adherents. From its inception the Christian faith was about change and about an unknown and yet vividly anticipated future. Dante's *Divine Comedy* is a classic representation of this spirit, and in its growing importance to George Eliot we can see evidence that her evolutionary perspective incorporates and develops ideas of the past. Crucial in these terms is the difference between the Catholic tradition that Dante represents and the Protestant tradition that predominated in England in George Eliot's time, represented most strongly in Milton. It is curious, I think, that when Daniel is furnishing an apartment for Mordecai he includes two busts, one of Dante and the other of Milton. Setting aside what Mordecai was to make of this pair, it is interesting to note the differing views of the future that each man implies. The Miltonic view, as seen in *Paradise Lost*, has to do with a Fall that ruins an otherwise perfect paradise; according to this view, were it not for the Fall, humanity would have continued in an already complete, static bliss. Out of this comes *felix culpa*, the notion that progress and change could come only after the loss of paradise. In Dante, by contrast, we find another view: that even in paradise as originally created, God's intention was for continuous growth and change. Here the Fall is a temporary detour corrected by Jesus, who takes humans back to where they were intended to be, to continue the process of developing humanity and creation.[8]

Dante's view, to put this in other terms, contains evolution as part of God's original creation, whereas Milton's view results in evolution being seen as a deviation from creation, a product of the Fall. I wonder if this might suggest one reason why, while we have many references in *Daniel Deronda* and in

Romola, as well as in George Eliot's journals and essays, to the *Inferno* and *Purgatorio*, she rarely refers to *Paradiso*.[9] I suspect that she did not quite know how to understand Dante's view of the future or how to incorporate it into her thinking. My contention is that Milton's worldview did not satisfy her, but its pervasiveness prevented her from seeing the future in anything but only vaguely hopeful terms. Furthermore, this could be another reason that a more fully developed Christian depiction of the cosmic future had to wait for another century.

For his part, Teilhard, in the "Epilogue" of *The Phenomenon of Man*, argues for Christianity as quintessentially "a religion of the future" in terms that would have found a resonance—though not entire agreement—with George Eliot. He cites its "rootedness in the past and ceaseless development"; he claims that in the context of evolution "interpreted as an ascent of consciousness," Christianity reflects a "trend towards a synthesis based on love"; and he asserts that Christianity "implies essentially *the consciousness of being in actual relationship* with a spiritual and transcendent pole of universal convergence."[10]

All of these terms find an echo in George Eliot's work (as well as in Dante's). In this chapter I want to draw from Teilhard's thought in order to suggest the contours and key elements of George Eliot's religious imagination. There are four ways in which Teilhard's ideas concerning what has come to be called evolutionary spirituality can help us to understand George Eliot's religious imagination. The first is their shared idea of the convergence of science and faith, which I will explore primarily through further discussion of *Daniel Deronda*; the second is their shared belief in the evolution of consciousness, which will take me to *Silas Marner*, the text in which this idea is most fully developed; the other two—radical perspectives on interpretation and suffering—are closely related to each other and are both related to Teilhard's notion of what Savary calls "continuous Incarnation."[11] These latter ideas are crucial throughout George Eliot's career, and I will explore them with reference to a number of her works.

The Convergence of Science and Faith: *Daniel Deronda* and the Theopoetic Imagination

Teilhard's notions of "universal convergence" and the possibility of relationship with "a spiritual and transcendent" power reflect George Eliot's intellectual hopes, and in her last novel she pursues with increased urgency and boldness the idea of converging forces and destinies pointing to an overarching pattern. When Daniel is engaging in a lengthy inward debate in which his reason argues with his feelings, intuitions, and wishes regarding his connection to Mordecai (whose destiny seems to be converging with his own), he wonders whether the old man's poverty necessarily precludes the presence of "some spiritual force within him" and whether his passionate ardor detracts from the possibility of "ennobling motive" and true wisdom.[12] In other words: could this poor strange old Jewish man really be a prophet with something important to say to Daniel? The narrator then follows Daniel's thoughts as he extends his reasoning to the realm of science:

> The inspirations of the world have come in that way too: even strictly-measuring science could hardly have got on without that forecasting ardour which feels the agitations of discovery beforehand, and has a faith in its preconception that surmounts many failures of experiment. And in relation to human motives and actions, passionate belief has a fuller efficacy. Here enthusiasm may have the validity of proof, and, happening in one soul, give the type of what will one day be general.[13]

This application of "faith" and "ardour" to scientific method and of "passionate belief" to human relations both implies a trial-and-error and future-oriented, evolutionary process as fundamental to all human endeavors and confirms the reliance of science on the "inspirations" of imagination.

Teilhard de Chardin is at the forefront of those scientists who are able to reconcile science and faith because he recognizes the dependence of all thinking on imagination and faith: "Neither in its impetus nor its achievements can science go to its limits without becoming tinged with mysticism and charged with faith."[14] In keeping with this, he argues that what he calls the "religion of science," which captivated rationalist thinkers of the eighteenth and nineteenth centuries, was limited by their materialist orientation. In response he formulates for the post-Enlightenment what I would call a theopoetics of science in which scientists acknowledge the need for a "re-integration, in a renewed form, of those very spiritual forces they claimed to be getting rid of."[15] Teilhard's work moves beyond the limits of rationalism and allows us to reconsider prescientific ways of understanding the world by providing a language that was unavailable even in George Eliot's time. He shows how the either/or of creation and evolution, of faith and reason, can now be reframed in terms of a rationally credible synthesis. As Père Daniélou notes: Teilhard "preserves the essentials" of Scholasticism—"the categories of personality, creation and God"—but "invents for it a new language expressive of modern science."[16]

Interestingly, Barbara Reynolds reinforces this view when, in arguing for the "relevance of Dante's allegory of heavenly life," she finds an affinity between his work and Teilhard's.[17] Elegantly and persuasively, Reynolds elaborates on several points of connection, notably their shared visual imagination, their similar reconciliation of the philosophical problem of the One and the Many, and their argument for Love as the universal and fundamental basis of life. She sums up: "At every essential point, the image or allegory which Dante's intuition has constructed upon the basis of his admittedly limited knowledge of the material world touches and joins hands with this recent structure assembled [by Teilhard] from the disparate elements of modern scientific discovery and thought."[18]

To see such an affinity is itself an exercise of "intuition," and thus a confirmation of the validity and power of analogical thinking. Relying on a similar intuitive sense, we can move from the affinity between Dante and Teilhard through George Eliot's knowledge of Dante to speculate about the affinity between George Eliot and Teilhard. For George Eliot, as for Teilhard, the categories noted by Daniélou—personality, creation, and God—were inescapable. As we noted in chapter 1, she accepted Darwin's account of the evolutionary processes pervading nature but (like Darwin himself) knew that this explanation did not account for the "mystery beneath the real." We know too that she was attracted for a time to Comte's positivist explanation of social evolution with its motto "Love as principle, order as basis, progress as end." But she was not satisfied with this essentially materialist explanation, which ultimately sacrificed the person to the system.[19] In many important ways, I think she would have welcomed Teilhard's way of synthesizing matter and spirit, science and faith.

In the first place, with her belief in the mystery of the natural world together with her deeply felt and variously demonstrated belief in the inward life of human beings, George Eliot would have been delighted and intrigued by Teilhard's affirmation that "*co-extensive with their Without, there is a Within to things.*"[20] She would also have grasped the importance of his assertion of the existence of spiritual energy as fundamental and of the relationship between external, physical energy and internal, spiritual energy. "Without the slightest doubt," he says, "*there is something* through which material and spiritual energy hold together and are complementary. In the last analysis, *somehow or other*, there must be a single energy operating in the world."[21] Teilhard pushes this idea to a point that would have seemed only logical, not only to Dante, but to George Eliot's poetic predecessors—Blake and the two Shelleys, and to that Jesuit poet of "inscape," Gerard Manley Hopkins. Teilhard works these ideas of mutual inherence into a theopoetic shape that these poets have already anticipated: "the first idea that occurs to us is that the 'soul' must be as it were the focal point of transformation at which, from all the points of nature, the forces of bodies converge, to become interiorized and sublimated in beauty and truth."[22]

Teilhard's affirmation of the soul in persons and in things as the radical center and ground of being ("the focal point of transformation at which, from all the points of nature, the forces of bodies converge") both affirms the inwardness of things and repositions "spiritual energy" as the source of material energy—just as William Blake did. We are not human beings having a spiritual experience, Teilhard famously said, but spiritual beings having a human experience. George Eliot's last novel is similarly radical as she situates its action in the soul of her characters and her readers. In this way she is refashioning the scope and shape of the serious novel to include a new aesthetic that harks back to ancient poetics from classical and Renaissance times.

This grand design of *Daniel Deronda* is signaled by many of the epigraphs, many written by George Eliot for the purpose. The epigraph to the novel as a whole is a short poetic piece that sounds a portentous warning to an unwary reader: "Let thy chief terror be of thine own soul," where "lurks vengeance" to ruin "captured joys" with "pallid pestilence." Having sounded this Gothic, sensational, or prophetic note, she introduces chapter 1 in a quite different tone with a self-reflexive, ironic, sophisticated comment that the inevitable "make-believe of a beginning" applies equally in the realm of Science and in that of "his less accurate grandmother Poetry." And yet even here, at the height of contemporary understanding ("No retrospect will take us to the true beginning"), her echo of Faust—"whether our prologue be in heaven or on earth"—spins the comment toward ultimate issues regarding the "soul" and to the sphere of imagination, where poetry meets science.

We can think of *Daniel Deronda* as George Eliot's attempt to capture in fiction the universe as she knew it—in all her vast range of knowledge in poetry, science, society, and psychology—as well as the universe of her own consciousness. In this venture, quite new in fiction, she is joining and advancing the tradition of cultural poetry modeled by Milton in *Paradise Lost*, Percy Shelley in his *Defence of Poetry*, and, particularly, Dante's *Divine Comedy*. The range of erudite (and at times playful) reference—from Aristotle to Copernicus to Jeremy Taylor to Jewish mysticism—suggests the sweep of Western culture and her interrogation of it. At the same time, the opening sentences of the novel proper—"Was she beautiful? . . . Was the good or evil genius dominant . . . ?"—invoke the peculiarly modern problem of interpretation that frames and energizes the whole interrogation.

There are three main ways in which George Eliot is shaping in *Daniel Deronda* what I would like to call a new cultural imaginary founded on a reconciliation of science and imagination. Each harks back to ways of thinking that have lost credibility at this time in the predominant rationalist environment that gives precedence to materialist, empiricist, secular viewpoints. The first is an appeal to a post-Enlightenment appreciation of the link between science and poetry; the second is an appeal to the Cabbala, the ancient Jewish understanding of destiny; the third is an appeal to the medieval, prescientific worldview of Dante.

The first of these appeals begins with the chapter 1 epigraph that challenges the precedence of Science and reminds us of its kinship with Poetry. While George Eliot has always pushed the boundaries of realism and reminded readers of the limitations of their own perspective and intelligence, here she makes "the inevitable makeshift of our human thinking" a central and repeated theme. She discourses at various points in the novel on the failings of "the unemotional intellect," suggesting that "perhaps an emotional intellect may have absorbed into its passionate vision of possibilities some truth of what will be."[23] Each term here is telling: she wants to champion passion and feeling, a vision that is more than physical and empirical, the importance of placing trust in possibilities as a way toward future truths. Daniel is her hero because he inwardly wrestles with the hegemony of rationalism and intuits the powerful energies that lie outside of its limits, and because he resists the sway of his own ego by "thinking himself imaginatively into the experience of others."[24]

The narrative affirms Deronda's "imaginative stirring"[25] by making his "wish-begotten belief in his Jewish birth"[26] and his romantic idealizing of his own destiny and of the beautiful damsel who will share it come true. Throughout Daniel's tale the narrator is conceding that her hero was "if you like, . . . romantic,"[27] but all the while George Eliot is asking the reader to think again about what we mean by "romantic" and to allow for the possibility that our limited view may be a function of our own "dulness of imagination."[28] This approach pervades the whole novel and shapes its structure: she invokes Aristotle in the epigraph to chapter 41 to ask us to rethink our conventional dismissal of coincidence and probability: "It is a part of probability that many improbable things will happen." She even goes so far as to suggest in the epigraph to chapter 44 that the "finer sense" and "lighter-clad intelligence" of "fairy-folk" may make their ears keener than ours.

Along with this appeal to imagination, Mordecai's belief in the Cabbala is the second way in which George Eliot tries to open her readers to new, countercultural perspectives. As suggested in the last chapter, George Eliot is intent to expand the reader's understanding of imagination to include religious perspectives that have lost currency in modern Europe. Far outside the standard contemporary English or European worldview is the Cabbala, which defines human temporal experience in terms of an ongoing process of reincarnation that will ultimately bring about "the Messianic time." As Mordecai explains:

> "In the doctrine of the Cabbala, souls are born again and again in new bodies till they are perfected and purified, and a soul liberated from a worn-out body may join the fellow-soul that needs it, that they may be perfected together, and their earthly life accomplished. Then they will depart from the mortal region, and leave place for new souls to be born out of the store in the eternal bosom."[29]

It is to George Eliot's enormous credit that Mordecai's expressed longing for this fellowship does not have the appearance of mere arcane eccentricity. Perhaps this is partly because his longing echoes her own in her beautiful poem—or, more aptly, hymn—"O May I Join the Choir Invisible." Here she expresses, with a fervor equal to Mordecai's, a longing to join "those immortal dead who live again / In minds made better by their presence" and to become one with those who "urge man's search / To vaster issues." She calls the mutual life of the living with the dead the "heaven" by which she longs to "inherit that sweet purity / For which we struggled, failed, and agonized." Like Mordecai's, her longing is charged with a belief in "that better self [that] shall live till human Time / Shall fold its eyelids, and the human sky / Be gathered like a scroll within the tomb / Unread for ever."

Dante's *Divine Comedy*, reflecting the standard late-medieval worldview, is the third way in which George Eliot challenges the imaginations of her contemporaries. While the reader encounters through Daniel a world of imaginative possibility, and through Mordecai a spirit of seemingly dauntless hope, Gwendolyn's story begins in the gambling casino, where emaciated, ghoulish, desperate figures of all shapes and types are united in a "dull, gas-poisoned absorption"[30] that foreshadows the Inferno she is to experience in her marriage. Religion exists and is attractive to humans primarily because they seek an explanation for and a way to deal with suffering, and throughout her depiction of Gwendolyn's ghastly marriage George Eliot invokes Dante's *Divine Comedy* to remind readers of the religious understanding that dominated the prescientific European world. George Eliot has often been accused of being unable to write about or really face "evil" because her empathetic ethic always compels her to urge sympathy even in the most unattractive specimens of humanity. In Grandcourt we find her considering the idea of unredeemed wickedness, a consummate egoism that does not see the world outside itself as comprised of anything but "admiring or envying spectators."[31]

George Eliot's reliance on Dante's images to anatomize and diagnose Gwendolyn's harrowing marital experience is striking, boldly taking the tale into a world unfamiliar in the "realist" novel. Grandcourt is described as a "lizard-like," "dangerous serpent," a modern Mephistopheles[32] whose psychological torture ranges from rigid "surveillance" to thumbscrews and the rack.[33] His treatment of his wife leads to comparisons to a colonizer who knows it is "safer to exterminate than to cajole" and to an "old time" husband who would consign his incompliant spouse to a lunatic asylum or a nunnery.[34] In keeping with the overall themes of the novel, it is noteworthy that his loathsomeness is said to be owing to failures of his imagination.[35] He is helped in his campaign of taking absolute control over his wife by the fact that, whereas it has become impossible for him to see any wrongdoing associated with himself, it has become impossible for her to dissociate herself from wrongdoing: fatally, she believes she is getting only what she deserves: "she felt she has sold herself . . . [,] her truthfulness and sense of justice."[36]

With deliberately religious language George Eliot invites us to "enter into the soul of this young creature": "She had a root of conscience in her, and the process of purgatory had begun for her on the green earth: she knew that she had been wrong."[37] Ironically, it is Gwendolyn's belief that she deserves to suffer that qualifies her for redemption and means that she can emerge from the hellish marriage, if only into purgatory. Her inner turmoil is so thoroughgoing and intense as to leave her questioning whether her murderous wishes are real or imagined. In another novel Gwendolyn might indeed have been driven mad, but with the help of Dante George Eliot represents her agonies as the waking dream of an all-too-sane woman, whose sufferings transform her grief into a religious experience—a psychic hell "as bad as nightmare,"[38] in which "fantasies moved within her like ghosts."[39] "In Gwendolyn's consciousness, Temptation and Dread met and stared like two pale phantoms";[40] but what makes her struggle redemptive is the fact that it is "her own wishes" and "her own hatred" that she fears, as much as and finally more than she fears her husband.[41]

Although Gwendolyn finds no help in churchgoing and is unable "to connect liturgy and sermon" with anything that matters,[42] it is telling that her desperation finds her falling back on not only the moral rhetoric of "remorse" and "punishment"[43] but the religious rhetoric of "atonement" and "penance."[44] And amidst the wealth of references that fill the text, it is the religious universe of Dante's *Divine Comedy* that most resonates with Gwendolyn's plight. Notably, the epigraph to chapter 64, after she has been pulled half-dead from the sea, provides an image from the *Purgatorio* that gives depth and credibility to the possibility of her struggling on into new life:

> "This mount is such . . . that to those
> Starting at the foot it's hard in the extreme;
> The more they climb, the easier it grows."[45]

It is interesting, then, that when George Eliot broadens her view in her last novel to consider more directly questions of ultimate meaning and destiny, she deliberately affirms the transformative power of imagination and turns to two ancient worldviews, the Cabbala and Dante's late-medieval Catholic view. She is as aware as any present-day psychiatrist that all of these perspectives—the imaginative sensibility that places stock in coincidence, perceives convergence in circumstances, and sees wishes coming true; Mordecai's passionate, intense belief in an invisible future and eternal destiny; Dante's interpretation of psychological, emotional struggles as spiritual battles for the soul—can as readily be seen as evidence of mental disorder and emotional distress. But she takes the risk in *Daniel Deronda* of opening up possibilities shaped by imagination and requiring an attitude of or resembling faith.

The Evolution of Consciousness: *Silas Marner* and the Origin of Personality

The second way in which Teilhard's understanding of evolutionary spirituality can help us understand George Eliot's religious imagination is to be found in his explanation of egoism and personality—the focus of so much of George Eliot's fictional attention—and the question of the One and the Many. Teilhard's fundamental idea is that "evolution is an ascent toward consciousness" and then to higher and higher levels of consciousness.[46] This is something George Eliot speculated upon and tried out in her "experiments in life."[47] Indeed, one could fruitfully analyze all of her works in terms of Teilhard's fundamental law of Complexity-Consciousness—the notion that increased complexity leads, in the one who welcomes it, to increased consciousness—along with the other two components, Attraction and Connection, which Teilhard understood to be the preliminary steps in this evolutionary process.[48]

Among the implications Teilhard draws out is the idea that the universe must be personal and that each of us is at once the center of our own world and at the same time being brought constantly "*into association with all the centres* surrounding it."[49] Teilhard proclaims that "the work of human works" can be meant only "to establish, in and by means of each one of us, an absolutely original centre in which the universe reflects itself in a unique and inimitable way" and that "those centres are our very selves and personalities," which will be reclaimed rather than dissolved at the end.[50] Individual consciousness is essential to existence and, moreover, according to the principle "*union differentiates,*" individual consciousnesses become more, not less, themselves "by convergence."[51] George Eliot would have exulted in hearing scientific arguments for a principle she reinforced in her fiction again and again:

> To be fully ourselves it is in . . . the direction of convergence with all the rest, that we must advance—towards the "other." The peak of ourselves, the acme of our originality, is not our originality but our person; and according to the evolutionary structure of the world, we can only find our person by uniting together. There is no mind without synthesis. . . . The true ego grows in inverse proportion to "egoism."[52]

Teilhard and George Eliot understand human consciousness and its development in ways that are mutually illuminating, as I would like now to explore using *Silas Marner*. In doing so I am deviating from my otherwise chronological account of George Eliot's career, but even this illustrates the fundamental evolutionary principle by which the seed may sometimes only latently reveal its potential and a fossil hold a record to be read by future explorers.

George Eliot's parable-like tale of 1861 marks a transition in her writing and can be seen in the current context as a kind of fossil recording her own evolution from the consciousness of her Midlands childhood and youth to that of mature urban adulthood. As Terence Cave shows in his excellent "Introduction" to the Oxford edition, *Silas Marner* is at several levels a study of the idea of human consciousness. For one thing, Silas's strange lapses of consciousness, by placing him "so precariously on the threshold of *un*consciousness," allow George Eliot "to give imaginative form to the Comtean notion of a gradual evolution of consciousness in human history."[53] "The structure of *Silas Marner*," notes Cave, "is the structure of a slow emergence into consciousness—very slow, minimal, yet crucial."[54] Further, Silas's move from the city to the countryside—even in its mirror inversion of George Eliot's own move from the country to the city at this time—as well as the story's source in a spontaneous childhood memory, link the tale to George Eliot's own development and that of society.[55] Just as the pervasive insect imagery plays on evolutionary models, so skeletons and linguistic dialects and cultural idioms appear as "fragments of human archeology."[56] In these ways this "anthropological study of pre-industrial village life"[57] is at the same time a study of the evolution of individual consciousness.

George Eliot invites this evolutionary analysis and even tells the reader that "Marner's inward life had been a history and a metamorphosis."[58] Indeed, we might say that Teilhard's analysis of the evolution of consciousness serves to "complexify" George Eliot's insights in a way that furthers consciousness in the reader. As George Eliot herself has often done, Teilhard shows that humans are on the one hand similar to animals and, on the other, absolutely different. What constitutes this difference is of course "reflection," which Teilhard defines fairly conventionally as "the power acquired by a consciousness to turn in upon itself."[59] He goes on to say that evolution would not occur—and indeed does not occur—where the advance toward consciousness is stayed or retarded. Crucially, "Life, being an ascent of consciousness, could not continue to advance indefinitely along its line without transforming itself in depth."[60] George Eliot seems to share this view, particularly in *Silas Marner*, as she explores various points at which the progress of human consciousness has stalled, waiting to be deepened by its response to complexity. In different ways she explores the liminal territory that marks what Teilhard calls the "*borders of intelligence*"[61]—points at which the distinction between animal and human consciousness is blurred. These are the periods of consciousness when a person or culture, rather than crossing what Teilhard calls "the threshold of reflection"[62] into thought, lingers in a state of instinctual or emotional stasis.

Silas is clearly stranded at "the threshold of reflection" by the betrayal he has experienced in Lantern Yard. But his potential for evolution is paradoxically manifest in a process of devolution as he begins "withering" more and more[63] until he is barely to be differentiated as a human being. As if anticipating Kafka's *Metamorphosis,* George Eliot's narrative dwells on the possibilities here as she describes Silas as "like the spider" weaving "from pure impulse, without reflection." Acting on physical needs alone, he gradually is able "to reduce his life to the unquestioning activity of a spinning insect."[64] Later, when Silas loses his gold, George Eliot describes his metamorphosis into "a plodding ant" that is stymied by a change to his habitual route.[65] Teilhard notes that what looks like thought in ants is "a paroxysm of consciousness" by comparison to the relative freedom of mammals; the insect's "unquestioning activity" is "the exact opposite of concentration."[66] George Eliot seems to represent in Silas at this stage the strange sight of a man who looks to be concentrating but is without reflection.

It is crucial for George Eliot, as for Teilhard, that a creature's absence of reflection is also an absence of love: Silas's work compensates for "the loveless chasms of his life," and when "thought was arrested," "affection seemed to have died."[67] But it is equally crucial that Silas has a "fervid," "intense nature"[68] that compels him to develop relationships with his guineas and his beloved pot: he believes they are "conscious of him, as his loom was."[69] As is the case for Robinson Crusoe, Silas's survival and eventual resumption of growth are a direct function of his ability to create consciousness and companionship in a barren world. Teilhard would see even his companioning of inanimate objects as evidence of an "interior life" by which an ego remakes the world into itself. "*So man becomes a person through personalization*," he writes.[70] But ultimately what awakens Silas from this long deathlike sleep is of course his love for Eppie. She is, as Silas suspects, a "message" from his past—the past before betrayal—but also an invitation to a future that is something other than a repetition of the present. The little girl frees him from the bondage that "the monotony of his loom and the repetition of his web" have become: "she called him away . . . re-awakening his senses . . . and warming him."[71] Teilhard would say that Eppie reactivates the development of his life by "transforming [it] in depth."

The transformation of Silas is clear, but I will mention just a couple of points that reinforce the evolutionary resonance. Eppie clearly makes a "link" for her adopted father to the social world of Raveloe, but just as crucially she revises his relationship to the natural world, "even to the old winter-flies."[72] George Eliot's descriptions of Eppie make clear that she attaches Silas to the human world but also that she frees him from his self-perception or, more accurately, his insect-like lack of self-perception, first by connecting him to the lives of animals. I don't think it is merely for the sake of sentimental appeal that George Eliot compares Eppie from the start to "a little starved robin" and "a small mouse" or that her play with her friends is compared to that of "little dogs."[73] And when the little girl is "talking to the winged things" in one breath and her father in the next, she is also weaving an alternative world for him in which he and she and the creatures around them are united.[74] George Eliot makes clear that "the little child had come to link him once more with the whole world"—and not just the human world. "There was love between him and the child that blent them into one, and there was love between the child and the world—from men and women with parental looks and tones, to the red lady-birds and the round pebbles."[75] Eppie indeed "personalizes" Silas to his world, transforming him from the "useful gnome or brownie" he has become into a person.[76]

Although Eppie's "refinement and fervour" make her what might be called more evolved than "a common village maiden,"[77] George Eliot nonetheless emphasizes her animal energy as we witness her "laughing and frisking" and playing with her dog and kitten.[78] As Teilhard puts it, a mammal departs from an insect in not being a prisoner of its physical being and instincts; it exhibits instead a sense of "exuberance of life and curiosity": "it takes interest, it flutters, it plays."[79] Even the fact that Eppie plays with the animals during dinner marks the change from Silas's previously physically determined existence: dinner is now more than a means to satisfy physical appetite. They are human persons, yes, but this means—rather paradoxically perhaps—they are also like animals and even like pebbles and plants: Silas learns to care lovingly for Eppie as if she were "a precious plant,"[80] and "as the child's mind was growing into knowledge, his mind was growing into memory" and reconnecting with his past. "As her life unfolded, his soul, long stupefied in a cold narrow prison"—like a seed long lying dormant in the cold ground—"was unfolding too, and trembling gradually into full consciousness."[81] George Eliot's unfolding of the evolution of Silas's consciousness as activated by love resonates with Teilhard's understanding. Fundamental to his analysis of the evolutionary process—as well as to Dante's explanation of the working of the cosmos—is the idea that love is the universal energy binding all creatures and all creation together. For Teilhard, love is the energy that directs the Attraction and Connection that precede and facilitate Complexity and Consciousness.

Evolutionary Spirituality, Incarnational Interpretation, and Subjective Knowing

The third idea that George Eliot shares with Teilhard has to do with their understanding of the evolution of language and interpretation in relation to the development of religious thought and feeling. In *Silas Marner* she is intent to demonstrate the paradoxical idea that Raveloe is at once inhabited by "our rural forefathers"[82] and utterly devoid of an inhabitant like us, since our development has necessitated movement away from this past and a consequent inability to know it. In this respect she is following the model of her revered Sir Walter Scott, but updating it in light of contemporary ideas on evolution. What is remarkable about *Silas Marner* is the way in which George Eliot tries to immerse readers in the culture of Raveloe in order to reproduce the slow, painful evolution of religious consciousness. When she moves Silas from one "little hidden world" to another,[83] the reader learns that every culture, while experienced by its inhabitants as comprehensive and even singular, is just such a little hidden world to anyone not belonging to it. Without Scott's typical "enlightened" character to provide perspective, and with its key outsider barely able to articulate his thoughts and feelings, the world of Raveloe seems to exist as a hermetically, and hermeneutically, sealed bubble and thus outside of the influence of evolution. In exactly this way, however, George Eliot is showing readers that this is their own past, and, crucially for my purposes, this is our religious heritage.

In a similar vein, Teilhard reminds his readers that in depicting the prehuman world and human nature as it evolved, he is by definition without the benefit of a "spectator" to interpret the processes, since these processes occurred before the move across the threshold of reflection brought the advent of thought. "What I depict is not the past *in itself*," he writes, "but as it must appear to an observer standing on the advanced peak where evolution has placed us." In other words, there is no human in this past and it is only as an observer, with the observer's advanced knowledge, that we can "picture" the past, as in a "film" in which we did not yet exist and we could not have survived. Nonetheless, Teilhard goes on, this "safe and modest method . . . suffices, through symmetry, to bring out ahead of us surprising visions of the future."[84]

Throughout *Silas Marner*, the narrator is sending the reader warnings not to prejudge the religious cultures of the past; in other words, to be careful how we interpret their efforts at interpretation. After Silas is betrayed by his Lantern Yard friends, for example, the narrator feels compelled to explain his immediate, utter despair and his lack of "independent thought" to her readers, whom she knows have themselves evolved—or think they have evolved—beyond such emotional, primitive habits of response: "To people accustomed to reason about the forms in which their religious feeling has incorporated itself, it is difficult to enter into that simple, untaught state of mind in which the form and the feeling have never been severed by an act of reflection."[85] Aside from the obvious irony here, the rhetoric is fascinating as George Eliot describes "reflection" as an act that "severs" form and feeling, which had once been "incorporated" together, causing a person to be analytical about his feelings and thus to separate out those feelings from the forms religion takes.[86] Likewise, when, in another demonstration of the link his "religious feeling" forges with "form," Silas sanctifies the hearth where Eppie came to him, the narrator is quick to warn readers to honor this religious impulse and acknowledge it as their own: "The gods of the hearth exist for us still; and let all new faith be tolerant of that fetishism, lest it bruise its own roots."[87]

The reader is challenged throughout to think again about how to define religious thought and feeling as George Eliot represents the evolution of religious consciousness in terms of Silas's relationship to language and the wary, tentative growth of his understanding of the relation of language to thought and feeling. Silas's evolution clearly entails a hermeneutical education for the "simple, untaught state of mind" that saw him take the drawing of lots at face value and then revert, in reaction to his betrayal and banishment, to a state of "benumbing unbelief."[88] Part of his unreflective, antisocial state is an attempt to recant the use of language altogether, but his reintegration into society necessitates language—even though it is "a stream that is almost sure to smack of a mingled soil"—just as it necessitates churchgoing, which is useful if only to provide a showcase for what the parish clerk deems "neighbourly" behavior.[89]

The integral relation of language and interpretation to the development of religious thought and feeling is most evident in Silas's relationship with his neighbor, Dolly Winthrop. To socialize Marner is a major reason for Dolly's efforts to get him to come to church, but she also expresses a sentiment religious enough to be called a "simple Raveloe theology." Dolly is hoping for a kind of conversion to sacramental religion in Silas, and she woos him with an appeal to his welfare: "You'd be a deal better, and you'd know which end you stood on, and you could put your trust i' Them as knows better nor we do." In a more sophisticated addition that is a match for any philosopher or theologian, she refers to "Them as we must all give ourselves up to at the last" and explains, "if we 'n done our part, it isn't to be believed as Them as are above us 'ull be worse nor we are, and come short o' Theirn."[90] As the narrator wryly notes, Dolly's use of the plural pronoun to designate the deity is not an indication of polytheism but merely her attempt to avoid "a presumptuous familiarity."[91] Still, George Eliot uses this odd turn of phrase not to mock Dolly but to emphasize the inadequacy of language and Silas's need to interpret this alien version of Christianity.

While Silas's poor vision, caused by his fearful, intense focus on his insect world, helps to convey the difficulty of seeing clearly or understanding anything beyond or even within one's range of sight, the scene involving the deciphering of the I.H.S. that Dolly has "pricked" into her cakes offers a metaphor for the coded world that every culture is, illegible to outsiders and taken for granted though often unread by those within. In the context of the development of religious traditions, the groping for connection in this scene between Silas and Dolly helps to bring to light issues of interpretation and mediation. Indeed, in our own day readers are likely to need the help of an explanatory note to understand I.H.S., and spell-check is likely to transliterate it into IRS or HIS, thereby confirming the overriding power of cultural codes. For his part, Silas has come from a religious sect that has rejected the state church and its clerical and liturgical forms in favor of a presumed firsthand reading of God's word in the Bible. And Dolly's illiteracy lends credence to the view that the adherents of the church do not actually *read* the prayer book that has come to replace the Bible as the institutionally sanctioned mediator between the people and God.

It is important of course that Dolly's efforts go beyond language: she brings cakes and practical help as well as well-meaning words, so that her genuine desire to nourish her neighbor is clear, and George Eliot makes the entangling of questions of spiritual nourishment and religious meaning explicit with their struggle over the meaning of the I.H.S. Neither Dolly nor Silas knows that the letters signify the first three letters of the name of Jesus in Greek, but Silas does at least recognize the letters, a feat that is beyond Dolly. Still, he is "unable to interpret them" as anything holding religious significance, while she believes they are "good letters" with a "good meaning," because they are found in church. Dolly does successfully convey to Silas the truly good meaning of the letters, however, in a way that upholds the key principle of George Eliot's religion: she succeeds because "there was no possibility of misunderstanding" the feeling behind her use of them.[92]

Even though Silas barely nibbles at Dolly's offerings, and whether or not we accept this as a Eucharistic scene and his neighbor as an unwitting priest, readers do witness here a feeding of the spirit. And while words are inadequate and the I.H.S. is indecipherable, he does nonetheless ingest the inscribed bread. Still, Dolly does not succeed in convincing Silas to come to church on Christmas Day, because, as this scene makes clear, she is still speaking a foreign language that "his imagination" cannot translate. Yet all of this prepares the way for the coming of Eppie, who will succeed, when all of the community's words and socializing gestures cannot, in unlocking what George Eliot calls here "the fountains of human love and divine faith." This notion is significant enough to compel her to rephrase it, to articulate more accurately the connection between faith and love, the human and the divine: in a rare change, it becomes in a later edition "human love and faith in a divine love."[93] It is important that instead of taking Silas to church George Eliot grants him what he truly needs—his own experience of incarnation in the person of a little child on New Year's Eve. For it is not by words and human efforts alone that he will be brought back to life. "What child is it?" ask several ladies.[94] "What child is this?" asks the Christmas hymn.

Dolly and Silas do actually connect, and Silas is actually restored to life because of the embodied, completely unexpected mediation of a child. In this, George Eliot is pointing to the limitations of even the best human efforts and perhaps honoring Dolly's respect for "Them as are above us." Certainly it is possible to see George Eliot's imitation of the Christian nativity narrative, particularly in the context of a culture in which the name of Jesus is unrecognizable, as a version of Comte's "religion of humanity"—an affirmation of Christian values without the need for Christ as anything but a fetish. But I would argue instead that the parable instructs us in matters of epistemology by reminding us of the importance of a kind of feeling knowledge that is manifest in incarnated and subjective knowing.

George Eliot's attention throughout her work to certain characters as readers helps draw *our* attention as readers to the hermeneutical task, which, as part of the evolutionary tide, had taken a new turn with the rise of scientific knowledge in her time. By alerting readers to a web of possibilities that have been written about for as long as humans have been reading (and may well have been talked about before that), *Silas Marner* points to the ongoing task of interpretation that predates any scientific perspective. It also makes clear that the human consciousness is by definition an interpretive consciousness regardless of its ability to read a literal text. Reading is of course a familiar convenient metaphor for understanding, which George Eliot makes complex use of throughout her career. It is central to George Eliot's conception of the religion of the future that readers must be doers, that the duality between word and action must be reframed in terms of an incarnational aesthetic that teaches readers how to act on what they learn.

That *Silas Marner* is frequently taken as a parable reminds us that the demand for readers or listeners to interpret and indeed act upon a story is an ancient ingredient in storytelling. In the wake of what is called the "higher criticism" of biblical texts, George Eliot reminds readers of a "lower" type of criticism that calls for a different but equally sophisticated and intelligent kind of interpretation. Here again it is helpful to remember George Eliot's reading of Dante. Dorothy L. Sayers reminds twentieth-century readers of *Purgatorio* that their Victorian forebears are responsible for creating the "partitioned-off personality" that threatens to prevent them from enjoying "the mixture of passion, mysticism, and science in one and the same poem." By contrast, she says, a medieval reader relished this integrated type of poetry, since "it would never occur to him that he ought to keep his head, his heart, and his religious experience in water-tight compartments."[95] A dangerous legacy of the Enlightenment is the arrogant dismissal of prescientific views as less intelligent, when they are more intelligently seen as earlier models from which our own evolve. As Barbara Reynolds puts it in her "Introduction" to *Paradiso*, "Modern science has not superseded medieval thought about the nature of creation, but only the physical picture which illustrated and accompanied it."[96] In terms of the hermeneutics of storytelling, George Eliot is helping to dismantle what Sayers calls the "Victorian bulkheads"[97] by reconnecting with the medieval imagination and incorporating key elements from it into our understanding of reading and thereby into the evolution of the human imagination itself.

We may look to biblical hermeneutics and to Dante for an understanding of the prescientific imagination that George Eliot is reworking for the contemporary reader. Firstly, in *Mimesis* Erich Auerbach famously shows that the distinctive contribution of biblical narrative to realism has to do with a paradoxical kind of authority that no longer holds sway after scientific criticism comes to the fore: "while, on the one hand, the reality of the Old Testament presents itself as complete truth with a claim to sole authority, on the other hand that very claim forces it to a constant interpretative change in its own content; for millennia it undergoes an incessant and active development with the life of man in Europe."[98] In other words, the Bible is part of a tradition that has always practiced evolutionary reading, a tradition that bases its authority on the expectation of continually changing interpretation. Further, Auerbach argues, while the Old Testament biblical narrative itself is seen to be developing in relation to its readers, biblical heroes too, unlike classical heroes, are "fraught with . . . development."[99] Their individuality and identity, won through intense suffering and hardship, give them a new kind of grandeur as true-to-life heroes. These two principles—the reverence for ordinary, indeed evolving, humanity and the understanding of readers and texts as evolving—form the basis for George Eliot's incarnational aesthetic.

Auerbach also writes of the "astounding paradox of what is called Dante's realism" by which he creates entirely human, mortal characters who inhabit and achieve their essence in an eternal, timeless sphere.[100] This "astounding" ability to make characters that are at once temporal and eternal, according to Reynolds, stymies post-scientific readers who are unable "to distinguish the figure from the thing figured."[101] Likewise, Hans Frei, in accounting for "the eclipse of Biblical narrative" with the rise of scientific criticism, speaks of the decline in credibility of figural interpretation and of narrative itself, a decline that is caused by a misguided correlation between truth and historical accuracy. In other words, we might say that the Bible lost credibility at this time largely because of readers' lack of imagination: stories were seen as merely contexts for truths that could be extracted, Frei says, when in fact, particularly in the case of the synoptic Gospels, "their narrative rendering, in effect a cumulative rendering of the theme, is indispensable."[102] Frei's point makes clear that the evolution of reading was a fundamental tenet of prescientific hermeneutics. Again, we may speak of this integral relation between story and subject matter as part of the incarnational aesthetic that George Eliot practices.

Indeed, it is not going too far to see George Eliot as demonstrating what is now called "story theology." Theologians in this group identify the problem Frei refers to of extracting the core and seeking the message, while forgetting that the story is essential. Story theology also reminds us of the oral, story form in which the Bible was experienced, especially by the nonliterate, and speaks of how signs and symbols of faith—stained glass windows, liturgical rituals, music, and, I daresay, letters pricked in cakes—speak without words. As Marcus Borg puts it, "Religious laws speak of how to behave; theology and doctrine speak of how to understand and what to believe; but stories appeal to the imagination, to that place within us where our images of reality, life, and ourselves reside. The great stories of the Bible image what the religious life is about."[103] Again, it seems to me that George Eliot in a similar way is reminding us of the role of imagination in awakening and developing the religious consciousness by demonstrating that it is both incarnational and evolving.

George Eliot's effort to reproduce the evolution of religious consciousness as a series of stories in which we are all immersed and entangled is part of a fuller effort to demonstrate the complexities of knowledge that are being revealed in her time, particularly with regard to subjectivity. Frequently, her narrator acknowledges that she herself and her readers are themselves subject to interpretative processes; she makes clear, in other words, that readers are interpreting but also being interpreted by what they read. Throughout her works, narrative "asides" are actually central in turning the text into a two-way mirror in which readers are continually asked to consider the "log" in their own eyes before judging characters in her stories or neighbors in real life. This ethical practice is grounded in philosophical and scientific knowledge concerning perception and self-knowledge. What might be called "the knowledge of knowledge" is constantly evolving at this time, for a key element in the crisis of knowledge that erupted in the nineteenth century is the problem of what may be summed up in the phrase "subjective knowing."

In regard to this, it is interesting that George Eliot shares with Teilhard a focus on sight. As many have noted, she uses the metaphor of seeing throughout her career to signal the problems associated with human egoism and its limitations. For his part, Teilhard entitles the foreword of *The Phenomenon of Man* "SEEING." Here he argues that the crisis provoked by evolution was a crisis about seeing. Scientists now had to acknowledge that their seeing was not objective but instead that their observations are "steeped" in preconceptions, that what they see may be "the reflection of their own thought," that "they are caught in their own net." In other words, in recognizing that knowledge could not but be shaped by the knower, scientists had to embrace the insight that philosophers and poets more readily appreciated: as Teilhard poetically phrases it, "Object and subject marry and mutually transform each other in the act of knowledge."[104] Or, in the words of Percy Bysshe Shelley in his *Defence of Poetry*, "All things exist as they are perceived: at least in relation to the percipient."

In this sense, the I.H.S. scene offers a beautifully explicit rendering of the complexities of the relation between subject and object: Dolly and Silas try to read the letters in a literal and in a religious sense and then go on to demonstrate their human meaning when Silas tastes the cake in which Dolly has pricked the letters. This scene, depicting a shift from the "what" of content to the "how" of embodied meaning, is one of many in which George Eliot explores the relationship between language and interpretation. Particularly, we can see linguistic dilemmas acted out in *The Mill on the Floss*, in which Mr. Tulliver, in a less benign rendition of Dolly's "theology," senses the power of language to overcome his enemies and give him a way to deal with the "puzzling," hostile world.[105] His children variously inherit his preoccupation: Tom is rather like Silas in learning the letters but being unable to interpret them in a way that renders them meaningful, while Maggie, with her passion for reading, imaginatively invests all texts with the potential to change her life. She looks for herself in texts, is discouraged at the version of selfhood she finds in Scott's novels, and then in desperation seeks for a "key" to living in Thomas à Kempis's *Imitation of Christ*. Her unlikely heir in this regard is Casaubon from *Middlemarch*, who invests his life's energy in finding the Key to all Mythologies and thereby his own vindication. In response, the dim-sighted Dorothea takes a lesson from the blind obsessiveness of her husband and invests her own faith in an embodied, lived-out quest for meaning.

All of these characters are caught in interpretative struggles involving the managing of the relationship between objective and subjective knowledge, and George Eliot has deep sympathy for the longing for subjective knowing, even in its most egoistic renderings.[106] As mentioned in chapter 1, Kierkegaard makes heavy philosophical weather of the idea that truth is in fact subjectivity. In his *Concluding Unscientific Postscript* he notes that objective truth—the "what" truth of content—can be made untrue by not being held subjectively as true. Only truth that is made inward by our "how" of enactment can be truly true. "Objectively the interest is focused merely on the thought-content," Kierkegaard argues, "subjectively on the inwardness. At its maximum this inward 'How' is the passion of the infinite, and the passion of the infinite is the truth. But the passion of the infinite is precisely subjectivity, and thus subjectivity becomes the truth."[107]

Kierkegaard goes so far as to connect the subjectivity of truth to the very existence of the individual: a person becomes an individual by making the truth inward, and it is this process that also makes her "subject to a dialectic with respect to time" by connecting her own inwardness in the present moment to the eternal.

> In the passionate moment of decision, where the road swings away from objective knowledge, it seems as if the infinite decision was thereby realised. But in the same moment the existing individual finds himself in the temporal order, and the subjective "how" is transformed into a striving, a striving which receives indeed its impulse and a repeated renewal from the decisive passion of the infinite, but is nevertheless a striving.[108]

This idea of a striving that both defines the person as an individual in time and affirms her or his relation to eternity could describe the dialectic underlying George Eliot's incarnational aesthetic. We could say that the search for a "key" by characters such as Maggie and Casaubon is based on a desire to experience the truth as subjective, and that characters such as Dorothea are more evolved (and blessed by their author) in being able to strive for the truth of subjectivity in a way that affirms their own relation with the infinite.

Central to Kierkegaard's thinking is the notion that a person only exists as an individual insofar as his activity is "transformed" by its relation to the infinite. He goes even further in arguing that God does not exist except in relation to this dialectic of inwardness. Kierkegaard's point is that God's invisibility in creation in any direct sense compels the believer to seek him by activating his own response; otherwise God remains what Richard Kearney might call a possibility. As Kierkegaard puts it: "He is in the creation, and present everywhere in it, but directly He is not there; and only when the individual turns to his inner self, and hence only in the inwardness of self-activity, does he have his attention aroused, and is enabled to see God."[109] God is everywhere, but seeing God requires a triangular dynamic of self-world-God. "Nature, the totality of created things, is the work of God. And yet God is not there; but within the individual man there is a potentiality (man is potentially spirit) which is awakened in inwardness to become a God-relationship, and then it becomes possible to see God everywhere."[110]

As paradoxically as he expresses it, Kierkegaard is restating a time-honored view regarding the subjectivity of faith that goes back to such a stalwart figure of orthodoxy as Augustine. Still, Kierkegaard reminds us of the need in the age of rationalism to reestablish the basis of faith in paradox and subjectivity. In this context we can say that whereas George Eliot is often understood to have moved beyond faith in a supernatural God, it is more accurate to see her in this tradition of what Teilhard might call a more complex kind of consciousness. When she depicts her heroine in "Janet's Repentance" seeing the ordinary "monotony" of the natural world as transformed after her conversion, for example, one might see a merely subjective experience:

> A very commonplace scene, indeed. But what scene was ever commonplace in the descending sunlight, when colour has awakened from its noonday sleep, and the long shadows awe us like a disclosed presence? Above all, what scene is commonplace to the eye that is filled with serene gladness, and brightens all things with its own joy?[111]

Rather, I would argue that George Eliot is here affirming the subjectivity of all knowing and confirming what she calls in *Daniel Deronda* "the emotional intellect" as a true guide. As Kierkegaard notes, it is mystery that both hides and reveals the presence of God. And it is for the percipient to see or not "the disclosed presence"—what Teilhard calls "the divine milieu"—in the world around her.

Evolutionary Spirituality and the Meaning of Suffering

These notions of embodied meaning and subjective knowing bring us to the fourth way in which George Eliot's religious imagination may be reframed in light of Teilhard's evolutionary ideas: their shared understanding of suffering. The interesting thing about emphasizing the interpretive role of the reader, as with emphasizing the role of the believer, is the risk of misinterpretation. Shifting the focus from doctrinal certainty to a dependence on the believer's engagement opens the faith to a number of dangers: the believer may misinterpret the doctrine, for one thing, or in turn may himself be interpreted as having no faith at all. This very riskiness is what constitutes evolutionary spirituality, according to Diarmuid O'Murchu, a Roman Catholic priest and writer who develops Teilhard's principles. In his book *Adult Faith*, O'Murchu highlights three main elements of evolutionary spirituality as it has evolved from Teilhard's original ideas: first, it is relational and emphasizes mutuality and co-creation; second, it is progressive; and third, it emphasizes imagination, feeling, and intuition. Identity, from this perspective, is built on an ancestral past but is always poised toward the future, thereby offering a faith stance for the person Susan Neiman calls the "grown-up idealist."[112]

When we consider George Eliot's fictional "experiments," we can identify several religious ideas to which she strove to give a "grown-up" response. Marian Evans's early preoccupations as the translator of Strauss and Feuerbach mirrored those of her contemporaries: the questions of the existence and the divinity of Jesus. For novelist George Eliot the focus shifts to Jesus as a model for humanity, as she turns from the question of his miracles to the practice of his ethics of love. As we have discussed, she speaks of being increasingly averse to "formulas" about beliefs and "more and more timid" about expressing her views except in her art:[113] in this way she is both demonstrating the ultimate truth of the incarnational aesthetic for herself and requiring the reader to respond in kind by interpreting the fictional embodied ideas in light of her or his own experience. In this way she is also illustrating David Richo's point about mature faith: "An adult does not possess a belief but follows on its endlessly provocative path. Faith is more like a path than a platform."[114]

Related to the perception of Jesus as miracle worker is the focus on his role as eliminator of suffering. Several aspects of this perception may inhibit or retard personal growth; for one thing, if Jesus is the one who eliminates suffering, one may denigrate the role of humans in striving to understand the causes of suffering and working to eliminate it. As O'Murchu points out, the celebration of Jesus as hero, both in miraculously healing pain and then in bearing all of the world's pain on the cross, may lead to a dualistic theology that pits goodness against an objective kind of evil, including scapegoats and devils and mega-corporations, and turns our attention away from our own complicity in injustice and our responsibility to work against it in the here and now.[115] At its worst, such an attitude turns the crucified Christ into a fetish or an idol for the kind of militant church that was Blake's target: the church that is more concerned about establishing its own power and identifying its enemies than alleviating the suffering of the poor, inside or outside of its walls.[116] The shift required here (as discussed in chapter 3) is from the notion of God suffering for us to a more mutual, adult understanding of God suffering alongside us and our fellows. This latter understanding pervades George Eliot's depiction of suffering, for the response she always promotes is empathy and sympathetic action. Just as Dinah comes alongside Hetty in the prison cell, so the reader is encouraged to come alongside, rather than to stand above, the foolish, inept Amos Barton, the vain, selfish Rosamond, the hypocritical, self-satisfied Bulstrode. In this way George Eliot is always asking her readers to stand in for the Jesus who loved and forgave sinners and stood against injustice and prejudice.

At the same time, all of these situations exemplify another essential element of George Eliot's view of suffering and of what O'Murchu refers to as "adult faith": that is, the conviction that suffering is an essential ingredient of life, without which there is no growth, no evolution. This is a far cry from the unhealthy kind of submission to evil that brings upon Christians the charge of disdain for the world and even collusion with the forces of death. In *The Divine Milieu* Teilhard works through a complex argument that redefines Christian resignation as an attitude that holds in tension an unflagging resistance to all forms of death and an acceptance of the will of God.[117] For Teilhard it is in this paradoxical attitude of active surrender that the Christian can achieve growth and contribute to the life of the world. We may compare this explanation to Kierkegaard's argument concerning the benefits of suffering that turns the sufferer "inward": "only inwardness in sufferings gains the eternal . . . When a person suffers and wills to learn from what he suffers, he continually comes to know only something about himself and his relationship to God; this is the sign that he is being educated for eternity."[118]

George Eliot likewise, as we have seen, treats with painstaking care this delicate question of the possibility of suffering as a necessary and potentially good thing, rather than something to be eliminated at any cost. This is part of the only partly comical burden of her poem "My Vegetarian Friend," as we saw in chapter 2, in which the narrator somewhat shamefacedly recognizes the value to him of other people's suffering. As mentioned earlier in reference to *Daniel Deronda*, religion exists because of suffering, and when Daniel advises Gwendolyn to "take the present suffering as a painful letting in of light,"[119] he is voicing George Eliot's own hard-won conviction of—or perhaps only hope in—the purposefulness of suffering and the ultimate goodness of the universe. She would understand, though not perhaps be able to affirm, Kierkegaard's belief that the universe is a "school of suffering"—variously imagined in the doctrine of the Cabbala and the Catholic doctrine of purgatory—that trains humans for eternity.[120] And if her appreciation of these faith-based explanations for suffering stopped short of certainty, the imaginative re-creations they generated in her fiction stand as testaments to her ongoing fascination with the "evidence of things not seen."

One of George Eliot's most thoughtful considerations of the problem of suffering comes in her first novel, when the narrator is working hard to justify Adam's evolution from the pain he has experienced with Hetty to his happiness with Dinah. Adam moves from love for Hetty to love for Dinah, the narrator wants us to know, not in spite of his sorrow or by forgetting his sorrow but by using his sorrow—by turning his sorrow inward. As Adam tells Dinah, when it comes to sorrow, as with love and happiness, "the more we know of it the better we can feel what other people's lives are or might be, and so we shall only be more tender to 'em, and wishful to help 'em. The more knowledge a man has the better he'll do 's work; and feeling's a sort o' knowledge."[121] George Eliot takes great pains in the denouement of the novel to convince the reader, while Adam works to convince Dinah, that their love does not diminish the value of Hetty or of their suffering. The narrator argues that Adam is not "the same man" as he was before he suffered and, rather than either insisting that he remain the same or bemoaning that change, she urges: "Let us rather be thankful that our sorrow lives in us as an indestructible force, only changing its form, as forces do, and passing from pain into sympathy—the one poor word which includes all our best insight and our best love."[122]

The idea that suffering exists for its value in producing wisdom and compassion is a familiar element of many religious traditions and philosophical schools of thought, but the conviction that we ought to "be thankful" for suffering is essentially bound up with an evolutionary understanding. Just as George Eliot proposes the idea of sorrow as "an indestructible force, only changing its form," so Teilhard proposes the value of sorrow as energy that is waiting to be transformed and redirected for good. As he writes in his essay "The Meaning and Constructive Value of Suffering," suffering is not a great mass of "waste"; rather it is "potential energy. In suffering is concealed, with extreme intensity, the world's power of ascension. The whole problem is to liberate it by making it conscious of what it means and what it can achieve."[123]

When George Eliot's narrator describes the process of the transformation of desire into submission, she could be quoting Teilhard: "For it is at such periods that the sense of our lives having visible and invisible relations beyond any of which either our present or prospective self is the centre, grows like a muscle that we are obliged to lean on and exert."[124] This sense of ongoing, relentless growth and change, with our selves as connected visibly and invisibly to centers of life beyond our own, is fundamental to Teilhard's evolutionary spirituality and to his own explanation of the cosmic meaning of suffering. We see in George Eliot's work her agreement with Teilhard that as evolutionary beings it is only by consciously working with suffering that we experience a "sense" of connection with the whole of life and contribute to its "ascension."

In this respect, it is interesting that in her last novel, George Eliot looks beyond Jesus and explores the religious experience of people whose Messiah has yet to come. This focus has significant implications for a perspective on suffering since, while Jewish people would like as much as anyone to avoid it, suffering is the story of their religious experience. For Daniel, this tradition offers a depth that is lacking in his high-society world. When he visits the synagogue in Frankfurt he "gave himself up" to the mere sounds of the "chanted liturgies," which, like Dolly with the I.H.S., he rather feels than understands, being ignorant of their "detailed verbal meaning."[125] Here George Eliot is reminding readers of the emotional, intuitive, imaginative appeal that can be lost in a preoccupation with seeking a literal, rationalistic basis for religious experience.

But her more important point emerges in the fact that the chanted liturgies resonate with, rather than satisfy, Daniel's yearning, as we notice when the narrator goes on to suggest that a mature religious attitude may come more readily to people who are steeped in a tradition full of stories of long waiting periods and centuries of promises:

> The most powerful movement of feeling with a liturgy is the prayer which seeks for nothing special, but is a yearning to escape from the limitations of our own weakness and an invocation of all Good to enter and abide with us; or else a self-oblivious lifting up of gladness, a *Gloria in excelsis* that such Good exists, both the yearning and the exultation gathering their utmost force from the sense of communion in a form which has expressed them both, for long generations of struggling fellow-men.[126]

George Eliot celebrates here the prayer that seeks, not to escape from this world, but "to escape from the limitations of our own weakness"; the prayer that asks not for a supernatural God-figure to rescue us out of this world but for "all Good . . . to enter and abide with us"; or, failing that, this prayer asks just to know that "such good exists," regardless of us and our needs, and finds satisfaction in sharing this "yearning" and "exultation" with fellow humans. Again, as in the language of *Adam Bede* above, George Eliot emphasizes the value of "a sense" that confirms "visible and invisible relations."

In her repeated affirmations of a knowledge that is comprised of feeling and for which words are a feeble adumbration, George Eliot is not only championing the primacy of feeling—sympathy, intuitive understanding, imaginative responsiveness—but discovering a key element of evolutionary spirituality. For just as learning to use reflection to direct the energy of the body and the passions was an essential step in the development of humanity, so now, in the wake of rationalism, learning to subjugate the objectifying intellectual processes is the next stage of human evolution. In terms of the religious imagination, this realization is a rediscovery of the meaning of incarnation, in that moving from complexity to consciousness in light of this new insight requires that humans learn how to reintegrate their minds and bodies together to produce a genuinely incorporated, "ensouled" version of humanity.[127]

Conclusion

✦

The Word Continuously Incarnated

"I can't help laughing at the imbecility of that pious dictum—that if Shelley had lived till now he would have been a Christian—that is, he would have been old woman enough for it by this time."[1] This biting comment from Marian Evans to her friend Sara Sophia Hennell in 1853 stands as a warning to anyone who dares to reopen the question of George Eliot's attitude to religion. But while I have suggested the possibility of George Eliot's return to a renewed understanding of religious faith in the "anatheistic" sense put forward by Richard Kearney, there would not be anything "old womanish" in the terms of her engagement. Rather, I have found throughout her writings evidence of an exploration of possible forms of religious consciousness that is pursued with the same rigorous skepticism that she expresses in this early comment.

As I have argued throughout, George Eliot considered her writing a religious vocation. From her first fictional work until the last, as well as in all of her poems, she is living out this calling in terms of an aesthetic that is incarnational: she creates characters, stories, and ideas in words that bring spirit to life by honoring and celebrating natural beings, including the human. And in doing so she invests the natural and the human with a sense of sacred value and significance.

George Eliot continues to develop this aesthetic practice throughout her career, as she continues to learn through her writing what it means that it is her holy calling to sanctify the ordinary. Such paradoxes abound in the mystical way of thinking, and it is this mystical practice that takes her aesthetic to a deeper level as she comes to question the distinction between the sacred and the secular and to experiment further with mystical ideas, particularly the holiness of everything and the ubiquitous presence of the sacred.

Daniel Deronda particularly is rife with experiments in mystical consciousness as she conjures with such nonrational concepts as coincidence, second sight, wish-fulfillment, and timely rescue. But this is only a bolder exploration of the kind of supranatural events and insights that appear throughout her writing. We need only think of little Eppie coming like an angel to save Silas. And in *The Mill on the Floss* we find the narrator urging readers to open themselves to a way of thinking that is beyond "maxims" and "general rules": "the mysterious complexity of our life is not to be embraced by maxims, and . . . to lace ourselves up in formulas of that sort is to repress all the divine promptings and inspirations that spring from growing insight and sympathy."[2] In human relations, as in our relations with nature—as we saw in her response to Darwin—mystery hints at the divine, if we would only not repress it.

As I argued in chapter 5, George Eliot is always and increasingly illustrating the essential role of interpretation in shaping consciousness and belief. Along with all the other approaches to religious thinking I mention here, her understanding of interpretation reflects what has come to be called "evolutionary spirituality." As I have tried to show, evolutionary spirituality both recovers ancient, often forgotten or overlooked ways of expressing religious thinking and points to an ever-evolving, ever-emergent "religion of the future" that is in constant need of reinterpretation. This understanding is based upon Teilhard's notion, as we noted in chapter 5, that evolution is "a general condition to which all theories, all hypotheses, all systems must bow and which they must satisfy henceforward if they are to be thinkable and true."[3]

This need for reinterpretation extends even to the key doctrines and texts of Christianity. Jesus himself models this mindset. For example, when the two disciples meet the resurrected Jesus on the road to Emmaus, he reveals his identity through the scriptures, showing them that they must reinterpret the text now that he has come. He then deepens their understanding by revealing himself in the ritual act of breaking the bread, offering himself as food for their journey, for they must continue to walk after he has left them. The truth becomes inward for them in a literal way when they eat the bread he has become. As Diarmuid O'Murchu says, he does not vanish into thin air when their eyes are opened—as if he is not meant to subsist in their more fully conscious perception—but rather he vanishes into them, becoming one with their consciousnesses, just as the bread becomes part of their bodies.

When these two disciples tell their story to the community they are acting on Teilhard's notion of what Savary calls "the continuous Incarnation of the great Christ body."[4] The resurrection appearances, particularly those recounted in Luke's stories and in John's account of Mary Magdalene's encounter with the risen Jesus at the tomb, emphasize that believers take up responsibility for telling the story and, by adding their contributions, transform both the story and themselves. They thus become part of the story; in this way future readers learn that they too must tell their story of God, that God's story cannot be told without them. More mysteriously still, they learn that they *are* God's stories, that they are the stories God tells. In this way they embody the continuous Incarnation of Christ.

Evolutionary spirituality explores the mysterious relationship between Christ and the believer by expounding the distinction between Jesus of Nazareth and the Christ whose body is comprised of believers. Louis Savary explains that, according to Teilhard, the traditional focus on an individualistic relationship between a believer and God must evolve into a spirituality that is "collective" and "relational" so as to participate in "the full emergence of Christ as a Cosmic Christ."[5] This evolutionary perspective can help us toward a fuller understanding of George Eliot's religious imagination. For whereas she has typically been understood as simply denying the divinity of Jesus, we might instead see her as dissatisfied with the traditional explanations. When in 1869 Renan's *Vie de Jésus*, a book that proposed to assert the human and minimize the Jewish identity of Jesus, was making quite a stir, George Eliot wrote to a friend that it "can furnish no new result":

> It seems to me that the soul of Christianity lies not at all in the facts of an individual life, but in the ideas of which that life was the meeting-point and the new starting-point. We can never have a satisfactory basis for the history of the man Jesus, but the negation does not affect the Idea of the Christ either in its historical influence or its great symbolic meanings.[6]

The distinction George Eliot makes here between "the man Jesus" and "the Idea of the Christ," rather than articulating an abstract spiritual concept, points instead to her sense that we must act on what we know—that is, as in the letter to Stowe cited at the beginning of chapter 5, "the difficulty of the human lot"—as we wait for what Teilhard would call "the full emergence of Christ as a Cosmic Christ." Even her affirmation of the "great symbolic meanings" of the Christ Idea, rather than an abstraction, is better seen in light of Coleridge's definition of the symbol as characterized "by the translucence of the Eternal through and in the Temporal" and as always partaking of "the Reality which it renders intelligible."

Six months before this letter, after hearing a performance of *Messiah*, George Eliot wrote to her friend Sarah Sophia Hennell of the "acme of poetry" achieved in Christianity in "the conception of the suffering Messiah" and "the final triumph 'He shall reign for ever and ever.'" She goes on: "The Prometheus is a very imperfect foreshadowing of that symbol wrought out in the long history of the Jewish and Christian ages."[7] While the explanations of evolutionary Christianity were unavailable to George Eliot, then, her imagination responded to "the Idea of the Christ" and its evolution as represented symbolically and poetically and musically. And as we have seen throughout, it is at this profound imaginative level that George Eliot's consciousness embraced deeply felt ideas.

NOTES

Preface

1. Pierre Teilhard de Chardin, *The Phenomenon of Man*, trans. Bernard Wall (1955; reprint, New York: Harper Perennial, 2008), 261, 259, 262; italics his.

2. Ibid., 219.

Introduction

1. George Eliot, "The Sad Fortunes of the Reverend Amos Barton," in *Scenes of Clerical Life* (Oxford: Oxford University Press, 1988), chap. 2, 14.

2. George Eliot, *Adam Bede* (Oxford: Oxford University Press, 2008), book 6, chap. 54, 472–73.

3. George Eliot, *The Works of George Eliot: Impressions of Theophrastus Such, Essays and Poems* (New York: A. L. Burt, n.d.), 111.

4. Ibid., 112.

5. Basil Willey, *Nineteenth-Century Studies* (London: Chatto and Windus, 1955), 238.

6. Barry Qualls, "George Eliot and Religion," in *The Cambridge Companion to George Eliot*, ed. George Levine (Cambridge: Cambridge University Press, 2001), 120.

7. Willey, 238.

Chapter 1

1. U. C. Knoepflmacher, *George Eliot's Early Novels: The Limits of Realism* (Berkeley: University of California Press, 1968), 160.

2. Lord Acton, Review of John Walter Cross's *George Eliot's Life* in *Nineteenth Century* (March 1885), xvii, 464–85; quoted in *George Eliot: The Critical Heritage*, ed. David Carroll (Cambridge: Cambridge University Press, 1992), 463.

3. Peter C. Hodgson, *The Mystery Beneath the Real: Theology in the Fiction of George Eliot* (Minneapolis, Minn.: Fortress, 2000), 1.

4. George Eliot's statement "With the ideas of Feuerbach I everywhere agree" is frequently and to my mind uncritically cited as evidence of her agreement with Feuerbach. George Eliot, *The George Eliot Letters*, ed. Gordon S. Haight, 9 vols. (New Haven, Conn.: Yale University Press, 1954), 2:153. I agree with Hodgson when, putting this statement back in the context of her comment on the "raw" Feuerbach that she subjected to her own "cooking," he opines that George Eliot could "everywhere agree" with "no single thinker." Hodgson, *The Mystery Beneath the Real*, 7. Further, she follows the remark with an assurance that she would "of course . . . alter the phraseology considerably," and for a writer to whom treatment was everything in fiction, as her publisher quickly found out when she declined to summarize the story she was writing, a disagreement on "phraseology" was a disagreement indeed.

5. In the same letter to Sara Sophia Hennell of 1843 in which George Eliot affirms "the *truth of feeling* as the only bond of union," she asks, "Ought we not on every opportunity to seek to have our feelings in harmony though not in union with those who are often richer in the fruits of faith though not in reasons, than ourselves?" (*George Eliot Letters*, ed. Haight, 1:162; italics hers). In a letter to Francois D'Albert-Durade in 1859 in which she explains her intimate knowledge of Evangelical Christianity, she writes, "I have not returned to dogmatic Christianity . . . but I see in it the highest expression of the religious sentiment that has yet found its place in the history of mankind, and I have the profoundest interest in the inward life of sincere Christians in all ages" (ibid., 3:231). A statement in a letter of 1860 to her friend Barbara Bodichon reflects her attitude of emotional sympathy balanced by intellectual skepticism: "As for the 'forms and ceremonies,' I feel no regret that any should turn to them for comfort, if they can find comfort in them: sympathetically, I enjoy them myself. But I have faith in the working-out of higher possibilities than the Catholic or any other church has presented, and those who have strength to wait and endure, are bound to accept no formula which their whole souls—their intellect as well as their emotions—do not embrace with entire reverence. The highest 'calling and election' is to *do without opium* and live through all our pain with conscious, clear-eyed endurance" (ibid., 3:366; italics hers). She enjoyed "churches and chapels" as places where "I can dream and think without risk of interruption" (ibid., 3:433). In a letter of 1861 describing a service at a Unitarian chapel, she expresses her love for the liturgy of the Church of England, relishing its "contrast" with the "borrowed washy lingo" of the preacher: "What an age of earnest faith, grasping a noble conception of life and determined to bring all things into harmony with it, has recorded itself in the simple pregnant, rhythmical English of those Collects and of the Bible!" (ibid., 3:442). Again to Mme. Bodichon in 1862: "Pray don't ever ask me again to rob a man of his religious belief, as if you thought my mind tended towards such robbery. I have too profound a conviction of the efficacy that lies in all sincere faith, and the spiritual blight that comes of No-faith, to have any negative propagandism in me. In fact, I have very little sympathy with Free-thinkers as a class, and have lost all interest in mere antagonism to religious doctrines. I care only to know, if possible, the lasting meaning that lies in all religious doctrine from the beginning till now" (ibid., 4:64–65).

6. Hodgson, *Mystery Beneath the Real*, 13, 152.

7. Ibid., 2.

8. Richard Kearney, *Poetics of Imagining: Modern to Post-Modern* (New York: Fordham University Press, 1998), 248.

9. Rosemary Ashton, *George Eliot: A Life* (London: Penguin, 1997), 25.

10. Ibid., 28.

11. See Rosemary Bodenheimer for an insightful analysis of the "Holy War" between Mary Anne Evans and her father; here as elsewhere Bodenheimer extends and develops suggestions of Ruby Redinger. Rosemary Bodenheimer, *The Real Life of Mary Ann Evans: George Eliot, Her Letters and Fiction* (Ithaca, N.Y.: Cornell University Press, 1994), 63ff.; Ruby Redinger, *George Eliot: The Emergent Self* (London: Bodley Head, 1976).

12. Ludwig Feuerbach, *The Essence of Christianity*, trans. George Eliot (New York: Harper and Row, 1957), chap. 8: 80.

13. In Carroll, ed., *George Eliot: The Critical Heritage,* 30.

14. *George Eliot Letters*, ed. Haight, 3:241.

15. In *George Eliot: Selected Essays, Poems and Other Writings*, ed. A. S. Byatt (London: Penguin, 1990), 265.

16. Ibid., 269.

17. Ibid., 270.

18. Ibid., 272–74.

19. Ibid., 272.

20. George Eliot's letters offer many examples of her sense that her fiction was following the evolution of her own experience. In 1859 she responds to her friend Mme. Eugene Bodichon's hope that more women come under George Eliot's influence by saying "at present my mind works with the most freedom and the keenest sense of poetry in my remotest past, and there are many strata to be worked through before I can begin to use *artistically* any material I may gather in the present" (*George Eliot Letters*, ed. Haight, 3:128–29). In a letter from the following year she chides Sara Sophia Hennell for not believing that "at least *some*" of her friends "share . . . the interest and hope you derive from the Doctrine of Development, with its geometrical progression towards fuller and fuller being" (ibid., 3:338; italics hers).

21. Ibid., 5:75–76. See also earlier letters to Sara Sophia Hennell in which George Eliot resolves not to try to discuss significant matters in letters because of the danger of being misunderstood.

22. Ibid., 3:227.

23. Gerald O'Collins, *Incarnation* (London: Continuum, 2003), 4–5.

24. Kathleen Norris, "A Word Made Flesh: Incarnational Language and the Writer," in *The Incarnation*, ed. Stephen T. Davis, Daniel Kendall, and Gerald O'Collins (Oxford: Oxford University Press, 2004), 303.

25. A. S. Byatt, "Introduction," in *George Eliot: Selected Essays, Poems, and Other Writings*, ed. Byatt, xxv.

26. In Byatt, ed., *George Eliot: Selected Essays, Poems, and Other Writings*, 262.

27. Gordon S. Haight, *George Eliot: A Biography* (New York: Oxford University Press, 1968), 58.

28. Lewes's decided yet discreet irreligious turn of mind can be deduced from his refusing to allow his children to be confirmed, thereby going against standard practice at their school.

29. See Sara Sophia Hennell's letter to George Eliot of June 26, 1859, for example, in which she writes of having learned that her friend is not pursuing work on the "Idea of a Future Life" that had once taken her attention but has instead become a fiction writer (*George Eliot Letters*, ed. Haight, 3:95–98); see also George Eliot's response to Sara Sophia Hennell's *Thoughts in Aid of Faith* (*George Eliot Letters*, ed. Haight, 3:144 [September 4, 1859]).

30. For a rich analysis of George Eliot's philosophical underpinnings, see Suzy Anger's essay, "George Eliot and Philosophy," in *The Cambridge Companion to George Eliot*, ed. George Levine (Cambridge: Cambridge University Press, 2001), 76–97.

31. In *George Eliot: Selected Essays, Poems, and Other Writings*, ed. Byatt, 58, 62; italics hers.

32. Ibid., 194, 199; italics hers.

33. Ibid., 59.
34. Ibid., 59–60.
35. Ibid., 206, 209.
36. Ibid., 142.
37. Ibid., 149; italics hers.
38. Ibid., 148.
39. Ibid., 154.
40. Ashton, *George Eliot: A Life*, 161.
41. Elizabeth Jay, *Religion of the Heart: Anglican Evangelicalism in the Nineteenth-Century Novel* (Oxford: Clarendon, 1979), 220.
42. This bears an interesting relation to Michael Polanyi's notion of "tacit knowledge" and the practice of "interiorization" that underlies knowing: "it is not by looking at things, but by dwelling in them, that we understand their joint meaning [i.e., the sum of the 'particulars']." Michael Polanyi, *The Tacit Dimension* (Gloucester, Mass.: Peter Smith, 1983), 17–18.
43. David Carroll expresses best the reason for the outraged reaction to the disclosure of George Eliot's identity: "the clerical gentleman who stressed so impressively the demands of duty in his vivid picture of a Christian society turned out to be a female atheist living with another woman's husband." In *George Eliot: The Critical Heritage*, ed. Carroll, 2.
44. Byatt, "Introduction," in *George Eliot: Selected Essays, Poems, and Other Writings*, ed. Byatt, xxv.
45. *George Eliot Letters*, ed. Haight, 2:377.
46. Ibid., 4:300.
47. In contrast to my interpretation of this remark, Byatt states: "Eliot saw her work as making *incarnate certain ideas* that she apprehended in the flesh, i.e., sensuously, materially, through feeling." Byatt, "Introduction," in *George Eliot: Selected Essays, Poems, and Other Writings*, xxix; italics hers.
48. Erich Auerbach, *Mimesis*, trans. Willard R. Trask (Princeton, N.J.: Princeton University Press, 1953), 72, 18.
49. George Eliot, Janet's "Repentance," in *Scenes of Clerical Life* (Oxford: Oxford University Press, 1988), 296.
50. George Eliot, *Adam Bede*, 4:27, 264.
51. Ibid., 4:30, 298.
52. The complex topic of narrative voice and its gender in George Eliot's novels is a subject of much critical discussion, but for my purposes it is important simply to accept the gender "George Eliot" bestows on "himself" at this point; once her true identity is known, George Eliot's narrative voice becomes female in my discussion.
53. George Eliot, *Adam Bede*, 2:17, 162.
54. Ibid.
55. Ibid.
56. George Eliot's letters abound with statements concerning the correlation between writing and religion. In a letter written before she became a novelist, she calls poetry and religion "the same thing," identifying the meaning the "soul" seeks in life as "poetry" (*George Eliot Letters*, ed. Haight, 1:263). "Writing is part of my religion," she writes in 1857 (ibid., 2:377). And, expressing what might be seen as her artistic credo in 1859, she writes,

> If Art does not enlarge men's sympathies, it does nothing morally. I have had heart-cutting experience that opinions are a poor cement between human souls; and the only effect I ardently long to produce by my writings, is that those who read them should be better able to *imagine and feel* the pains and the joys of those who differ from themselves in everything but the broad fact of being struggling erring human creatures. (ibid., 3:111; italics hers)

George Eliot's sense of the deep link between a religious sense and an artistic sense is evident when she remarks that "low conceptions of art" exist alongside "ignorant views of religious history and religious life." She goes on, "*Truth* in art is so startling, that no one can believe in it as art; and the specific forms of religious life which have made some of the grandest elements in human history are looked down upon as if they were not within the artist's sympathy and veneration and intensely dramatic reproduction" (ibid., 3:184–85).

57. Ibid., 4:300.

58. George Eliot, *Adam Bede*, 2:17, 163.

59. In *George Eliot: Selected Essays, Poems, and Other Writings*, ed. Byatt, 282.

60. George Eliot, *Adam Bede*, 1:6, 67.

61. Ibid., 6:54, 472–73.

62. Feuerbach, *Essence of Christianity*, 5, 62–63.

63. George Eliot, *Adam Bede*, 2:17, 165 (*sic*).

64. Ibid., 1:3, 34.

65. Ibid., 6:52, 456.

66. When he seeks to account for the modern decline in interest in the incarnation, for example, O'Collins begins by noting that "much Western culture finds little meaning and purpose in suffering" (O'Collins, *Incarnation*, 114).

67. In a letter to John Chapman in 1856, George Eliot expresses curiosity about a story called "Compensation" and continues: "I have long wanted to fire away at the doctrine of Compensation, which I detest, considered as a theory of life." *George Eliot Letters*, ed. Haight, 2:258. In *Adam Bede*, she permits Adam to "fire away" bitterly at this doctrine.

68. George Eliot, *Adam Bede*, 4:35, 327.

69. *George Eliot Letters*, ed. Haight, 1:206.

70. Feuerbach, *Essence of Christianity*, 5, 64.

71. Thomas C. Oden, "Introduction," in *Parables of Kierkegaard* (Princeton, N.J.: Princeton University Press, 1978), xv.

72. John Shea, *Stories of Faith* (New York: Thomas More, 1980), 11.

73. George Eliot, *Adam Bede*, 1:3, 34.

74. The human lack of self-knowledge is a theme that runs from George Eliot's first story to her final fictional essays in *Theophrastus Such*, whose narrator is named after an apostle of Aristotle. A representative expression of the idea comes from "The Sad Fortunes of the Reverend Amos Barton":

> Thank heaven, then, that a little illusion is left to us, to enable us to be useful and agreeable—that we don't know exactly what our friends think of us—that the world is not made of looking-glass, to show us just the figure we are making, and just what is going on behind our backs! By the help

of dear friendly illusion, we are able to dream that we are charming—and our faces wear a becoming air of self-possession; we are able to dream that other men admire our talents—and our benignity is undisturbed; we are able to dream that we are doing much good—and we do a little. (2, 14)

75. George Eliot expresses her deep commitment to the idea of individuality, along with a number of important ideas about her faith stance, in a letter to Charles Bray in 1857: "I dislike extremely a passage . . . in which you appear to consider the disregard of individuals as a lofty condition of mind. My own experience and development deepen every day my conviction that our moral progress may be measured by the degree in which we sympathize with individual suffering and individual joy. The fact that in the scheme of things we see a constant and tremendous sacrifice of individuals is, it seems to me only one of the many proofs that urge upon us our total inability to find our own natures a key to the Divine Mystery. I could more readily turn Christian and worship Jesus again than embrace a Theism which professes to explain the proceedings of God. But I don't feel at all wise on these matters. I have a few strong impressions which serve me for my own support and guidance but do not in the least qualify me to speak as a theorist" (*George Eliot Letters*, ed. Haight, 2:402–3). While one might hear in this a claim of atheism, I would see it as evidence of George Eliot's engagement in an ongoing process of religious exploration. I would argue that we see here an openness that will lead to the "anatheism" that Richard Kearney proposes as characteristic of those who wrestle with issues of faith. See my chapter 3.

76. Charles Taylor, *Sources of the Self: The Making of Modern Identity* (Cambridge, Mass.: Harvard University Press, 1989), 130–31.

77. Ibid., 134.

78. Feuerbach, *Essence of Christianity*, xxxiii–xxxiv; italics his.

79. Ibid., xxxix.

80. Ibid., 1, 11.

81. Ibid., 25, 242.

82. Søren Kierkegaard, *Concluding Unscientific Postscript to Philosophical Fragments* (1846; reprinted, Princeton, N.J.: Princeton University Press, 1992), 223.

83. Ibid., 187, 195.

84. Søren Kierkegaard, *Upbuilding Discourses in Various Spirits: Part Three: The Gospel of Sufferings, Christian Discourses*, trans. Howard V. Hong and Edna H. Hong (1857; reprinted, Princeton, N.J.: Princeton University Press, 1993), 256; Søren Kierkegaard, *Purity of Heart Is to Will One Thing* (1847; reprinted, New York: Harper, 1965), 190; italics his.

85. *George Eliot Letters*, ed. Haight, 3:230–31.

86. Ibid., "Introduction," 1:xliii.

87. George Eliot, *Adam Bede*, 1:15.

88. One of the most delicate renderings of religious consciousness occurs when George Eliot takes Dinah, Adam, and his brother Seth on a walk through the countryside (always for these working folk a purposeful journey, rather than a tour of nature). Adam expresses his preference for walking "to work by a road that 'll take me up a bit of a hill" so that he has a sense of the world as a "big place" with "other men working in it with their heads and hands besides yourself." His dreamy, pious brother prefers the hills on a cloudy day, when he feels

"as if that was heaven where there's always joy and sunshine, though this life's dark and cloudy." In contrast to both, Dinah says she can't find God in nature if it means turning her back on the urban poor. "It's very blessed on a bleak cold day, when the sky is hanging dark over the hill, to feel the love of God in one's soul, and carry it to the lonely, bare, stone houses, where there's nothing else to give comfort" (George Eliot, *Adam Bede*, 1:11, 109). With such comments George Eliot subtly adumbrates a complex sense of religious inwardness.

89. Along with Polanyi's sense of "interiorization," George Eliot's sense of what I will call "feeling knowledge" resonates with contemporary discussions of the meaning of sympathy. See, for example, Bartky's analysis of the work of Max Scheler, who defines "fellow-feeling" as "a genuine *out-reaching* and entering into the other person and his individual situation, a true and authentic *transcendence* of one's self." Quoted in Sandra Lee Bartky, *Sympathy and Solidarity and Other Essays* (Lanham, Md.: Oxford University Press, 2002), 79; italics hers.

90. *George Eliot Letters*, ed. Haight, 2:378.

91. Of many comments in her letters, I select two: "I can only go on writing what I feel, and waiting for the proof that I have been able to make others feel" (ibid., 2:335); "Writing is part of my religion, and I can write no word that <does not clothe my [deep?] faith.> is not prompted from within" (ibid., 2:377 [*sic*]). And from her journal a remark that includes a reference (with biblical echoes) to her positive valuation of "compensation": "At present I value [these comments on her success] as grounds for hoping that my writing may succeed and so give value to my life—as indications that I can touch the hearts of my fellow men, and so sprinkle some precious grain as the result of the long years in which I have been inert and suffering" (ibid., 2:416).

92. The trope of confession has provoked a variety of comments. Richard Simpson, a Roman Catholic writing in 1863, sees in "the persevering way in which George Eliot indicates confession" the deepest sign of a "Christian anthropology, without the basis of Christian theology" (quoted in *George Eliot: The Critical Heritage*, ed. Carroll, 247). Redinger pathologizes the frequent confessional scenes as a sign of George Eliot's frustrated "haunting need to confess" (Redinger, *George Eliot: The Emergent Self*, 108). George Eliot teases with an interesting distinction in a letter to Sara Sophia Hennell from 1843, which includes the often-quoted celebration of the "*truth of feeling* as the only universal bond of union": "Those who can write, let them do it as boldly as they like, and let no one hesitate at proper seasons to make a full *con*fession (far better than *pro*fession)" (*George Eliot Letters*, ed. Haight, 2:162).

93. *George Eliot Letters*, ed. Haight, 2:335–36.

94. George Eliot, "Janet's Repentance," 10, 229; 22, 270, 271.

95. Ibid., 18, 258.

96. Ibid., 25, 289.

97. Søren Kierkegaard, *The Sickness Unto Death* (1849; reprinted, Princeton, N.J.: Princeton University Press, 1992), 43–44.

98. See Terence Cave's excellent introduction to the Oxford World's Classics edition of the novel. Terence Cave, "Introduction," in George Eliot, *Silas Marner* (Oxford: Oxford University Press, 1998).

99. As Bodenheimer notes, "piety about the past became a persistent theme in Marian's letters to Cara Bray" (*Real Life of Mary Ann Evans*, 99); it is of course

a persistent theme in her fiction and an obsessive one in *The Mill on the Floss*. Bodenheimer quotes a letter of 1858 in which George Eliot comments that, while the past may be irrecoverable, there is nothing to "hinder the past from being sacred and belonging to our religion." *George Eliot Letters*, ed. Haight, 8:199–200; quoted in Bodenheimer, *The Real Life of Mary Ann Evans*, 100.

100. George Eliot, *Adam Bede* (Oxford: Oxford University Press, 1996), 2:20, 199; italics hers.

101. For what is perhaps the most stimulating discussion of this story, see Sandra Gilbert and Susan Gubar, *The Madwoman in the Attic* (New Haven, Conn.: Yale University Press, 1979); see also Jennifer Uglow, *George Eliot* (London: Virago, 1987), chap. 7.

102. *George Eliot Letters*, ed. Haight, 3:227.

103. George Eliot, *Middlemarch* (Oxford: Oxford University Press, 1997), 3:20, 192.

104. *George Eliot Letters*, ed. Haight, 3:269.

105. George Eliot, *The Mill on the Floss*, 4:1, 273.

106. Ibid., 7:1, 484.

107. Frank Kermode, *The Sense of an Ending* (New York: Oxford University Press, 1967), 67.

108. Michel Foucault, "What Is an Author?" in *Modern Criticism and Theory: A Reader*, ed. David Lodge (1969; reprinted, London: Longman, 1988), 197.

109. *George Eliot Letters*, ed. Haight, 4:64.

110. Kearney, *Poetics of Imagining*, 234.

Chapter 2

1. *The Journals of George Eliot*, ed. Margaret Harris and Judith Johnston (1998; reprinted, Cambridge: Cambridge University Press, 2000), 333.

2. Frederick Karl, *George Eliot: Voice of a Century: A Biography* (New York: Norton, 1995), 372, 436.

3. George Eliot, *The Mill on the Floss*, 2:1, 150.

4. Ibid., 2:1, 138.

5. *George Eliot Letters*, ed. Haight, 3:366.

6. Ibid., 3:363–64.

7. Ibid., 4:71.

8. Ibid., 4:64–65.

9. Ibid., 4:472.

10. *Journals of George Eliot*, ed. Harris and Johnston, 92.

11. In her *Diary*, George Eliot records that she is working on this poem, "the matter of which was written in prose 3 or 4 years ago." *Journals of George Eliot*, ed. Harris and Johnston, 122 (Sunday, January 8, 1865).

12. George Eliot, "A Minor Prophet," in *The Works of George Eliot*, 343–51, line 17. Subsequent references will include line numbers in the body of the text.

13. Lewes reports his wife crying so much and so intensely as she wrote the death of Maggie that he feared for her health (*George Eliot Letters*, ed. Haight, 3:227).

14. George Eliot, "'A Fine Excess': Feeling Is Energy," *Leaves from a Note-Book,* in *The Works of George Eliot*, 222.

15. Ibid., 222–23.
16. Ibid., 223.
17. Ibid., 222.
18. Upon seeing great works of art in Florence, for example, George Eliot writes to the publisher John Blackwood that she is "thrown into a state of humiliating passivity" but rallies when she thinks of the evident "rarity" of "great and truthful art." "Every hand is wanted in the world that can do a little genuine, sincere work" (*George Eliot Letters*, ed. Haight, 3:294).
19. George Eliot, *The Mill on the Floss*, 4:1, 273.
20. For astute psychological readings of George Eliot's early works, see Redinger, *George Eliot: The Emergent Self*; for equally astute readings of all of George Eliot's works in relation to her life, see Bodenheimer, *Real Life of Mary Ann Evans*.
21. Byatt, "Introduction," in *George Eliot: Selected Essays, Poems, and Other Writings*, xxv.
22. Ashton, *George Eliot: A Life*, 288.
23. *George Eliot Letters*, ed. Haight, 4:300.
24. Ibid., 4:286.
25. Ibid., 4:300.
26. *Journals of George Eliot*, ed. Harris and Johnston, 109, 108; George Eliot, *Diary* 1863, 1862. A sampling of George Eliot's comments during her writing of *Romola* in 1862 gives a sense of her intense struggles: "I have been ailing all this last week and have worked under impeding discouragement. I have distrust in myself, in my work, in others' loving acceptance of it which robs my otherwise happy life of all joy . . . Will it ever be finished? Ever be worth anything?" (February 26, *Journals of George Eliot*, ed. Harris and Johnston, 109–10); "protracted headache and discomfort" (March 24, 110); "My head very infirm" (April 1, 111); "very ailing for a fortnight and more" (April 16, 111); "A dreadful palsy has beset me for the last few days" (July 10, 112); "wretched headache" (November 28, 113); "violent attack of sick headache" (December 9, 113); "I am extremely spiritless—dead, and hopeless about my writing. The long state of headache and disordered liver has left me in depression and incapacity" (December 17, 114). It comes as something of a surprise after all this to hear her summing up the year with this comment: "I have had more than my average amount of comfortable health until this last month . . ." (December 31, 115).
27. *George Eliot Letters*, ed. Haight, 4:300, 301.
28. Ibid., 4: 354–55.
29. George Eliot, *Adam Bede*, 4:35, 327.
30. It is interesting that while, as Byatt notes, George Eliot began her essay "Silly Novels by Lady Novelists" as a review of a novel called *Compensation* in order to "fire away at the doctrine of Compensation, which I detest" (*George Eliot Letters*, ed. Haight, 2:258; quoted in Byatt, "Introduction," in *George Eliot: Selected Essays, Poems, and Other Writings*, xvi), she later had Adam Bede fire away at the doctrine on her behalf.
31. Critical commentary on or even acknowledgment of "Self and Life" is rare. There is some speculation that it was published in 1878, making it one of George Eliot's last works.
32. George Eliot, "Self and Life," in *The Works of George Eliot*, 388–90.

33. Among the critics who have explored this topic, see especially Bodenheimer, *Real Life of Mary Ann Evans*. Frederick Karl's comments on this are also interesting; see Karl, *George Eliot: Voice of a Century*.

34. Paul Ricoeur, *Oneself as Another*, trans. Kathleen Blamey (Chicago: University of Chicago Press, 1992), 162.

35. Paul Ricoeur, "Narrative Identity," in *On Paul Ricoeur: Narrative and Interpretation*, ed. David Wood (London: Routledge, 1991), 198–99; italics his.

36. *Journals of George Eliot*, ed. Harris and Johnston, 289.

37. Ibid.

38. Carroll, ed., *George Eliot: The Critical Heritage*, 20.

39. *Journals of George Eliot*, ed. Harris and Johnston, 141, 145.

40. Ibid., 147.

41. *George Eliot Letters*, ed. Haight, 4:139; italics hers.

42. Again, Bodenheimer's analysis is most astute and suggestive. See Bodenheimer, *Real Life of Mary Ann Evans*.

43. *George Eliot Letters*, ed. Haight, 2:343.

44. *Journals of George Eliot*, ed. Harris and Johnston, 72.

45. *George Eliot Letters*, ed. Haight, 2:64.

46. Paul Ricoeur, "Life in Quest of Narrative," in *On Paul Ricoeur: Narrative and Interpretation*, ed. David Wood (London: Routledge, 1991), 32.

47. Alexander Welsh, among others, has analyzed how the two secrets—her authorship and her non-marriage to Lewes—worked together. The anguish that might have marked what Welsh calls the "open secret" of her liaison with Lewes (*George Eliot and Blackmail*, 123) was instead transferred to the jealously guarded secret of her authorship, while the pride of authorship was proclaimed instead in her relationship. Alexander Welsh, *George Eliot and Blackmail* (Cambridge, Mass.: Harvard University Press, 1985).

48. *Journals of George Eliot*, ed. Harris and Johnston, 283.

49. Ibid., 284.

50. *George Eliot Letters*, ed. Haight, 4:40.

51. Ibid., 4:49.

52. Richard Holt Hutton, Unsigned Review of *Romola, Spectator* (18 July 1863), xxxvi, 2265–7 in *George Eliot: The Critical Heritage*, ed. Carroll, 205.

53. *George Eliot Letters*, ed. Haight, 4:97.

54. Ibid., 4:103–4.

55. Ibid., 4:465, 462.

56. Ibid., 4:472.

57. In the letter to Hennell quoted above, George Eliot refers to her "deep delight" over the "conduct" towards her of the respected clergyman F. D. Maurice, confiding in her the "interest in certain relations between conduct and religious belief which has been urged on my notice by the experience of the last eight years [presumably the years of her liaison with Lewes]." (*George Eliot Letters*, ed. Haight, 4:104). Years before, she has made clear that "writing is part of my religion" and consecrated her own work as part of a religious effort (*George Eliot Letters*, ed. Haight, 2:377).

58. Ibid., 4:104.

59. George Eliot, *Romola* (Oxford: Oxford University Press, 1998), 1:11, 112.

60. Ibid., 1:11, 113.

61. Ibid., 1:11, 112.
62. Ibid., 1:15, 48.
63. Ibid., 1:15, 155.
64. Ibid., 1:17, 172.
65. Ibid., 1:20, 190, 194.
66. Ibid., 2:32, 269.
67. Ibid., 2:27, 235.
68. Ibid., 2:36, 305.
69. Ashton, *George Eliot: A Life*, 276. As Ashton puts it in relation to the way that George Eliot limits the power of her heroine in *Adam Bede*, Dinah Morris: "Feminists then and now have been frustrated by her limiting end choices for her heroines" (207). For a subtle and insightful analysis of the complexities of George Eliot's response to questions regarding women's role, see Alexis Easley, "Authority, Gender and Identity: George Eliot in the 1850s," *Women's Writing* 3, no. 2 (1996): 145–60.
70. George Eliot, *Romola*, 2:36, 309.
71. Ibid., 2:37, 313.
72. Ibid., 2:36, 310.
73. Ibid., 2:40, 339.
74. Ibid., 2:40, 344.
75. Ibid., 2:40, 343.
76. Ibid., 2:40, 344.
77. Ibid., 2:41, 348. See Bodenheimer's excellent analysis of George Eliot's pattern of compelling her heroines to go back. Bodenheimer, *Real Life of Mary Ann Evans*.
78. George Eliot, *The Mill on the Floss*, 7:2, 497.
79. George Eliot, *Romola*, 3:55, 431.
80. Ibid., 3:56, 442.
81. Ibid., 3:56, 442.
82. Richard Holt Hutton, Unsigned Review of *Romola*, *Spectator* (18 July 1863), xxxvi, 2265-7 in *George Eliot: The Critical Heritage*, ed. Carroll, 205.
83. George Eliot, *Romola*, 3:66, 509; 3:71, 541.
84. Richard Holt Hutton, Unsigned Review of *Romola*, *Spectator* (18 July 1863) xxxvi, 2265-7 in *George Eliot: The Critical Heritage*, ed. Carroll, 205.
85. George Eliot, *Romola*, 3:66, 509.
86. Ibid., 3:71, 541; italics hers.
87. George Eliot, "Notes on *The Spanish Gypsy* and Tragedy," in *A George Eliot Miscellany: A Supplement to Her Novels*, ed. F. B. Pinion (London: Macmillan, 1982), 126.
88. George Eliot, *The Spanish Gypsy*, in *The Works of George Eliot*, book 4, p. 225.
89. For a helpful survey of the critical response to the piece, see *The Spanish Gypsy by George Eliot*, ed. Antonie Gerard van den Broek (London: Pickering and Chatto, 2008).
90. In *A George Eliot Miscellany*, ed. Pinion, 127.
91. Ibid., 128.
92. George Eliot, *The Spanish Gypsy*, book 1, p. 110.
93. In *A George Eliot Miscellany*, ed. Pinion, 127.

94. Ibid., 127.
95. George Eliot, *Felix Holt, the Radical* (London: Penguin, 1995), 2:30, 291.
96. In *A George Eliot Miscellany*, ed. Pinion, 128–29.
97. George Eliot, *The Spanish Gypsy*, book 4, p. 206.
98. Ibid., book 4, p. 214.
99. Ibid., book 1, pp. 100–101,
100. Ibid., book 4, p. 215.
101. Kearney, *Poetics of Imagining*, 229.
102. Ibid., 230.
103. Ibid., 233.
104. Ibid., 234.
105. George Eliot, "Epilogue," in *Romola*, 547.
106. Ibid.
107. In one of the few critical studies of Eliot's poetry, *George Eliot and the Landscape of Time: Narrative Form and Protestant Apocalyptic History* (Chapel Hill: University of North Carolina Press, 1986), Mary Wilson Carpenter does a fascinating analysis to show that George Eliot's 1874 volume of poetry was a woman's response to Keble's *Christian Year* and other patriarchal models. "Instead of meditating on the life of Christ, George Eliot meditates on the life and death of the visionary artist" (189).
108. George Eliot, "O May I Join the Choir Invisible," in *The Works of George Eliot*, 399–400.

Chapter 3

1. George Eliot, "Prelude," in *Middlemarch*, 3.
2. Haight, *George Eliot: A Biography*, 420, 432.
3. Joan Bennett, *George Eliot: Her Mind & Art* (1948; reprinted, London: Cambridge University Press, 1966), 161, 162.
4. See the entry "Jubal" in *A Dictionary of Biblical Tradition in English Literature*, gen. ed. David Lyle Jeffrey (Grand Rapids, Mich.: Eerdman, 1992), 417.
5. As I noted in chapter 2, Carpenter contends that George Eliot's 1874 verse collection is a response to Keble's *Christian Year*; she argues that George Eliot "replaces Christian doctrine with humanist ideals" and revises his "patriarchal and elitist perspectives with poems that reexamine the value of womanhood and celebrate the community rather than the progress of the individual soul" (Carpenter, *George Eliot and the Landscape of Time*, 154). Carpenter shows how George Eliot's plan, in starting with "Jubal" and ending with "O, May I Join the Choir Invisible," "begins with the creation and proceeds to the apocalyptic 'end,' or purpose, of both visionary art and artist" (157).
6. George Eliot, "The Legend of Jubal," in *The Works of George Eliot*, 250.
7. Ibid., 251.
8. Ibid., 252.
9. Ibid., 255.
10. Ibid., 253.
11. Ibid., 250.
12. Ibid., 258.
13. Ibid., 269.
14. Ibid., 270.

15. Ibid., 271.

16. Two examples from George Eliot's letters of 1857 will serve to illustrate her complex range of feelings with regard to her work: in June, she writes to a friend of her tentative hope that all the suffering she has undergone "has probably been a preparation for some special calling"; in another letter in October she clarifies to E. F. S. Piggott that her refusal to write a review is not based on vanity: "Do not think me an ordinary conceited woman who is flattering herself that her work is of importance to the world. It is nothing but a sense that my work is important as a matter of every day advantage, that gives me courage to write at all" (*George Eliot Letters*, ed. Haight, 2:343, 398).

17. George Eliot, "Armgart," in *The Works of George Eliot*, scene 1, p. 286.

18. Ibid., 1, 286.

19. Ibid., 1, 290.

20. Ibid., 1, 291.

21. Ibid., 1, 293.

22. Ibid., 1, 292.

23. Ibid., 2, 299, 300.

24. Ibid., 4, 314.

25. Ibid., 4, 318.

26. Ibid., 4, 319.

27. Ibid., 4, 322.

28. Ibid.

29. Ibid., 4, 317.

30. George Eliot, *Felix Holt*, 1:3, 50.

31. George Eliot, *Middlemarch*, 8: "Finale," 821.

32. George Eliot, *Felix Holt*, 2:30, 291.

33. Ibid., 2:27, 265.

34. Ibid., *Appendix B*, "Address to Working Men, by Felix Holt," 498, 497, 499.

35. George Eliot, *Middlemarch*, 2:12, 116.

36. Ibid., 2:20, 192.

37. Ibid., 2:15, 147.

38. Ibid., 2:15, 146.

39. Ibid., 3:24, 248. George Eliot uses Caleb Garth, a character usually seen as partly based on her memory of her father, to speak of her own regard for work and its potential for sacredness. The narrator tells us that his "sublime labour" has had the power of poetry and philosophy and religion over him since he was young. "But it would be difficult to convey to those who never heard him utter the word 'business,' the peculiar tone of fervid veneration, of religious regard, in which he wrapped it, as a consecrated symbol is wrapped in its gold-fringed linen" (*Middlemarch*, 3:24, 249, 248).

40. R. A. Solway, *Prelates and People: Ecclesiastical Social Thought in England 1783–1852* (Toronto: University of Toronto Press, 1969), 279.

41. Ibid., 17.

42. Ibid., 17–18.

43. W. M. Jacob, *The Clerical Professions in the Long Eighteenth Century 1680–1840* (Oxford: Oxford University Press, 2007), 9.

44. Ibid.

45. Hugh McLeod, *Religion and Society in England, 1850–1914* (London: Macmillan, 1996), 14.
46. J. R. H. Moorman, *A History of the Church in England* (1953; reprinted, London: Adam and Charles Black, 1961), 333.
47. Ibid.
48. Jacob, *The Clerical Professions*, 9.
49. Ibid., 12.
50. George Eliot, *Felix Holt*, 1:3, 45.
51. Ibid., 1:3, 48.
52. Ibid., 1:3, 45.
53. Solway, *Prelates and People*, 17.
54. George Eliot clearly has a soft spot for the Dissenting minister, Rufus Lyon, such that he could be seen to rank among those glorious failures discussed in the last chapter. In part he is a victim of timing since he believes that "the fight for religious and political liberty" is "God's cause," unlike the unbelieving men such as Felix who are fighting for it (*Felix Holt*, 1:5, 65). She also sets him in the context of ongoing evolutionary processes over which he can have no control: "Mr. Lyon will perhaps seem a very simple personage, with pitiably narrow theories; but none of our theories are quite large enough for all the disclosures of time, and to the end of men's struggles a penalty will remain for those who sink from the ranks of the heroes into the crowd for whom the heroes fight and die" (ibid., 1:6, 86). She speaks out on behalf of the "little man" with the "heroic heart" who "found in his Christian faith a reason for clinging the more to one who had not a large party to back him" (ibid., 3:37, 355). And she allows her narrator to personalize her regard: "I confess to smiling myself. . . . but I never smiled at Mr Lyon's trustful energy without falling to penitence and veneration immediately after." She further claims that it is our vision that is truly "narrow" and fragmented compared to his "wider vision of past and present realities" (ibid., 2:16, 184).
55. Solway, *Prelates and People*, 48.
56. George Eliot, "Amos Barton," 1, 7.
57. George Eliot, *Middlemarch*, 1:6, 58.
58. Ibid., 8:84, 802.
59. Ibid., 1:6, 57.
60. Ibid., 5:50, 487.
61. Ibid., 5:50, 488.
62. Ibid., 5:50, 487.
63. Ibid., 1:9, 75.
64. Ibid., 1:4, 38.
65. Solway, *Prelates and People*, 164.
66. George Eliot, *Middlemarch*, 1:2, 22.
67. Ibid., 1:4, 35.
68. Carpenter analyzes George Eliot's fiction in terms of her lifelong quest for order: "George Eliot's narratives construct 'fictions' of history through reference to various formal and symbolic systems of codification" (Carpenter, *George Eliot and the Landscape of Time*, xi). As early as 1839 the young Mary Anne Evans was engaged in "compiling a Chart of Ecclesiastical History," which she abandoned in six months when someone else beat her to it (Haight, *George Eliot: A Biography*, 24).

69. George Eliot, *The Mill on the Floss*, 4:3, 290–91.
70. George Eliot, *Middlemarch*, 4:41, 412.
71. Ibid., 1:6, 56.
72. George Eliot, "Prelude," *Middlemarch*, 3.
73. George Eliot, *Middlemarch*, 1:3, 24.
74. Ibid., 1:1, 7.
75. Ibid., 1:3, 24.
76. Ibid., 1:3, 28.
77. Ibid., 1:3, 28; 1:4, 38; 1:3, 28.
78. Ibid., 1:3, 28.
79. Ibid., 1:5, 49.
80. Ibid., 1:10, 84.
81. Ibid., 1:1, 10.
82. Ibid., 1:7, 62.
83. Ibid., 1:7, 62–63.
84. Ibid., 1:2, 18.
85. Ibid., 1:7, 63.
86. Ibid., 1: 10, 84–85.
87. Ibid., 3:28, 272.
88. Ibid., 1:5, 49.
89. George Eliot, "Address to Working Men, by Felix Holt," 497.
90. George Eliot, "Prelude," *Middlemarch*, 3.
91. George Eliot, *Middlemarch*, 1:2, 22.
92. Ibid., 6:54, 529.
93. Ibid., 8: "Finale," 820.
94. Ibid., 5:46, 455.
95. Ibid., 8: "Finale," 822.
96. George Eliot, *The Mill on the Floss*, 6:8, 426.
97. George Eliot, *Middlemarch*, 8: "Finale," 822.
98. Ibid., 822.
99. Richard Kearney, *Anatheism: Returning to God after God* (New York: Columbia University Press, 2010). Kearney quotes Michel de Certeau on what Kearney calls "the importance of the mystical experience in the West as a cross-over point between the religious and irreligious, the secular and the sacred" (9): "Mysticism is less a heresy or liberation from religion than an instrument of unveiling, *within* religion itself, a truth that would first be formulated in the mode of a margin inexpressible in religion to orthodox texts and institutions, and which would then be able to be exhumed from beliefs. The study of mysticism . . . gives rise, in the historical relation of the West to itself, to a reintegration that eradicates the past without losing its meaning" ("Mysticism," *Diacritics* 22, no. 2 [Summer 1992]: 24; quoted in *Anatheism*, 9; italics his). I am arguing that in *Middlemarch* and *Daniel Deronda*, George Eliot accomplishes from the outside, through mysticism, an engagement with a truth that is inside religion, suggesting the possibility of such a return to the truth from the inside by a process of "reintegration."
100. Kearney, *Anatheism*, 3.
101. George Eliot, "Evangelical Teaching: Dr Cumming," in *George Eliot: Selected Essays, Poems, and Other Writings*, ed. Byatt, 59–60.

102. Bodenheimer, *Real Life of Mary Ann Evans*, 99.
103. George Eliot, *Adam Bede*, 4:35, 327.
104. George Eliot, *Middlemarch*, 5:48, 468.
105. Ibid., 5:48, 469.
106. Ibid., 2:20, 192.
107. Ibid., 4:41, 421.
108. Ibid., 4:41, 422.
109. Ibid., 5:50, 485.
110. Ibid., 5:50, 487.
111. Ibid., 5:50, 488.
112. Ibid., 5:50, 488.
113. Ibid., 5:50, 488–89.
114. Dorothea's only partly articulate sense of her religious longing beautifully signals her renunciation of previous desires for perfection. Thus we can see George Eliot exemplifying an early version of Kearney's "anatheism" which, he says, "resists perfect Origins and Ends" and rather than enacting a nostalgic return to the past is returning into the future: "We are, to borrow from Kierkegaard, not concerned with a 'recollection' *backward* but with a 'repetition' *forward*. The *ana* signals a movement of return . . . to an inaugural instant of reckoning at the root of belief" (Kearney, *Anatheism*, 7; italics his).
115. George Eliot, *Middlemarch*, 5:50, 488.
116. George Eliot, *The Mill on the Floss*, 6:9, 435.
117. Karl Rahner, *The Mystical Way in Everyday Life: Sermons, Prayers, and Essays* (Maryknoll, N.Y.: Orbis Books, 2010), xx.
118. Ibid., xxii.
119. Ashton, *George Eliot: A Life*, 307, 335.
120. George Eliot, *Adam Bede*, 6:52, 456.
121. George Eliot, *Daniel Deronda* (1995; London: Penguin, 2003), 6:41, 514.
122. Kearney, *Anatheism*, 86.
123. George Eliot, "Finale," *Middlemarch*, 8: 822.

Chapter 4

1. George Eliot's complex exploration of time here reminds us again of Richard Kearney's notion of anatheism, which is, in Kierkegaard's terms, "not concerned with a 'recollection' *backward* but with a 'repetition' *forward*" (Kearney, *Anatheism*, 7).
2. *George Eliot Letters*, ed. Haight, 6:318.
3. Ibid., 6:216.
4. Sara Sophia Hennell, *Present Religion as a Faith Owning Fellowship with Thought* (1865; reprinted, https:archive.org/details/presentreligion03henngoog), 9.
5. Ibid., 11–12.
6. Matthew Arnold, *God and the Bible: A Review of Objections to "Literature and Dogma"* (1874; reprinted, https:/archive.org/details/literatureanddog028325mbp), chap. 1, 52; italics his.
7. *George Eliot Letters*, ed. Haight, 6:87.
8. Ibid., 6:87.
9. Ibid., 6:310.
10. Ibid., 6:53–54.

11. Ibid., 6:64–65.
12. Ibid., 6:99.
13. Ibid., 6:286–87.
14. Ibid., 6:287.
15. Ibid., 6:310.
16. Ibid., 6:287.
17. Ibid., 6:216.
18. Ibid., 6:216–17.
19. Ibid., 6:167.
20. Ibid., 6:120; quoted from J. W. Cross, *George Eliot's Life as Related in Her Letters and Journals* (Arranged and Edited by Her Husband, J. W. Cross), 3 vols. (Edinburgh: W. Blackwood and Sons, 1885), 3:253.
21. *George Eliot Letters*, ed. Haight, 6:125.
22. George Eliot, *Adam Bede*, 6:52, 456.
23. While comparable to other George Eliot heroines, Gwendolyn is as revolutionary a construction as Daniel in being not simply a spoiled rich girl but instead a young woman who has a sense of her own inadequacy and, even more striking, a deep "world-nausea," which, while self-indulgent and only partly genuine, suggests an existential angst that is more than a personal failing (George Eliot, *Daniel Deronda*, 3:24, 272).
24. George Eliot, *Daniel Deronda*, 5:35, 415, 418.
25. Ibid., 4:29, 332.
26. Ibid., 5:35, 415; italics hers.
27. Ibid., 5:35, 411.
28. Ibid., 5:35, 423.
29. Ibid., 5:35, 430.
30. Ibid., 5:35, 430.
31. Ibid.
32. George Eliot, *Daniel Deronda*. Gwendolyn expresses her desire to do "what she likes" repeatedly; see, for example, 1:4, 39; 1:7, 69; 2:11, 124; 2:13, 136, 138. Fleishman convincingly argues that George Eliot's characterization of Gwendolyn is in part a response to Arnold's critique in *Culture and Anarchy* of the Philistine attitude of extreme individualism, as well as "a systematic study of the difficulty of knowing what one likes (that is, what will give lasting satisfaction) and of doing it when associated with others who do only what they like." Avrom Fleishman, *George Eliot's Intellectual Life* (Cambridge: Cambridge University Press, 2010), 196.
33. George Eliot, *Daniel Deronda*, 5:36, 445, 449.
34. Ibid., 8:65, 766–67.
35. Ibid., 5:36, 446.
36. Ibid., 5:36, 438–39.
37. Ibid., 5:36, 446.
38. Ibid., 5:36, 451.
39. Ibid., 5:36, 452.
40. Ibid., 5:36, 452–53.
41. Ibid., 5:36, 453.
42. Ibid., 6:45, 563; 6:48, 589.
43. Ibid., 6:48, 609.

44. Ibid., 7:57, 700, 701.
45. Ibid., 8:65, 769.
46. Ibid., 8:65, 771.
47. Ibid.
48. Ibid., 8:69, 795.
49. Ibid., 8:69, 805–6.
50. Ibid., 8:69, 807.
51. George Eliot dwells at length upon the "crisis" that is only beginning for Gwendolyn as she struggles to exchange egoism for "duty." Recalling ideas on martyrdom and renunciation from previous novels and poems, the narrator speaks of how "there comes a terrible moment to many souls when the great movements of the world . . . enter like an earthquake into their own lives." She describes the eruption as like warfare requiring enormous sacrifice and making "visible" the "Invisible Power that has been the object of lip-worship and lip-resignation." In such crises martyrs "live reviled" and die with "no angel" taking notice. "Then it is that the submission of the soul to the Highest is tested . . . and a religion shows itself which is something else than a private consolation" (*Daniel Deronda*, 8:69, 803–4). She invokes Old Testament imagery to conjure the enormous soul-shattering powers that burst forth when Gwendolyn is fighting even to begin to move from egoism to altruism.
52. Ibid., 5:40, 496.
53. Terence Cave, "Introduction" and "Notes" in George Eliot, *Daniel Deronda*, 844.
54. Ibid., xxiv.
55. Ibid., xxx.
56. Ibid., 5:38, 471.
57. See Michael Davis, *George Eliot and Nineteenth-Century Psychology: Exploring the Unmapped Country* (Aldershot, Eng.: Ashgate, 2006). Whereas Davis in his study of the relationship between religious experience and psychology in George Eliot's novels argues that her theological language "draws not on God but on the possibilities of the mind" (163), I would argue that her theological language does both, showing the relation between God and the mind and increasingly, as we see particularly in *Daniel Deronda*, a conviction of the wider range of theological language and the relation of "God" to everything. I agree with his understanding of the way that George Eliot draws on imagination and nonrational mental processes to explore religious experience, but I would broaden the notion beyond the "unconscious," which is his main focus. My contention is that George Eliot is constructing a language for religious experience in her time that has become familiar in our own time. This is particularly the case in *Daniel Deronda*, where she includes the very structure of the novel in this exploration so that elements such as coincidence, intuition, and imagination are given a credibility that is not usually allowed in serious fiction or in life. Her sense of a spiritual life that is different from spiritualism and from conventional Christianity's understanding is evident, for example, in her exploration of the idea of "emotional intellect" (George Eliot, *Daniel Deronda*, 6:41, 514), in Daniel's intuitive sense of kinship with Mordecai, in Gwendolyn's experience of "the judgment of the Invisible and Universal" (ibid., 8:64, 763), and her feeling of "a vast mysterious movement" and "something spiritual and vaguely tremendous"

(ibid., 8: 69, 804). I would posit George Eliot's sense of a wide range of nonrational ways of engaging experience that are connected to religious experience. For further discussion of these matters, see Diarmuid O'Murchu, *Ancestral Grace: Meeting God in our Human Story* (New York: Orbis Books, 2008). In O'Murchu's words: "Beyond the experience of life based on the immediacy of our senses is an alternative worldview opening up realms of mystery and fascination for the intuitive imagination, that sphere of human living so pauperized by the excessive rationalism of recent centuries" (O'Murchu, *Ancestral Grace*, 26–27). For further exploration of the idea of coincidence, see also Miriam Therese Winter, *Paradoxology: Spirituality in a Quantum Universe* (Maryknoll, N.Y.: Orbis Books, 2009). Even the structure of *Daniel Deronda* testifies to George Eliot's sense that, in M. T. Winter's words, "coincidence is a trademark of the Spirit in our daily lives" (Winter, *Paradoxology*, 101).

58. George Eliot, *Daniel Deronda*, 5:35, 416.
59. Ibid.
60. Ibid., 5:35, 417.
61. Ibid., 5:35, 420.
62. Ibid., 5:35, 422.
63. Ibid.
64. Ibid., 4:32, 366.
65. Ibid., 4:32, 364.
66. Ibid., 4:32, 363.
67. Ibid., 4:32, 365.
68. Ibid., 6:43, 545.
69. Ibid., 6:42, 532.
70. Ibid., 5:38, 472.
71. Ibid., 6:43, 546.
72. Ibid., 7:55, 685.
73. Ibid., 5:40, 495.
74. Ibid., 8:63, 750.
75. Ibid., 5:40, 496.
76. Ibid., 5:40, 498.
77. Ibid., 6:43, 540.
78. Ibid., 8:63, 748.
79. Ibid., 6:41, 514.
80. Ibid., 6:43, 546.
81. Ibid., 2:18, 196.
82. Ibid., 2:18, 197.
83. Ibid., 5:39, 481.
84. Ibid., 3:20, 210.
85. Ibid., 4:33, 391.
86. Ibid., 4:34, 396.
87. Ibid., 5:35, 411.
88. Ibid., 8:60, 721.
89. Ibid., 4:32, 366.
90. Ibid., 3:19, 205.
91. Ibid., 4:33, 381.
92. Ibid., 5:38, 474.

93. Terence Cave, "Introduction" and "Notes," George Eliot, *Daniel Deronda*. As Cave notes, George Eliot has Mordecai recite a poem that imitates the style of this "major medieval Jewish poet" (note, p. 833) whom she acknowledges in the text, but it is telling that she has her own poet teaching his work to a boy whose imitation can only be clownish. Mordecai seems in his poetic nature to be seeking something beyond a modeling of the past.

94. George Eliot, *Daniel Deronda*, 5:38, 480.

95. *George Eliot Letters*, ed. Haight, 6:89.

96. Ibid., 6:124.

97. Ibid., 6:89.

Chapter 5

1. *George Eliot Letters*, ed. Haight, 5:30.

2. Louis M. Savary, *The New Spiritual Exercises: In the Spirit of Teilhard de Chardin* (New York: Paulist, 2010), 14.

3. Ibid., 16.

4. Teilhard de Chardin, *Phenomenon of Man*, 219.

5. Ibid., 218; italics his.

6. It is interesting to find in George Eliot's letter to Harriet Beecher Stowe quoted above a rare explicit reference to the evolution of her own "religious point of view . . . I do not find my temple in Pantheism, which, whatever might be its value speculatively, could not yield a practical religion, since it is an attempt to look at the universe from the outside of our relations to it (the universe) as human beings. As healthy, sane human beings we must love and hate—love what is good for mankind, hate what is evil for mankind. For years of my youth I dwelt in dreams of a pantheistic sort, falsely supposing that I was enlarging my sympathy. But I have travelled far away from that time" (*George Eliot Letters*, ed. Haight, 5:30).

7. Ibid., 6:120; quoted from *George Eliot's Life*, ed. Cross, 253.

8. In her notes to the Images of *Purgatorio,* Dorothy Sayers explains the important distinction of Dante's medieval theology that has become lost in her time: "In the *allegory*, the Earthly Paradise is the state of *innocence*. It is from here that Man, if he had never fallen, would have set out upon his journey to the Celestial Paradise which is his ultimate destination; but because of sin, his setting-out is from that other Forest which is the degraded and horrifying parody of this one. His whole journey through Hell and Purgatory is thus a *return* journey in search of his true starting-place—the return to original innocence. Natural innocence is not an end in itself, but the necessary condition of beginning: it was never intended that unfallen Adam should remain static, but that he should progress from natural to supernatural perfection. . . . Dante's Earthly Paradise . . . represents the recovery of that original perfection of human nature which was impaired by the Fall. Once we remember that Eden is, and was always meant to be, a starting-place and not a stopping-place, we shall have little difficulty in finding a consistent and intelligible significance for the allegory." Dorothy L. Sayers, "Introduction" and "Notes," in Dante, *The Divine Comedy 2: Purgatory* (Harmondsworth, Eng.: Penguin, 1955), 293–94; italics hers.

Reinforcing this point, Barbara Reynolds, in her "Notes" for *Paradiso*, emphasizes: "for Dante, the perfected life, which is the eternal vision of God, does not mean that further progress is impossible; on the contrary, eternal life means an endlessly deepening vision of the inexhaustible." Barbara Reynolds, "Introduction" and "Notes," in Dante, *The Divine Comedy 3: Paradise* (Harmondsworth, Eng.: Penguin, 1962), 25, note 3.

9. As we noted in chapter 3, Armgart saw her artistry as winning her a place as "a happy spiritual star" in Dante's vision of the celestial Paradise, where she imagines great artists as moving in the midst of "a sublime necessity of good." George Eliot, "Armgart," 1, 292.

10. Teilhard de Chardin, *Phenomenon of Man*, 298; italics his.

11. Louis M. Savary, *Teilhard de Chardin—"The Divine Milieu" Explained: A Spirituality for the 21st Century* (New York: Paulist, 2007), 88.

12. George Eliot, *Daniel Deronda*, 6:41, 513.

13. Ibid., 6:41, 513.

14. Teilhard de Chardin, *Phenomenon of Man*, 284.

15. Ibid., 285.

16. Pierre Teilhard de Chardin, *Human Energy*, trans. and intro. J. M. Cohen, foreword by N. M. Wildiers (New York: Harcourt Brace Jovanovich, 1969), 15.

17. Reynolds, "Introduction" in Dante, *The Divine Comedy 3: Paradise*, 29.

18. Ibid., 33.

19. George Eliot's affiliation with Positivists is well known, but she never counted herself as one of Comte's school. In 1866 she reads Comte's *Système de politique positive, ou Traité de sociologie, instituant la religion de l'humanité* and writes in a letter to her friend Mrs. Richard Congreve, whose husband is a convinced Positivist: "My gratitude increases continually for the illumination Comte has contributed to my life. But we both of us study with a sense of having still so much to learn and to understand" (*George Eliot Letters*, ed. Haight, 4:333). Fleishman argues convincingly for the greater influence of J. S. Mill over Comte on George Eliot. See especially chapter 3, and his analysis of George Eliot's critique of Comte in her brief essay "Historic Guidance" (Fleishman, *George Eliot's Intellectual Life*, 232–33).

20. Teilhard de Chardin, *Phenomenon of Man*, 56; italics his.

21. Ibid., 73; italics his.

22. Ibid., 73. Diarmuid O'Murchu, among others who have developed Teilhard's thinking, argues for an evolutionary model that rejects the soul vs. body dualism and sees "soulfulness" as an integral element of creation that manifests the energy of God:

> Instead of our preoccupation with the soul within the body, we are invited to engage with the notion of the body within the soul. God's primary embodied presence in creation is in the cosmos itself, ensouled with the creative energy of God's Holy Spirit. That same inspired life-force imbues the creation and evolution of our home planet at every stage of its coming into being. And long before humans evolved, . . . the planet was populated with bacteria whose intelligent, creative behavior has only been understood in recent decades and clearly witnesses to a soul-filled vitality. Diarmuid O'Murchu, *Consecrated Religious Life: Paradigms in Decline* (Maryknoll, N.Y.: Orbis Books, 2005), 68–69.

23. George Eliot, *Daniel Deronda*, 6:41, 514.

24. Ibid., 6:41, 511.
25. Ibid., 4:32, 366.
26. Ibid., 6:41, 512.
27. Ibid., 6:41, 515.
28. Ibid., 6:41, 513.
29. Ibid., 6:43, 540.
30. Ibid., 1:1, 9.
31. Ibid., 6:48, 585.
32. Ibid., 6:48, 587; 7:54, 672; 6:48, 596.
33. Ibid., 6:48, 587; 7:54, 680.
34. Ibid., 6:48, 594, 595.
35. Ibid., 6:44, 555; 7:54, 671.
36. Ibid., 7:54, 669.
37. Ibid.
38. Ibid., 7:54, 674.
39. Ibid., 6:48, 606.
40. Ibid., 7:54, 674.
41. Ibid., 7:54, 681.
42. Ibid., 6:48, 604.
43. Ibid., 5:36, 449.
44. Ibid., 6:48, 602; 7:57, 700.
45. Dante, *The Divine Comedy 2: Purgatory*, trans. Dorothy L. Sayers (Harmondsworth, Eng.: Penguin, 1949), 4:88–90.
46. Teilhard de Chardin, *Phenomenon of Man*, 258.
47. *George Eliot Letters*, ed. Haight, 6:216.
48. Savary, *New Spiritual Exercises*, 17.
49. Teilhard de Chardin, *Phenomenon of Man*, 259; italics his.
50. Ibid., 261.
51. Ibid., 262; italics his.
52. Ibid., 263.
53. Terence Cave, "Introduction" and "Notes" in George Eliot, *Silas Marner* (Oxford: Oxford University Press, 1998), xvii; italics his. Cave reinforces the idea, expressed elsewhere, that "George Eliot never espoused the systems of Feuerbach, Comte, Spencer, Darwin, and the rest wholesale; she had a sharply critical mind, and her novels should be read as an exploration of these ideas and their limits rather than as an application of them." He goes on to illustrate this point with references to the work of William Myers, Nancy Paxton, Susan Cohen, Sally Shuttleworth, and David Carroll (xx–xxi).
54. Ibid., xvii.
55. Ibid., xvii, xxv.
56. Ibid., xxvii.
57. Ibid., xxx.
58. George Eliot, *Silas Marner*, 1:1, 7.
59. Teilhard de Chardin, *Phenomenon of Man*, 165.
60. Ibid., 166.
61. Ibid., 167; italics his.
62. Ibid., 164.
63. George Eliot, *Silas Marner*, 1:2, 19.

64. Ibid., 1:2, 15.
65. Ibid., 1:10, 74.
66. Teilhard de Chardin, *Phenomenon of Man*, 155.
67. George Eliot, *Silas Marner*, 1:2, 15.
68. Ibid., 1:1, 7; 1:2, 18; see also. 2:19, 159.
69. Ibid., 1:2, 18–19.
70. Teilhard de Chardin, *Phenomenon of Man*, 172; italics his.
71. George Eliot, *Silas Marner*, 1:14, 124.
72. Ibid., 1:14, 124.
73. Ibid., 1:14, 119, 126, 129.
74. Ibid., 1:14, 124.
75. Ibid., 1:14, 129.
76. Ibid., 1:14, 128.
77. Ibid., 2:16, 142.
78. Ibid., 2:16, 136.
79. Teilhard de Chardin, *Phenomenon of Man*, 155.
80. George Eliot, *Silas Marner*, 1:14, 129.
81. Ibid., 1:14, 124.
82. Ibid., 1:3, 29.
83. Ibid., 1:1, 8.
84. Teilhard de Chardin, *Phenomenon of Man*, 35; italics his.
85. George Eliot, *Silas Marner*, 1:1, 12–13.
86. We might relate this development, whereby Silas painfully learns to reconcile form and feeling and eventually to come to integrate his maternal heritage into his adult social self, to what Lacan calls the movement from the mirror stage to the symbolic order. In the present context we might also see it as an illustration of Kearney's anatheism, the process of returning to religious feeling by continually adapting its forms.
87. George Eliot, *Silas Marner*, 1:14, 127.
88. Ibid., 1:1, 13.
89. Ibid., 1:10, 77.
90. Ibid., 1:10, 81.
91. Ibid., 1:10, 82.
92. Ibid., 1:10, 80–81.
93. Ibid., 1:10, 84; note p. 186.
94. Ibid., 1:8, 113.
95. Sayers, "Introduction" in Dante, *The Divine Comedy 2: Purgatory*, 13.
96. Reynolds, "Introduction" in Dante, *The Divine Comedy 3: Paradise*, 22.
97. Sayers, "Introduction" in Dante, *The Divine Comedy 2: Purgatory*, 13.
98. Auerbach, *Mimesis*, 16.
99. Ibid., 18.
100. Ibid., 191.
101. Reynolds, "Introduction" in Dante, *The Divine Comedy 3: Paradise*, 23.
102. Hans Frei, *The Eclipse of Biblical Narrative: A Study in Eighteenth- and Nineteenth-Century Hermeneutics* (New Haven, Conn.: Yale University Press, 1974), 13.
103. Marcus J. Borg, *Meeting Jesus Again for the First Time: The Historical Jesus & the Heart of Contemporary Faith* (San Francisco: Harper, 1994), 121.

104. Teilhard de Chardin, *Phenomenon of Man*, 32.

105. George Eliot, *The Mill on the Floss*, 1:2, 10.

106. In a letter to Harriet Beecher Stowe in 1870, George Eliot writes, "I fear that Casaubon-tints are not quite foreign to my own mental complexion. At any rate I am very sorry for him" (*George Eliot Letters*, ed. Haight, 5:322).

107. Kierkegaard, *Concluding Unscientific Postscript to Philosophical Fragments*, 181.

108. Ibid., 182.

109. Ibid., 218.

110. Ibid., 220–21.

111. George Eliot, "Janet's Repentance," 26, 296.

112. Quoted in Diarmuid O'Murchu, *Adult Faith: Growing in Wisdom and Understanding* (New York: Orbis Books, 2010), 86.

113. *George Eliot Letters*, ed. Haight, 6:216–17.

114. Quoted in O'Murchu, *Consecrated Religious Life*, 126.

115. Diarmuid O'Murchu, *Reclaiming Spirituality* (New York: Crossroads, 1998). O'Murchu spells out some of the implications of this focus on the heroic Jesus at the expense of his mission and that of his followers:

> By individualising Jesus into the unique, divine hero sent by God, the story of God's New Reign on Earth, for which Jesus is the primordial disciple, quickly becomes the Jesus Story; the very context that gives prophetic edge, spiritual originality and cultural impact to the story is gradually undermined and virtually eroded. All the powerful narratives, e.g. miracles, become potentially 'proof-texts' to establish the divinity of this one, unique hero. The fact that the miracles are the first signs and tangible evidence for a new world becomes a secondary consideration.
>
> Gradually, the major events, e.g., crucifixion, become isolated experiences whose actual historicity we seek to establish to substantiate the existence of this one important person; we lose the archetypal meaning of crucifixion as a dynamic force that underpins so many processes in our daily lives and in our evolving world. (*Reclaiming Spirituality*, 147)

116. See O'Murchu's discussion of these issues, for example in *Quantum Theology: Spiritual Implications of the New Physics* (New York: Crossroads, 1998), 133–34; and in O'Murchu, *Ancestral Grace*, 132.

117. In his explanation of Teilhard's *Divine Milieu*, Savary notes:

> True resignation demands that we fight sincerely and with all our strength, 'in union with the creative force of the world,' to drive evil away so that nothing in creation is diminished . . . For the Christian, says Teilhard, this noble human quest is also an essential part of our striving with the rest of humanity to realize the earth's potential for higher consciousness. (Savary, Teilhard de Chardin: *"The Divine Milieu" Explained,* 115).

Savary explains that Teilhard teaches the Christian "how to live in submission to God in *an active way*" by confronting evil and what he calls "diminishments" with a resignation that is the opposite of passive (ibid.,116).

118. Kierkegaard, *Upbuilding Discourses in Various Spirits*, 256–57.

119. George Eliot, *Daniel Deronda*, 5:36, 452.

120. Kierkegaard, *Upbuilding Discourses in Various Spirits*, 256.
121. George Eliot, *Adam Bede*, 6:52, 456.
122. Ibid., 6:50, 435–36.
123. Teilhard de Chardin, "The Meaning and Constructive Value of Suffering," in *Teilhard de Chardin: Pilgrim of the Future*, ed. Neville Braybrooke, trans. Noël Lindsay (New York: Seabury, 1964), 26.
124. George Eliot, *Adam Bede*, 6:50, 436.
125. George Eliot, *Daniel Deronda*, 4:32, 367.
126. Ibid.
127. In *Consecrated Religious Life*, Diarmuid O'Murchu elaborates on the non-dualistic idea that sees all of the created world as "soulful" and all the more worthy of liberation:

> Instead of reserving the holy to a spiritualized realm within the human body alone, we are invited to contemplate the holy in all that has been born of, and touched by, the living spirit of God. Instead of identifying spirituality with the soul that can transcend the body, the earth, and all created things, we are invited to engage gracefully with the holy that is immanent in the whole of creation. Instead of identifying salvation with the soul inhabiting the heavenly realm, we are invited to work together for the soulful liberation of all who live on this earth burdened with the injustice of man-made oppression. (*Consecrated Religious Life*, 68)

Conclusion

1. *George Eliot Letters,* ed. Haight. 2:126.
2. George Eliot, *The Mill on the Floss,* 7:2, 498.
3. Teilhard de Chardin, *Phenomenon of Man*, 219.
4. Louis Savary, *The New Spiritual Exercises*, 88, 27.
5. Ibid., 27.
6. *George Eliot Letters*, ed. Haight, 4:95.
7. Ibid., 4:71.

BIBLIOGRAPHY

Anger, Suzy. "George Eliot and Philosophy." In *The Cambridge Companion to George Eliot*, edited by George Levine, 76–97. Cambridge: Cambridge University Press, 2001.

Arnold, Matthew. *God and the Bible: A Review of Objections to "Literature and Dogma."* 1874. Reprint. https://archive.org/details/literatureand dog028325mbp.

Ashton, Rosemary. *George Eliot: A Life*. London: Penguin, 1997.

Auerbach, Erich. *Mimesis: The Representation of Reality in Western Literature*. Translated by Willard R. Trask. 1946. Reprint. Princeton, N.J.: Princeton University Press, 1953.

Bartky, Sandra Lee. *Sympathy and Solidarity and Other Essays*. Lanham, Md.: Oxford University Press, 2002.

Bennett, Joan. *George Eliot: Her Mind & Art*. 1948. Reprint. London: Cambridge University Press, 1966.

Bodenheimer, Rosemary. *The Real Life of Mary Ann Evans: George Eliot, Her Letters and Fiction*. Ithaca, N.Y. Cornell University Press, 1994.

Borg, Marcus J. *Meeting Jesus Again for the First Time: The Historical Jesus & the Heart of Contemporary Faith*. San Francisco: Harper, 1994.

Byatt, A. S. "Introduction." In *George Eliot: Selected Essays, Poems, and Other Writings*, edited by A. S. Byatt. London: Penguin, 1990.

Carpenter, Mary Wilson. *George Eliot and the Landscape of Time: Narrative Form and Protestant Apocalyptic History*. Chapel Hill: University of North Carolina Press, 1986.

Carroll, David. *George Eliot and the Conflict of Interpretations*. Cambridge: Cambridge University Press, 1992.

———, ed. *George Eliot: The Critical Heritage*. London: Routledge and Kegan Paul, 1971.

Cave, Terence. "Introduction" and "Notes." In *Daniel Deronda*, by George Eliot. 1995. Reprint. London: Penguin, 2003.

———. "Introduction" and "Notes." In *Silas Marner*, by George Eliot. Oxford: Oxford University Press, 1998.

Cross, J. W., ed. *George Eliot's Life as Related in Her Letters and Journals*. 3 vols. Edinburgh: W. Blackwood and Sons, 1885.

Cunningham, Valentine. *Everywhere Spoken Against: Dissent in the Victorian Novel*. Oxford: Clarendon, 1975.

Dante. *The Divine Comedy, 1: Hell*. Translated by Dorothy L. Sayers. Harmondsworth, Eng.: Penguin, 1949.

———. *The Divine Comedy, 2: Purgatory*. Translated by Dorothy L. Sayers. Harmondsworth, Eng.: Penguin, 1955.

———. *The Divine Comedy, 3: Paradise*. Translated by Dorothy L. Sayers and Barbara Reynolds. Harmondsworth, Eng.: Penguin, 1962.

Davis, Michael. *George Eliot and Nineteenth-Century Psychology: Exploring the Unmapped Country*. Aldershot, Eng.: Ashgate, 2006.

Davis, Stephen T., Daniel Kendall, and Gerald O'Collins, eds. *The Incarnation*. 2002. Reprint. Oxford: Oxford University Press, 2004.

Easley, Alexis. "Authorship, Gender and Identity: George Eliot in the 1850s." *Women's Writing* 3, no. 2 (1996): 145–60.

Eliot, George. *Adam Bede*. Oxford: Oxford University Press, 2008.

———. *Daniel Deronda*. 1995. Reprint. London: Penguin, 2003.

———. *Essays of George Eliot*. Edited by Thomas Pinney. New York: Columbia University Press, 1963.

———. *Felix Holt, the Radical*. London: Penguin, 1995.

———. *The George Eliot Letters*. Edited by Gordon S. Haight. 9 vols. New Haven, Conn.: Yale University Press, 1954.

———. *A George Eliot Miscellany: A Supplement to Her Novels*. Edited by F. B. Pinion. London: Macmillan, 1982.

———. *The Journals of George Eliot*. Edited by Margaret Harris and Judith Johnston. 1998. Reprint. Cambridge: Cambridge University Press, 2000.

———. *The Lifted Veil and Brother Jacob*. London: Penguin, 2004.

———. *Middlemarch*. Oxford: Oxford University Press, 1997.

———. *The Mill on the Floss*. Oxford: Oxford University Press, 1996.

———. *Romola*. 1994. Reprint. Oxford: Oxford University Press, 1998.

———. *Scenes of Clerical Life*. Oxford: Oxford University Press, 1988.

———. *Selected Essays, Poems, and Other Writings*. Edited by A. S. Byatt. London: Penguin, 1990.

———. *Silas Marner*. Oxford: Oxford University Press, 1998.

———. *The Works of George Eliot: Impressions of Theophrastus Such, Essays and Poems*. New York: A. L. Burt, n.d.

Fleishman, Avrom. *George Eliot's Intellectual Life*. Cambridge: Cambridge University Press, 2010.

Feuerbach, Ludwig. *The Essence of Christianity*. Translated by George Eliot. 1854. Reprint. New York: Harper and Row, 1957.

Foucault, Michel. "What Is an Author?" In *Modern Criticism and Theory: A Reader*, edited by David Lodge, 196–210. 1969. Reprint. London: Longman, 1988.

Frei, Hans W. *The Eclipse of Biblical Narrative: A Study in Eighteenth- and Nineteenth-Century Hermeneutics*. New Haven, Conn.: Yale University Press, 1974.

Gilbert, Sandra, and Susan Gubar. *The Madwoman in the Attic*. New Haven, Conn.: Yale University Press, 1979.

Haight, Gordon S. *George Eliot: A Biography*. New York: Oxford University Press, 1968.

———, ed. *The George Eliot Letters*. 9 vols. New Haven, Conn.: Yale University Press, 1954.

Harris, Margaret, and Judith Johnston, eds. *The Journals of George Eliot*. 1998. Reprint. Cambridge: Cambridge University Press, 2000.

Hennell, Sara Sophia. *Present Religion as a Faith Owning Fellowship with Thought*. 1865. Reprint. https://archive.org/details/presentreligion03henngoog.

Hodgson, Peter C. *The Mystery Beneath the Real: Theology in the Fiction of George Eliot*. Minneapolis, Minn.: Fortress, 2000.

Jacob, W. M. *The Clerical Professions in the Long Eighteenth Century 1680–1840*. Oxford: Oxford University Press, 2007.

Jay, Elizabeth. *Religion of the Heart: Anglican Evangelicalism in the Nineteenth-Century Novel*. Oxford: Clarendon, 1979.

Jeffrey, David Lyle, general ed. *A Dictionary of Biblical Tradition in English Literature*. Grand Rapids, Mich.: Eerdmans, 1992.

Karl, Frederick. *George Eliot: Voice of a Century: A Biography*. New York: Norton, 1995.

Kearney, Richard. *Anatheism: Returning to God after God*. New York: Columbia University Press, 2010.

———. *The God Who May Be: A Hermeneutics of Religion*. Bloomington: Indiana University Press, 2001.

———. *Poetics of Imagining: Modern to Post-Modern*. New York: Fordham University Press, 1998.

Kermode, Frank. *The Sense of an Ending*. New York: Oxford University Press, 1967.

Kierkegaard, Søren. *Concluding Unscientific Postscript to Philosophical Fragments*. 1846. Reprint. Princeton, N.J.: Princeton University Press, 1992.

———. *Parables of Kierkegaard*. Edited by Thomas C. Oden. Princeton, N.J.: Princeton University Press, 1978.

———. *Purity of Heart Is to Will One Thing*. 1847. Reprint. New York: Harper, 1965.

———. *Repetition* and *Fear and Trembling*. 1843. Reprint. Princeton, N.J.: Princeton University Press, 1983.

———. *The Sickness Unto Death*. 1849. Reprint. Princeton, N.J.: Princeton University Press, 1992.

———. *Upbuilding Discourses in Various Spirits: Part Three: The Gospel of Sufferings, Christian Discourses*. Translated by Howard V. Hong and Edna H. Hong. 1857. Reprint. Princeton, N.J.: Princeton University Press, 1993.

Knoepflmacher, U. C. *George Eliot's Early Novels: The Limits of Realism*. Berkeley: University of California Press, 1968.

Levine, George, ed. *The Cambridge Companion to George Eliot*. Cambridge: Cambridge University Press, 2001.

McLeod, Hugh. *Religion and Society in England, 1850–1914*. London: Macmillan, 1996.

Moorman, J. R. H. *A History of the Church in England*. 1953. Reprint. London: Adam and Charles Black, 1961.

Norris, Kathleen. "A Word Made Flesh: Incarnational Language and the Writer." In *The Incarnation*, edited by Stephen T. Davis, Daniel Kendall, and Gerald O'Collins, 303–12. 2002. Reprint. Oxford: Oxford University Press, 2004.

O'Collins, Gerald. *Incarnation*. 2002. Reprint. London: Continuum, 2003.

Oden, Thomas C. "Introduction." In *Parables of Kierkegaard*. Princeton, N.J.: Princeton University Press, 1978.

O'Murchu, Diarmuid. *Adult Faith: Growing in Wisdom and Understanding.* New York: Orbis Books, 2010.

———. *Ancestral Grace: Meeting God in Our Human Story.* New York: Orbis Books, 2008.

———. *Consecrated Religious Life: Paradigms in Decline.* Maryknoll, N.Y.: Orbis Books, 2005.

———. *Quantum Theology: Spiritual Implications of the New Physics.* 1997. Reprint. New York: Crossroads, 1998.

———. *Reclaiming Spirituality.* New York: Crossroads, 1998.

Perkin, J. Russell. *Theology and the Victorian Novel.* Montreal: McGill-Queen's University Press, 2009.

Polanyi, Michael. *The Tacit Dimension.* Gloucester, Mass.: Peter Smith, 1983.

Qualls, Barry. "George Eliot and Religion." In *The Cambridge Companion to George Eliot*, edited by George Levine, 119–37. Cambridge: Cambridge University Press, 2001.

Rahner, Karl. *The Mystical Way in Everyday Life: Sermons, Prayers, and Essays.* Maryknoll, N.Y.: Orbis Books, 2010.

Redinger, Ruby. *George Eliot: The Emergent Self.* London: Bodley Head, 1976.

Reynolds, Barbara. "Introduction" and "Notes." In Dante, *The Divine Comedy, 3: Paradise.* Harmondsworth, Eng.: Penguin, 1962.

Ricoeur, Paul. "Life in Quest of Narrative." In *On Paul Ricoeur: Narrative and Interpretation*, edited by David Wood, 20–33. London: Routledge, 1991.

———. "Narrative Identity." In *On Paul Ricoeur: Narrative and Interpretation*, edited by David Wood, 188–99. London: Routledge, 1991.

———. *Oneself as Another.* Translated by Kathleen Blamey. Chicago: University of Chicago Press, 1992.

Savary, Louis M. *The New Spiritual Exercises: In the Spirit of Teilhard de Chardin.* New York: Paulist, 2010.

———. *Teilhard de Chardin—"The Divine Milieu" Explained: A Spirituality for the 21st Century.* New York: Paulist, 2007.

Sayers, Dorothy L. "Introduction" and "Notes." In Dante, *The Divine Comedy, 1: Hell.* Harmondsworth, Eng.: Penguin, 1949.

———. "Introduction" and "Notes." In Dante, *The Divine Comedy, 2: Purgatory.* Harmondsworth, Eng.: Penguin, 1955.

———. "Notes." In Dante, *The Divine Comedy, 3: Paradise.* Harmondsworth, Eng.: Penguin, 1962.

Shea, John. *Stories of Faith.* New York: Thomas More, 1980.

Solway, R. A. *Prelates and People: Ecclesiastical Social Thought in England 1783–1852.* Toronto: University of Toronto Press, 1969.

Strauss, D. F. *The Life of Jesus Critically Examined.* Translated by George Eliot.1846. Reprint. Mifflintown, Penn.: Sigler Press, 1994.

Taylor, Charles. *Sources of the Self: The Making of Modern Identity.* Cambridge, Mass.: Harvard University Press, 1989.

Teilhard de Chardin, Pierre. *The Divine Milieu.* Translated by Bernard Wall. 1957. Reprint. New York: Harper Perennial, 2001.

———. *Human Energy.* Translated by J. M. Cohen, foreword by N. M. Wildiers. 1962. Reprint. New York: Harcourt Brace Jovanovich, 1969.

———. "The Meaning and Constructive Value of Suffering." In *Teilhard de Chardin: Pilgrim of the Future*, edited by Neville Braybrooke, translated by Noël Lindsay. New York: Seabury, 1964.

———. *The Phenomenon of Man*. Translated by Bernard Wall. 1955. Reprint. New York: Harper Perennial, 2008.

Uglow, Jennifer. *George Eliot*. London: Virago, 1987.

Underhill, Evelyn. *Essential Writings*. Edited by Emilie Griffin. Maryknoll, N.Y.: Orbis Books, 2003.

Van den Broek, Antonie Gerard, ed. *"The Spanish Gypsy" by George Eliot*. London: Pickering and Chatto, 2008.

Welsh, Alexander. *George Eliot and Blackmail*. Cambridge, Mass.: Harvard University Press, 1985.

Wildiers, N. M. "Foreword." In Teilhard de Chardin, *Human Energy*, translated by J. M. Cohen. 1962. Reprint, New York: Harcourt Brace Jovanovich, 1969.

Willey, Basil. *Nineteenth-Century Studies*. London: Chatto and Windus, 1955.

Winter, Miriam Therese. *Paradoxology: Spirituality in a Quantum Universe*. Maryknoll, N.Y.: Orbis Books, 2009.

INDEX